✳ How much of e-mo scepticism is inherited from sextus, & how much is it anticipating, or @ least pointing toward, Levine?

✳ contingency, in the victorian context, seems to become "alterity". radical contingency → radical alterity.

✳ Question — when does 'suspense' transition from connotations of tranquility to agitation? Foglevine, it seems to be this agitating quality of suspense that allows it to contribute to a discourse of Narrative form.

Do we see suspense in Baconian experiment? If so, is it fraught w/ pleasurable anxiety?

The Serious Pleasures of Suspense

Victorian Literature and Culture Series
Jerome J. McGann and Herbert F. Tucker, Editors

The Serious Pleasures of Suspense

Victorian Realism
and Narrative Doubt

Caroline Levine

UNIVERSITY OF VIRGINIA PRESS
Charlottesville and London

University of Virginia Press
© 2003 by the Rector and Visitors of the University of Virginia
All rights reserved
Printed in the United States of America on acid-free paper
First published 2003

9 8 7 6 5 4 3 2 1

LIBRARY OF CONGRESS CATALOGING-IN-PUBLICATION DATA
Levine, Caroline, 1970 –
   The serious pleasures of suspense : Victorian realism and narrative
doubt / Caroline Levine.
      p.   cm. — (Victorian literature and culture series)
Includes bibliographical references and index.
   ISBN 0-8139-2217-8 (alk. paper)
   1. English fiction—19th century—History and criticism.
2. Suspense fiction—History and criticism.   3. Suspense in
literature.   4. Realism in literature.   5. Narration (Rhetoric)
I. Title. II. Series.
PR878.S87 L48 2003
823'.8353 — dc21   2003000797

For my parents

Contents

Acknowledgments

This is a book about the pleasures of reading, which have always been precious to me. I am glad to say that the pleasures of writing have been equally intense, but without the many students, colleagues, and friends who were willing to think with me, they would not have been pleasures at all.

When it comes to suspense, my students are the group to whom I owe the most immediate thanks, since they are the ones who have reaffirmed for me—semester after semester—that the delays of nineteenth-century suspense continue to feel delicious and exciting, that readerly guesses and forecasts are more often wrong than right, and that not knowing is a surprisingly meaningful pleasure.

My thanks also extend well beyond the classroom. I am grateful to *Victorian Literature and Culture* and its publisher, Cambridge University Press, for permission to reprint revised versions of chapters 1 and 3: "Harmless Pleasure: Gender, Suspense, and *Jane Eyre*" *Victorian Literature and Culture* 28: 2 (September 2000), 275–86; and "Visual Labor," *Victorian Literature and Culture* 28: 1 (March 2000), 73–86. I wish to thank *Women's Writing* and Ashgate Publishing Ltd. for allowing me to reprint portions of chapters 5 and 7, both now substantially altered: "Women or Boys? Gender, Realism, and the Gaze in *Adam Bede*," *Women's Writing* 3

(1996), 113–27; and "The Prophetic Fallacy: Foreshadowing and Narrative Knowledge in *Romola*," in *From Author to Text*, ed. Caroline Levine and Mark W. Turner (Aldershot, UK: Ashgate, 1998). And thanks are due to Blackwell for permission to reprint an article that formed the groundwork for a part of chapter 2: "Seductive Reflexivity: Ruskin's Dreaded *Trompe l'Oeil*," *Journal of Aesthetics and Art Criticism* 56 (Fall 1998), 366–75.

One of my most lasting obligations is to the British Marshall Commission, which funded the research I undertook as a graduate student at the University of London. Since that time, I have received valuable assistance from research funds at Wake Forest University and Rutgers University. And I have been offered generous moral support from colleagues at those institutions and at the University of Wisconsin. I am particularly grateful to Carol Singley for her unstinting enthusiasm.

Recently, two scholars have come to epitomize the intellectual ideal for me: they combine generosity of spirit, liveliness of intellect, and profound integrity. Both Carolyn Williams and Maria DiBattista put their faith in this project when its future seemed bleakest, and both offered their encouragement when I felt most forsaken and isolated.

A few crucial conversations have transformed this project. My thanks to Elizabeth Deeds Ermarth, Seth Koven, George Levine (who is no relation), Patrick O'Malley, Denise Quirk, and Rebecca Walkowitz for comments that got me thinking along wholly new tracks. Isobel Armstrong alone knows how much she has contributed to my scholarly development and to the progress of this book. The anonymous reader and series editors at the University of Virginia Press made astute and invaluable suggestions, which I am only too glad to have taken. I am also very much obliged to Cathie Brettschneider of the Press for her resourcefulness and hard work. Erin O'Connor's comments have always been right on the mark—unerringly perceptive and at times quite dazzlingly so. All errors, without a doubt, are my own.

Perhaps my greatest good fortune has come in the shape of gifted, stimulating, loyal, loving, and compassionate friends. Two exceptional Victorianists—Jan Caldwell and Lisa Sternlieb—will always be treasured. From our trip to Darwin's house to our disputes over Charlotte Brontë, they made scholarship and happiness indistinguishable. Amanda

Claybaugh's sharpness of mind is endlessly invigorating, and her companionship has enriched my life. Rachel Harmon's gift for weaving philosophical reflection into the fabric of everyday experience has long been a source of delight and sustenance. I am also deeply grateful for the friendship of Winifred Amaturo, Rick Caldwell, Richard Falkenrath, Louise Keely, Jonathan Marks, Ina Jo McKenzie, Martin Puchner, Julian Sheather, Henry Turner, Rebecca Walkowitz, and Matt Werdegar. I will always be indebted to John Allen and John Snyder, whose wisdom and insight have repeatedly opened up new channels of thought and feeling. And Mark W. Turner—best of colleagues, best of friends—has been there since the beginning. Mark taught me the intense pleasures of intellectual collaboration, and the brilliant sunlight he has brought into my life has seen me through many a dark passage.

I have enjoyed the company of Peter, Laura, Kate, and Hannah more than I can say, and I cannot thank them enough for their warm hospitality. My debt to my extraordinary parents—to whom this book is dedicated—is simply immeasurable.

As for Jon McKenzie—my brilliant companion, my sweet love—he is the most serious pleasure of my life.

The Serious Pleasures of Suspense

Introduction

Narrative suspense did not fare well in critical circles in the twentieth century. In *Aspects of the Novel,* E. M. Forster described suspense as a literary technique that appealed particularly to "tyrants and savages."[1] "The primitive audience," he wrote, "was an audience of shock-heads, gaping round the camp fire, fatigued with contending against the mammoth or the woolly rhinoceros, and only kept awake by suspense."[2] If for Forster suspense was primeval and barbaric, boorish and low, for Roland Barthes it was just the opposite: too civilized—too much the product of nineteenth-century bourgeois culture. In *S/Z* and *The Pleasure of the Text,* Barthes argues that the texts of suspense kindle a desire for ideologically consoling conclusions, offering an "organized set of stoppages" on the way to endings that resolve contradictions and repress possibilities.[3] Suspenseful strategies are found in "the text that comes from culture and does not break with it"; they are "linked to a *comfortable* practice of reading."[4]

Forster and Barthes might have pictured the audience for suspenseful narratives in dramatically different contexts, but they have this much in common: for both, suspense produces credulity and obedience—*passivity.* Whether manipulated by barbarous tyrants or produced by modern capitalism, suspense emerges as a literary instrument of social control.

Critics in the past few decades have largely accepted the claim that narratives of suspense encourage a political submissiveness. Catherine Belsey, for example, asserts that the nineteenth-century novel introduces social contradictions, but it always successfully suppresses them, structurally, through what she sees as its inexorable movement toward reassuring closure.[5] Similarly, D. A. Miller reads Victorian suspense as a temporary volatility designed to provoke the reader's desire for order, and particularly for the powerful social regulation that eludes the supervision of the police.[6] In the wake of Barthes, Belsey, and Miller, it has become something of a commonplace to presume that suspense fiction reinforces stability, activating anxiety about the social world only in order to repress that anxiety in favor of unambiguous disclosures and soothing restorations of the status quo.[7]

But it was not always so. This book makes the case that Victorian writers and readers understood suspenseful narrative as a stimulus to active speculation. For a startling array of nineteenth-century thinkers—from John Ruskin and Michael Faraday to Charlotte Brontë and Wilkie Collins—the experience of suspense was not a means of social regulation, but a rigorous political and epistemological training, a way to foster energetic skepticism and uncertainty rather than closure and complacency. Suspense fiction was all about teaching readers to suspend judgment. And I will argue, here, that the nineteenth century was not wrong about suspense: the classic readerly text was indeed far more writerly—dynamic, critical, questioning, and indeterminate—than Barthes ever tempts us to imagine.[8]

Victorian novels are inclined to flaunt their secrets. Conspicuously withholding crucial pieces of knowledge, they invite the ravenous readerly curiosity we call "suspense." Suspense happens when children do not know their parents and when husbands disappear, when objects are stolen and banknotes mislaid. Suspense happens in *Jane Eyre* when Rochester announces that he must pay a visit to the third story but does not tell us why. Suspense happens in *Great Expectations* when Pip learns that he is forbidden to know the name of his benefactor. And in so many Victorian fictions, the secret, when it finally emerges, turns out to be entirely different from what we have been invited or expected to imagine. Readers and characters may put forward a range of guesses and conjectures, but narrative mysteries remind us that even the plentiful range of our guesses may be narrow when compared with the hidden truth. And so, as we read suspenseful plots, we learn to doubt and guess, to speculate and hypothesize, to pause in the knowledge that we do not know.

Nineteenth-century scientists and philosophers insisted that a doubtful pause was absolutely essential to the pursuit of knowledge. If we were not compelled to suspend judgment, they argued, we would simply rush to assume that our prejudices were true and right, and we would fail to open ourselves up to the possibility of unexpected truths and surprises. From this epistemological perspective, novelistic suspense performed a critical cultural role: narrative enigmas and delays could help to foster habits of hesitation and uncertainty. In the space between the mystery and its revelation, audiences were forced to wait and wonder, unable to say for sure whether their assumptions would fit the facts. Novelistic mysteries thus seemed to demand a kind of cultural and ideological self-restraint: they asked readers to ready themselves for the potential failures of belief and tradition when set against the surprising, unconventional otherness of the world.

In this context, suspense became the perfect vehicle for a new aesthetic that writers in the 1850s began to call "realism." For these thinkers, the real was that which did not belong to the mind—that which stood separate from patterns of thought and belief. In order to grasp the fundamental alterity of the world, it was necessary to put aside one's own intellectual habits and presumptions. The mind must come to know its own limits. Realism came to mean the suspending of assumption and belief, and narrative suspense emerged as the realist strategy par excellence.

Given this insistence on skepticism and doubt, it is perhaps no surprise that a number of radical thinkers in the mid-Victorian period welcomed both realism and narrative suspense. For them, the startling otherness of the real seemed capable of undermining entrenched habits of thought and conservative convictions. The real itself was radical. And since suspenseful narrative entailed the reining in of received opinions and conventional wisdom, the doubtful delays of suspense appeared to be an ideal instrument of unorthodox thought. A surprisingly broad spectrum of progressive thinkers recommended the skeptical pause of suspense: not only liberal political philosophers such as George Henry

Lewes and John Stuart Mill, but a whole mixed bag of anti-conventional minds—Christians, atheists, socialists, and feminists, from Charles Dickens to John Tyndall and from Charlotte Brontë to T. H. Huxley. Suspense seemed to be on the side of anyone who wanted to disrupt the deadening routines of the status quo.

But suspense had its detractors in the period, too. Was suspense indeed the best method for approaching alterity? Some writers, such as George Eliot, found something politically alarming in the demand to suspend desire and expectation, since the pressure to restrain the self seemed to reinforce an oppressive model of femininity. If the "angel in the house" was expected to suspend herself in order to serve her masculine counterparts, then an ideal of self-suspension could only work to restrict women still further. Other writers, such as Henry James, called attention to the sheer impossibility of suspending judgment, since the self inevitably projected itself onto the world. This book identifies three theoretical moments in the nineteenth-century debate around suspense: first the articulation of suspense as a proper ethical and epistemological model for approaching the world; then a series of focused critiques of the claims of suspense; and finally the replacement of suspenseful narrative with anti-suspenseful forms.

Victorian Suspense: Science, Politics, and Pleasure

Whether they praised or undermined suspenseful narrative, a whole host of nineteenth-century thinkers argued that the suspension of judgment was a necessary stage in the pursuit of knowledge. Scientists were among the most vocal champions of this skeptical model. And what they shared with novelists and philosophers was a method that I call the "realist experiment."

Although scientific thinkers argued passionately about the proper course of the scientific method in the Victorian period, virtually all agreed that Francis Bacon's notion of pure induction had proved itself an impossibility.[9] One could not gather facts without relying on some kind of theoretical framework to guide the process. Thus theory—and in particular the hypothesis—was indispensable to science.[10] In a review of a new edition of Bacon's works in 1857, William Whewell wrote: "Bacon and all who, like him, try to devise technical methods of extracting sciences from facts, make the mistake of overlooking the great truth, that the process of discovery necessarily involves invention—mind—genius."[11] By 1878, the entry on Bacon in the *Encyclopedia Britannica* condemned him for not recognizing the "true scientific procedure," which was "by hypothesis followed up and tested by verification."[12]

Jonathan Smith argues that the growing insistence on the hypothesis lent a new importance to the power of the imagination.[13] Scientists confessed that one could not know the world without indulging in conjectures, speculations, even dreams. As Stanley Jevons put it in 1873, "Fertility of the imagination and abundance of guesses at truth are among the first requisites of discovery."[14] But scientists and philosophers of science also recognized dangers in letting the imagination run wild. T. H. Huxley claimed that although the imagination was essential to science, it must be kept "in due and rigid subordination." Jevons warned that Descartes and Leibniz "fell into excess in the use of hypothesis." And even the radical John Tyndall, who was famous for promoting the "scientific use of the imagination," advocated a "hard discipline which checks licentiousness in speculation."[15]

But if it was true that the imagination had to be restrained, what was the appropriate way to bring it under control? The answer, according to the most prominent nineteenth-century scientists, was to *experiment*—to test the imagination's fertile possibilities against the evidence of the world. Thus Michael Faraday—perhaps the most famous of nineteenth-century experimenters—exhorted his audience to "let the imagination go . . . holding it in and directing it by experiment."[16] Jevons claimed that the scientist "must hold [his guesses] as worthless until they are verified by experiment," and Huxley warned his readers to beware of the seductions of the mind, when "our deductions carry us beyond the reach of [the] great process of verification."[17] The message was clear enough: since the imagination was a necessary but disorderly force in science, the activity of experimentation alone could ensure that it was put to good use.

The most radical version of this position held that all belief, all speculation, all prejudice could be submitted to a rigorous process of testing. As Huxley wrote in 1866: "The improver of natural knowledge refuses to acknowledge authority, as such. For him, scepticism is the highest of duties; blind faith the one unpardonable sin. . . . The man of science has learned to believe in justification, not by faith, but by verification."[18] To be sure, Huxley, an agnostic Darwinist, represented an extreme position on the spectrum of nineteenth-century science, but many others joined him in what he called the scientist's "duty to doubt."[19] The devoutly religious Faraday wrote to the *Times* in 1853 to berate those who imagined that the spiritualists' "table-turning" worked by electricity. He castigated "the great body" of the public who "know nothing" of electricity and magnetism and yet leap to conclusions of all kinds, "rather than suspend their judgment."[20] In place of this credulity, Faraday offered the evidence of an experiment. Similarly, Jevons claimed that the act of "suspending judgment" was necessary to the development of science, affirming that the wisest scientists were those who realized how little they knew.[21]

For the most prominent Victorian scientists and philosophers of science, then, the suspension of judgment marked the appropriate epistemological relationship between mind and world. The imagination, set free, would offer nothing but frenzied dreams and wild imaginings, but there was no access to the otherness of the world unmediated by the labor of the mind. Thus scientists had to strike a balance between indulging hypotheses and constraining them, between liberating the mind and checking its unruly speculations against the evidence offered up by the alterity of the world. The metaphor of "suspending" captured the uneasy experience of this provisional position, and the scientific experiment put it into practice.[22]

It is not far, I want to suggest, from the suspension of judgment to the workings of narrative suspense. Indeed, the experiment provided both a formal paradigm and an epistemological purpose for suspense fiction in the Victorian period. Formally speaking, the experiment always implied a narrative of suspense: experimenters might mobilize the most convincing hypotheses about the hidden facts of the world, but they were always required to wait to see how the world would respond. Experimentation meant an anxious delay between the excitement of conjecture and the appearance of more certain knowledge. As far as epistemology was concerned, the suspenseful pause between hypothesis and results bespoke a rigorous set of constraints on both dogma and desire. Thus G. H. Lewes insisted on the test as the only way to limit the impulses of prejudice:

> Who has not observed, even in himself, the eagerness with which some argument is snatched at, and some statement credited,

when these seem to confirm his own view of the case? To sub-
mit our own conclusions to the vigorous test of evidence, and to
seek the truth irrespective of our preconceptions, is the rarest
and most difficult of intellectual virtues.[23]

Testing, Lewes warned, would bring "the unrest of doubt," but such
anxiety was essential to legitimate knowledge seeking.[24] Similarly, we
find Faraday, torn by doubts about one of his experiments, writing of
his determination to "hold [his] judgment in suspense."[25] And Tyndall
championed suspenseful hesitation as essential to a judicious science:
"there are periods when the judgment ought to remain in suspense, the
data on which a decision might be based being absent."[26]

   To treat suspense as a trivial phenomenon, then, is to miss the fact
that it encouraged a thoroughgoing skepticism that satisfied even the least
frivolous of Victorian thinkers. Scientists and philosophers took seriously
the uneasy delay, the confession of ignorance, the intellectual labor of
careful guesswork, speculation, and doubt. And suspense was especially
appealing to progressives such as Lewes, Tyndall, Huxley, and John Stuart Mill because it entailed the suspension of both authority and convention.[27] For radical skeptics, it was important to learn to hover between
speculations and a recognition that those speculations might be proved
wrong; one must acquire the habit of guessing and waiting, both using
and restraining the imagination, poised to encounter the new. In short,
the experiment not only modeled an anxious experience of suspense; it
also gave suspense a clear epistemological and political value.

   The importance of the back-and-forth movement between hypothesis and verification did not remain confined to the discourse of the natural sciences. In 1855 a young Fitzjames Stephen defended novel reading
as a serious activity for young men on eminently scientific grounds:

> What we call knowledge of the world is acquired by the same
> means as other kinds of knowledge, and consists not in the mere
> acquaintance with maxims about life, but in applying appro-
> priate ideas to clear facts. . . . This arrangement is effected, to a
> very great degree, by guesses and hypotheses. . . . No one will
> be able to make any use of his experience of life, or to classify it
> in such a manner as to add to his real knowledge, unless he is
> provided in the first instance with some schemes or principles of

classification, which he starts with, and which he enlarges, narrows or otherwise modifies as he sees cause. . . . Novels, perhaps, offer a greater number of such hypotheses than are to be derived from any other source.[28]

Narrative fiction emerges, here, as a particularly effective way to introduce readers to the activity of hypothesizing and testing in order to come to knowledge.[29]

The suspension of judgment also became a political model, a way to unsettle prevailing beliefs and inherited conventions. In *The Stones of Venice,* John Ruskin offered his most pointed critique of market economics and industrialization. To this end, he condemned the arrogant complacency of contemporary culture, insisting that partial knowledge was the only proper human condition:

That man is always happy who is in the presence of something which he cannot know to the full, which he is always going on to know. This is the necessary condition of a finite creature with divinely rooted and divinely directed intelligence; this, therefore, its happy state,—but observe, a state, not of triumph or joy in what it knows, but of joy rather in the continual discovery, of new ignorance, continual self-abasement, continual astonishment. Once thoroughly our own, the knowledge ceases to give us pleasure. . . . It is dead; the wonder is gone from it, and all the fine colour which it had when first we drew it up out of the infinite sea.[30]

Here, Ruskin invokes the greatness of a perfect God in order to diminish human claims to progress and preeminence. We must learn to doubt our own knowledge, to celebrate our own ignorance. Only when we are humbled may we come to examine social life skeptically and critically. Thus Ruskin invites us to enjoy the possibilities of the new and the unconventional, to ready ourselves for shifts and surprises.

It may strike us as strange to find Ruskin insisting that ignorance brings happiness. Surely his "self-abasement" seems more like a harsh discipline, a reining in of inclination and desire. Indeed, George Levine has argued that the Victorian call for "scientific disinterest" brings such stringent demands for the erasure of the self that it is tantamount to death

dependence on an imagined future

itself: "that ultimate Victorian virtue—self-annihilation."[31] But my own work points to a rather different conclusion. Scientific experimentation, radical politics, and suspenseful storytelling all rely on the act of imagining a future—a future that, despite our best guesses, may or may not come to pass. And if Ruskin is right, as we wait, suspended, to see whether or not the future will bear out our suppositions and desires, we experience a vital, vibrant *pleasure*. This pleasure in ignorance is precisely the pleasure familiar to readers of fictional plots: those readers who keenly look forward to a future that is postponed, enjoying the experience of doubt, the pleasures of what Ruskin calls "going on to know." Against rigid convention and inflexible orthodoxy, readers of suspenseful plots take pleasure in the very anxiety that events to come may not fit their expectations or fulfill their desires. And as any reader of suspense fiction will confirm, the self is not obliterated in the process: it is only humbled by the prospect of an unknowable future, a humility that is itself curiously pleasurable. Thus it is not the torture of self-annihilation but the joy of self-suspension that haunts Victorian knowledge seeking.

Radical doubt, rigorous testing, and narrative pleasure: it is George Eliot who brings the assorted strands together in the single figure of the scientific experiment. In a fragmentary essay called "Storytelling," she compares the interest of narrative suspense to the interest of an experiment in chemistry:

> Indirect ways of arriving at knowledge are always the most stirring even in relation to impersonal subjects. To see a chemical experiment gives an attractiveness to the definition of chemistry, and fills it with a significance which it would never have had without the pleasant shock of an unusual sequence such as the transformation of a solid into gas, or *vice versa*. . . . Curiosity becomes the more eager from the incompleteness of our first information.[32]

To illustrate the absorbing nature of narrative, George Eliot invokes the scientific experiment. And as in Ruskin, what excites our interest is the knowledge that we do not know.

As Eliot makes clear, scientific experimentation provokes a stimulating narrative curiosity: the enforced pause, the stirring up of unsettling doubts, the anticipation of "pleasant shocks," the lurking possibility of surprise. But even more disquieting, the suspense of the experiment also implies a relationship between mind and world that is crucial to a new and skeptical realist epistemology. The scientist imagines a hypothesis about the world and sets it up to be tested against the facts of that world. The world, separate from the experimenter, then gives back its truths. The initial hypothesis imagines a correspondence between the world and our images of it, but then the progress of the experiment demands that we pause, wait, and suspend judgment, all the while compelled to acknowledge that the world may not in fact fit our visions of it. And the pleasure of this pause is, at least in part, an excitement about the fact that the world may defy convention, resist authority, elude familiar representations. Thus we actually come to enjoy the split between world and mind, delighted to imagine that we do not know. Suspenseful narratives teach us to take pleasure in the activity of stopping to doubt our most entrenched beliefs, waiting for the world to reveal its surprises, its full unyielding otherness. The pleasures of suspense are, then, remarkably serious pleasures.[33]

Victorian Realism

At the center of this book is the claim that suspense and realism were inseparable in the context of mid-Victorian England. To be precise, a cluster of British thinkers self-consciously theorized a new aesthetic in the 1850s. They borrowed their model of perception from scientific experimentation, putting their most serious emphasis on testing and the suspension of judgment. They called this project "realism."

In the past half century, French realism has typically been understood as the source and exemplar of all nineteenth-century realisms, with British realism characterized as a latecomer, or imitator, of the French model.[34] French realism has seemed clear and coherent—purposefully launched in the 1850s with debates about Courbet's painting and the emergence of a journal called *Le réalisme*—while British realism has emerged as more inchoate and plural, resisting both a consensual definition and a common canon of examples. For example, George Levine's *Realistic Imagination* describes Mary Shelley and D. H. Lawrence as integral to a realist tradition that valorized the ordinariness of social life over the excesses and monstrosities of romance, while Elizabeth Deeds Ermarth, in her *Realism and Consensus in the English Novel,* casts Defoe,

Richardson, Austen, Eliot, Dickens, and James as representatives of a realism of spatio-temporal coordinates that found its roots as far back as
Descartes. If U. C. Knoepflmacher sees George Eliot's early fiction as
part of a struggle to copy "the circumstances of external life faithfully,"
Fredric Jameson argues that Scott's historical novels represent the "first
great realism" of the British tradition because they are "characterized by
a fundamental heterogeneity in . . . raw materials and by a corresponding
versatility in . . . imaginative apparatus." Harry Shaw has recently invited
us to think of Austen, Scott, and Eliot as realists because of their attention to history. Nancy Armstrong includes the figures of Emily Brontë,
Dickens, Lewis Carroll, and Rider Haggard in her account of a realism
concerned with reproducing visual appearance, and Patrick Brantlinger
reads Trollope and Thackeray as the best representatives of a realism that
relies on money "as the measure of all values." [35]

Was realism one aesthetic or many? Did it describe all theorizations
of mimesis in the nineteenth century—all models of truth or accuracy
in representation? Or was it a single school or style or method? Taken
together, what the critical literature reveals is that practices of representation in nineteenth-century Britain were rich, numerous, sophisticated,
and complex—and cannot easily be reduced to a single clear paradigm.
In this complex context, however, I want to suggest that we can isolate
"realism" as a distinctly new and self-conscious phenomenon. My own
research shows that the term "realism" did not apply to all mimetic en-
deavors in the nineteenth century—or even to all notions of truth in
representation. Victorian uses of the word "realism" referred to a critical aesthetic project that midcentury thinkers worked to formulate and
define explicitly.

I start with a reading of the influential work of John Ruskin, who was
not only one of the first writers to use the term "realism" in English but
also one whose work inspired other early uses of the word. In *Modern
Painters* (1843–60), Ruskin urged the scientific experiment as the most
effective approach to cultural images, inviting his readers to test the representations around them against the reality of their own experience.
The consequence of this method, he argued, was that the most revered
images would show themselves to be disappointingly unreal, exposing
their stylistic conventions and ideological investments. Teaching his readers to test all images and assumptions, Ruskin painstakingly explained

how to mistrust the pictures of the world put forward by tradition. Thus "realism," in its earliest articulation, was a form of cultural critique.

Ruskin's method came as a shock to his readers. As we will see, his contemporaries both bemoaned and celebrated what they described as his unsettlingly novel approach to representation. But today, too, Ruskin's theorization of realism might hold some surprises. If contemporary critics have been inclined to define realism as an epistemological faith in the appearances of things,[36] in Ruskin's work "realism" emerges first and foremost as a skeptical method. Indeed, Ruskin's insistence on experimentation results precisely from the *failures of mimesis:* there would be no need to test hypotheses if knowledge were self-evident and if truth lay in surfaces that could be translated into clear images of the world. Thus the realist call to experimentation arises from the possibility that a given image, or a particular hypothesis, or an established convention *might not fit the world.* The realist experiment is not about putting our faith in representation. It is about putting mimesis to the test.

Adopting the scientific experiment as his paradigm, Ruskin offers the vigilant suspension of judgment as the only fair and appropriate relationship between mind and world. Indeed, it is *Modern Painters* that leads me to propose that Victorian realism required the doubts and anxieties of narrative suspense—and vice versa. When we read the suspenseful form of the nineteenth-century novel through the lenses of Ruskin's aesthetics, the most popular Victorian novels—including *Jane Eyre, Great Expectations,* and *The Moonstone*—show themselves as realist narratives in the Ruskinian sense, urging their readers into the wary suspension of judgment.

Plotting Victorian Realism

In the chapters that follow, I trace the contours of a largely forgotten Victorian idea: the union of a skeptical realist epistemology with a suspenseful narrative form. This book does not aim to offer a historical survey of Victorian representational practices or a general theory of suspense; instead, it proposes what I would characterize as a *historical heuristic.* That is, through readings of a series of historically interconnected texts, I uncover a particular conceptual model. This model is portable: it has the potential to move across genres and disciplines of knowledge and across time and space. But it is also, at least in its beginnings, culturally specific, linked to the discourses and practices of a particular context. In the following chapters, I focus on the complex articulation of this model as it is worked out in a series of highly theoretical Victorian texts. My emphasis on a specific theoretical paradigm will, I hope, have two effects: firstly, it will allow Victorian writers to emerge as serious thinkers whose sophisticated aesthetic, philosophical, ethical, and political reflections have not always been given their due; and secondly, it will permit me to offer a mobile, adaptable interpretive paradigm that can extend well beyond the works I read in the ensuing chapters. Thus although I do not track the many passages of the realist experiment myself, I intend the readings I introduce to provide a heuristic—a model for reading any number of examples.

I use "theory" here in its broadest sense. Since suspense is a narrative problem, much of the most sophisticated thinking about it happens in novels themselves. Indeed, the unorthodox collection of texts amassed in this book—including art criticism, scientific theory, highbrow and popular fiction—emerges from their shared interest in epistemology and, specifically, from their concern with one particular formal model of gathering knowledge. Thus in the chapters that follow, fictional texts appear alongside nonfiction prose to reveal an intensive nineteenth-century engagement with the experimental method and its demand to suspend judgment.

The first two chapters of this book show Ruskin bringing the model of the scientific experiment to the arts. Chapter 1 traces the roots of the English term "realism" to *Modern Painters*. Taking Ruskin as a kind of inaugural theorist of realism, I show how he works to differentiate his model from traditional aesthetics. Crucially, he shifts the aesthetic project away from the creation of harmonious beauty and toward the difficult work of testing representation's claims to truth. Insisting on the active work of experimentation, Ruskin asks us to attend carefully to the otherness of nature in order to free ourselves both from the formulaic, repetitive habits of mind we have inherited from the past and from the growing tyranny of industrial labor. Thus Ruskin's realism leads directly to his socialism, the new society he imagines in *The Stones of Venice*.

Ruskin's rebellious experiments had implications not only for politics but for narrative, providing a careful justification for a new and suspenseful model of knowledge seeking. In chapter 2, we see that Ruskin puts forward two narratives in *Modern Painters,* one cast as unethical and complacent, the other as unsettling and anti-conventional. The pernicious narrative is the story of our experience of trompe l'oeil painting, a kind of mimesis that starts by fooling the eye and ends by unveiling the trick. This is representation that teaches us to enjoy our own sense of mastery, urging us into a smug readerly self-congratulation at having spotted the ruse. By contrast, the plot of experimental science leads to a humble skepticism. We are too easily inclined to trust authoritative and established representations, according to Ruskin, and so we must learn to set images against the world they claim to represent—only to discover, all too often, that the representations fail. Thus the experiment teaches us to stop and doubt, to become relentlessly suspicious of mimesis. If the verisimilitude of trompe l'oeil leads us to enjoy our command of representation and the world, the realist experiment shows us that our knowledge is partial and our representations always disposed to fail.

Chapters 2, 3, and 4 show nineteenth-century novelists putting suspenseful experiments to serious ethical, political, and epistemological ends. In *Jane Eyre,* Charlotte Brontë sets up numerous conventional images of femininity and allows them to collapse in the face of more surprising alternatives thrown up both within the novel and outside the novel's bounds. Jane speculates and tests her conjectures about gender and sexuality repeatedly against the evidence, only to find that the truth lies beyond her conventional guesses. Brontë also invites readers to speculate about the gender of the author of *Jane Eyre,* calling on her audience to test their own assumptions about women's writing. Edgar Allan Poe and Charles Dickens give us characters whose most important ethical and epistemological lesson is that they cannot trust their own desires and prejudices to paint a proper picture of the otherness of the world. Pip's ethical failure lies in his unwillingness to test his presumptions, a failure set against the success of his alter ego, Biddy, the self-denying woman who solves some of the novel's mysteries by suspending judgment. And most explicitly of all, perhaps, Wilkie Collins's characters in *The Moonstone* exonerate the hero by performing a scientific experiment that upsets the most resistant conservatives called to witness it, in a tense and anxious process that is carried over dozens of pages. In all three novels, suspenseful testing calls for a willingness to attend to alterity, to imagine unconventional answers, and to usher in the new. I want to suggest, too,

Suspense here is still a technique for gaining knowledge.

that these texts are not only of interest in themselves: they are defining moments in the launching of the popular nineteenth- and twentieth-century genres of detection and romance, typifying the patterns of modern suspense fiction.

With Ruskin, Brontë, Dickens, and Collins, then, we have what I call the first moment of the realist experiment, when the skeptical patterns of scientific inquiry prompted the suspenseful plots of Victorian realism. But trouble was brewing. In the second moment of the realist experiment, Victorian writers began to turn a wary eye on the experiment and on the apparently happy alliance of suspense and realism.

George Eliot is the first thinker to begin to unravel the claims of suspense. First, she worries about the consequences of suspenseful realism for the feminine subject. The experiment demands a suspension of personal inclination and desire, which, as George Levine suggests, might be tantamount to self-annihilation. And if this self-annihilation is held up as a cultural ideal for women in particular, then perhaps suspense exercises a kind of repressive political power of its own. In *Adam Bede,* Eliot asks whether the model of self-suspension reinforces the conservative image of the feminine angel in the house, the figure who always acts ethically because she never allows herself to impose her own desires on the other. According to this paradigm, women are seen as better readers of the otherness of the world only because they know how to deny their preferences and suppress their inclinations. Eliot questions both suspenseful plotting and feminine self-denial and mobilizes, in their place, her own redefinition of realism, which calls for a return of the feminine self and for a balanced, mutual recognition of self and other. In *The Lifted Veil,* published immediately after *Adam Bede,* Eliot then takes on the ethics of Ruskinian realism, suggesting that suspense does not necessarily lead to an anti-conventional appreciation of alterity. And in *Romola* she shows that suspenseful narrative fails in its claims to a knowledge of otherness: it simply cannot bring us to know the alterity of the world. On political, ethical, and epistemological grounds, the realist experiment begins to lose its radical force.

But Eliot's critique of Ruskin also closes down some of realism's disruptive potential. By focusing attention on the consequences of the realist experiment specifically for desiring female subjects, Eliot takes up the cause of individual self-assertion and equality and abandons the pleasures of suspended judgment. Thus *Adam Bede* closes not with the longing for new social relationships but with the creation of a capitalist and strictly gendered heterosexual family. Disenchanted with suspense, Eliot then shifts the focus of realist narrative away from its role as a skeptical method for approaching alterity. By the time she writes *Romola,* she has come to frame narrative not as the process by which we learn to come to know the otherness of the world but as itself a mimetic image of reality. With George Eliot, then, comes the beginning of a new critique of suspenseful realism—the critique that knows realism not as a skeptical, experimental practice but as a failed attempt to replicate the world's truths.

The third moment of the realist experiment builds on Eliot's skepticism about suspense, as writers grew increasingly interested in the rhetorical construction of plotted narrative. Henry James's experimental short story "Travelling Companions" was written as a direct and critical response to Ruskin. The story sets two kinds of plots in motion in the same text: the first is the suspenseful plot of desire—the love story—and the second is the itinerant time of the tourist, moving from site to site according to the recommendations of a guidebook. James suggests that the tourist plot, with its episodic arbitrariness, reflects the experience of actual travelers and is therefore a more accurate mimetic image of the ways that experience unfolds over time than its suspenseful other. And in this mimetic context, suspenseful narrative looks manipulative and controlling. James, using the guidebook to structure his hero's experience, critiques the artful and contrived character of realism's plotted mysteries.

In "Travelling Companions," James also extends Eliot's critique of the implicit politics of Ruskin's realist epistemology. His story suggests that all consensus among tourists about the substance of Italy comes not from the alterity of the real but from a collective experience and identity that is carefully constructed—managed and directed—by the representations of the guidebook, and it is an experience that is guided by clear political interests and identities. With James, our access to the real is shown to be inevitably mediated by the texts of culture. Thus we can no longer separate convention from tested truth. And if we cannot test representations and hypotheses against the real on the grounds of truth or falsehood, James urges us to ask, instead, how representations shape our experience and arrange our world for understanding. In the Jamesian narrative, we are invited not to cast off convention but rather to recognize the value-laden grounds and consequences of our inevitably conventional ways of knowing the world.

Walter Pater and Oscar Wilde push the nineteenth-century critique of realism to its final stage by taking apart the ways that the narrative of the experiment constructs the world for consciousness. In *The Renaissance,* Pater's essays never privilege the alterity of the real as the stable site of meaning and value but suggest, instead, that the real is understood only in light of its representations, while representations take on their meaning only in light of the real. Thus Pater moves us back and forth between image and reality, but he does not focus our attention on the outcome of the comparison; instead, he urges us to attend to the gap itself between representation and the world. Pater's work comes surprisingly close to the plotted skepticism of Ruskinian realism but crucially transfers our interest to the middle of the story—shifting from the promise of knowledge to the breaks crucial to the rhetorical production of understanding. Following in Pater's footsteps, Oscar Wilde then inverts the relations between hypothesis and evidence, revealing that each is defined against its opposite. In *The Picture of Dorian Gray,* he blithely turns the realist experiment on its head, switching the conventional roles of suspended stillness and narrative motion to draw attention to the artifices of narrative representation.

Stretching from Ruskin to Wilde, the story that unfolds here suggests that a self-conscious British realism never attempted to replicate the world: it involved neither a struggle for a transparent mimesis nor an attempt at unqualified referentiality. The realists worked, first, to gesture to the radical otherness of the world, and they did so by pointing to the failures of representation. But this effort to acknowledge alterity slowly yielded to a sense of the impossibility of getting at an otherness outside of the languages of representation—and the realist experiment turned inward, to investigate its own rhetorical practices. Although at first glance this narrative might seem like a movement from reference to self-reference, the shift is, I think, slighter and subtler than that. Ruskin's realism was itself a reflexive project, emerging from an awareness of the limits of mimesis, appearance, and belief and interrogating both the artifices and the materiality of representation—attempting always to mark both the possibilities and the constraints involved in knowledge.

Thus, although Ruskin labored to find a reliable epistemological method, and Wilde flaunted the artfulness of art, these writers shared a theoretical paradigm. Tracing an arc that extended from *Modern Painters* to *Dorian Gray,* from a socialist epistemology to a celebration of narrative self-reflexivity, the realist experiment concentrated a set of skeptical Victorian concerns about representation, convention, and knowledge. Linking philosophy to painting and science to fiction, the experimental method established suspense as a defining strategy of nineteenth-century knowledge gathering. And as Victorian texts, both high and low, dispersed the model of the experiment—working and reworking it, unraveling it, condemning it, and even putting it to the test—suspense emerged as an essential critical instrument of nineteenth-century intellectual culture.

PART I

Ruskin and the
Suspension of Judgment

Ruskin's Radical Realism

Critics have been complaining about Ruskin's inconsistencies since his work first began to appear. In 1856, Elizabeth Rigby wrote contemptuously of Ruskin's "crotchety contradictions and peevish paradoxes." Marshall Mather lamented in 1897 that the critic's "so-called inconsistencies roused the laughter and sneer of superficial readers." By 1933, R. H. Wilenski simply affirmed that "Ruskin's art criticism . . . is an appalling muddle." And in our own time, scholars as various as John Rosenberg, Elizabeth Helsinger, and Gary Wihl have pointed not so much to the connections as to the shifts, gaps, and breaks that interrupt the succession of Ruskin's first nine major volumes—*Modern Painters, The Seven Lamps of Architecture,* and *The Stones of Venice.*[1]

But it is worth noticing, surely, that Ruskin's first massive works on art are all interwoven, picking up recurrent themes, cross-referencing one another, and even intersecting chronologically. He wrote the first two volumes of *Modern Painters,* stopped to write the *Seven Lamps,* which, it turned out, was a brief version of the three volumes of *The Stones of Venice,* which then followed; and then, curiously, he returned to *Modern Painters,* to write three more volumes of it, all before 1860. And far from framing the later texts of *Modern Painters* as a new and separate project from the earlier volumes, Ruskin carefully invites readers to see the whole work as a single venture, interrupted by a long delay. In the preface to the final volume, he insists on his thoroughgoing consistency: "In the main aim and principle of the book, there is no variation from its first syllable to its last" (*Works* 7: 9). And at the beginning of the third volume, he asks us to try to make sense of the whole: "In taking up the clue of an inquiry, now intermitted for nearly ten years, it may be well to do as a traveller would, who had to recommence an interrupted journey in a guideless country; and, ascending, as it were, some little hill beside our road, note how far we have already advanced, and what pleasantest ways we may choose for farther progress" (5: 17). If it seems as if we have been without a guide and have lost our way in the confusing landscape of *The Seven Lamps of Architecture* and *The Stones of Venice,* Ruskin assures us that we may discover where we have been and where we are bound—simply by looking around us at the lay of the critical land. We should be able to trace the "progress" we have made from *Modern Painters* 1, through *The Stones of Venice,* even so far as to foresee the substance of the later volumes of *Modern Painters.* If Ruskin is reassuringly there to offer us some helpful hints in the third volume, so much the better, but the implication is that we are capable of making sense of the route all by ourselves.

Taking a cue from the sage Ruskin, we might try to make sense of the journey. It is my contention that it is indeed fruitful to read *The Stones of Venice* as flanked on both sides by the five volumes of *Modern Painters* and to take seriously the fact that within the texts themselves Ruskin works to integrate, rather than to separate, the two projects. It is true that the crucial concerns of the two texts look remarkably different on first reading. If *The Stones of Venice* is best remembered for its emphasis on humanizing labor, *Modern Painters* teaches us how to look at nature and evaluate landscape painting. *Stones* is politically radical and sensitive to the forces of historical change, while *Modern Painters* is apparently concerned with the more transcendent—and perhaps more dubious—categories of nature, truth, and representation. *Stones* had a lasting impact on nineteenth-century socialist thought; *Modern Painters* participated in a Victorian discussion of realism. Despite these apparently contradictory concerns, however, the works insistently cite one another. Indeed, as if his readers had unrestrained access to all of his works and could look easily from one to another, Ruskin refers to volumes from different works as integral parts of his argument and refuses to relegate such references to the footnotes.[2] *Modern Painters* is woven into the text of *The Stones of Venice,* just as *Stones* makes numerous appearances in the final volumes of its painterly counterpart.[3]

This chapter begins by investigating Ruskin's groundbreaking use of the word "realism" in *Modern Painters*. It then turns to the political vision Ruskin articulated in *The Stones of Venice*. Setting the two in dialogue, it uncovers vital links between the realism defined in *Modern Painters* and the socialism of *The Stones of Venice*. I want to make the case here that the close intertwining of Ruskin's iconoclastic aesthetics with his radical political principles should challenge us to rethink the politics of Victorian realism more generally.

Ruskinian Realism

Critics have typically characterized nineteenth-century realism as a mediating aesthetic—as an attempt to bridge the gap between self and world. Lukacs championed bourgeois realism as literature that represented the contradictory relations between individuals and their social and historical environment.[4] Later scholars of realism have followed Lukacs in attending to realism's mediating role, but they have seen the images themselves as the mediating forces—working to bring the reader into contact with the world. George Levine, John P. McGowan, Katherine Kearns, and Tom Lloyd all characterize Victorian realism as the attempt to use language to get at a reality beyond language—whether to a prior, unmediated experience of the world or to materiality itself.[5]

Nancy Armstrong points to a paradox in this model:

> To mediate, according to the epistemology of realism, fiction has to record the interaction between the individual and his or her social-historical milieu without significantly modifying either one. The logic of the photograph reveals the paradox informing this assumption. It suggests that the immediacy of certain experiences in fiction is a function of mediation: the obtrusive and pervasive substitution of visual forms of objectification for things and people themselves.[6]

To gain immediate access to the real, we rely on particular forms of mediation—forms that must seem to erase themselves in the very moment of their mediating activity. The purpose of the representation's appearance is, it would seem, to disappear. And since the realist mediating apparatus never does dissolve, realist art has more often than not been deemed a failure. Thus Elena Russo argues that critics have given up on realism because they have been disappointed in the failures of the "union mistica," the perfect correspondence between language and the real: "to know is to know directly and without mediation; this is not possible; therefore, the world is unknowable."[7]

But what this postmodern paradox overlooks is the keen Victorian interest in the practice itself of mediation. Knowing full well that representation and the world were at odds, nineteenth-century theorists of realism nonetheless wanted to articulate a *process* by which they might judiciously and respectfully approach the realities of the world. As George Eliot wrote to the painter Frederic Leighton: "Approximate truth is the only truth attainable, but at least one must strive for that, and not wade into arbitrary falsehood."[8] Victorian writers claimed social and ethical value for the work of creating the representation—valuing not so much mimetic immediacy as the very activity of mediation. Thus Victorian realism's own theorists focused less on the verisimilitude of the product than on the *labor* that went into its making. George Eliot's famous formulation of realism in *Adam Bede* stresses the hard work of truthful representation: "Falsehood is so easy, truth so difficult. The pencil is conscious of a delightful facility in drawing a griffin—the longer the claws, and the larger the wings, the better; but that marvellous facility which we mistook for genius is apt to forsake us when we want to draw a real unexaggerated lion." In the opening paragraphs of *Shirley,* Charlotte Brontë addresses us as if reading realist fiction were like everyday labor: "Something real, cool, and solid lies before you; something unromantic as Monday morning, when all who have work wake with the consciousness that they must rise and betake themselves thereto." And as G. H. Lewes explained in his *Principles of Success in Literature* in 1865: "when you write in your own person you must be rigidly veracious. . . . This vigilance may render Literature more laborious; but no one ever supposed that success was to be had on easy terms."[9]

It was Ruskin, of all the Victorian theorists, who was most insistent that seeing and representing the world demanded serious and significant work. "Two lines are laid on canvas; one is right and another wrong. . . . One person feels it,—another does not; but the feeling or sight of the one can by no words be communicated to the other: it would be unjust if it could, for that feeling and sight have been the reward of years of labor" (*Works* 3: 609–10). Here, even feeling and sight—faculties that we might think of as spontaneous, natural, unmediated—are the fruits of long and arduous work.[10] In the first volume of *Modern Painters,* Ruskin urges young artists, whom he always calls "workmen," never to avoid difficult labor: "Their work should be full of failures; for these are the signs of efforts" (623).[11] To see and represent the reality of the natural world calls for self-denial, rigorous discipline, "necessary labour." Ruskinian realism, in other words, is a *laboring aesthetic.*

Surprisingly, Ruskin's importance to British realism has not attracted much critical attention. A look at the 1850s suggests that the very beginnings of Victorian realism are closely associated with *Modern Painters.* The very first uses of the word are connected with Ruskin's writing in the 1840s and 1850s.[12] In 1856, when George Eliot reviewed the third volume of *Modern Painters,* she pointedly emphasized her use of the new aesthetic term: "The truth of infinite value that [Ruskin] teaches is *realism*—the doctrine that all truth and beauty are to be attained by a humble and faithful study of nature, and not by substituting vague forms, bred by imagination on the mists of feeling, in the place of definite, substantial reality."[13] In this early use of the word "realism," Eliot conspicuously calls for "humble and faithful *study*"—not for a style or effect of mimesis, but for the laborious act of attending to the world.

If Ruskin's role in the formulation of "realism" has rarely been acknowledged, the kind of realism he defines has likewise failed to attract serious critical notice. His is a realism that calls not for a particular kind of content or mode of representation, but for a new understanding of the active, complex work required to get at the visual truths of the world.[14] This struggle is arduous, Ruskin explains, because Victorian life is saturated with deceptive images that have corrupted the culture's capacity to see. He writes:

> How many people are misled, by what has been said and sung of the serenity of Italian skies, to suppose they must be more *blue* than the skies of the north, and think that they see them so. . . . When people see in a painting what they suppose to have been their impressions, they will affirm it to be truthful, though they

feel no such impression resulting from it. Thus, though day after day they may have been impressed by the tone and warmth
of an Italian sky, yet not having traced the feeling to its source
and supposing themselves to be impressed by its *blueness,* they
will affirm a blue sky in a painting to be truthful, and reject the
most faithful rendering of all the real attributes of Italy as cold
or dull. (*Works* 3: 144)

The inherited conventions of representation lull us into complacency,
blinding us to the actual appearance of the world. Ruskin insists that we
must learn to push past the formulas of culture. But the power of pre-
existing images and judgments is so strong that we cannot perceive the
world unless we labor to throw off our preconceptions: "We are . . . constantly missing the sight of what we do not know beforehand to be visible; and painters, to the last hour of their lives, are apt to fall in some
degree into the error of painting what [they assume] exists, rather than
what they can see" (145). And so Ruskin argues that we must *experiment*—relentlessly putting images and expectations to the test, setting
them against the world to see where they correspond and where they fail.
The labor of realism involves learning to resist the weight of authority
and tradition by carrying out a rigorous set of tests.

To give just one example—among literally hundreds in *Modern
Painters*—Ruskin instructs us to undertake the following experiment:

> Take any important group of trees, I do not care whose—
> Claude's, Salvator's, or Poussin's—with lateral light. . . . Can it
> be seriously supposed that those murky browns and melancholy
> greens are representative of the tints of leaves under full noon-
> day sun? I know that you cannot help looking upon all these pic-
> tures as pieces of dark relief against a light wholly proceeding
> from the distances; but they are nothing of the kind, they are
> noon and morning effects with full lateral light. Be so kind as to
> match the colour of a leaf in the sun (the darkest you like) as
> nearly as you can, and bring your matched colour and set it be-
> side one of these groups of trees, and take a blade of common
> grass, and set it beside any part of the fullest light of their fore-
> grounds, and then talk about the truth of colour of the old mas-
> ters! (*Works* 3: 283)

Comparing the representation to the leaf it represents, we are invited to perceive the extent of the difference. If we protest that Claude wanted to paint a dark environment, Ruskin explains that the picture is internally contradictory: misleading either in its use of color or in its placement of the sun. Confronted with the discrepancy between the real and its images, we are urged to throw off our passive faith in the Old Masters in favor of a radical skepticism, ready, thanks to the experiment, to test the most orthodox of representations.

We will turn to the forms and aims of Ruskin's experiments again in the next chapter, but for now it is important to note that his refusal to accept traditional aesthetic authority came as a shock to Victorian readers. *The Churchman* was surprised at Ruskin's willingness to overturn conventional assumptions: "it is no common mind that can soar above the mists and delusions of traditionary prejudice." A review in *Blackwood's* had it that the young writer "has not the slightest respect for the accumulated opinions of the best judges for these two or three hundred years." The *Athenaeum* bewailed his "heterodox criticism," while the radical Walt Whitman praised Ruskin's work for its "fresh ideas," and Elizabeth Rigby was provoked by the "strange and new doctrines" set forth in *Modern Painters*. As early as 1846, *Fraser's* was calling *Modern Painters* "perhaps the most remarkable book which has ever been published in reference to art." [15]

If Ruskin's new method of judging artistic representation was heterodox, it was also widely read. The censorious Rigby was none too pleased by "Mr. Ruskin's popularity," accounting for it as the fashionable devotion to the new. [16] But it was no passing fad. Thirty years later, *Modern Painters* seemed to have ushered in an influential revolution in the history of aesthetics. In 1874, J. J. Jarves looked back on its publication as a world-shattering moment: "there suddenly appeared on the aesthetic horizon a youthful critic of remarkable flow of language, startling novelty of ideas . . . who, at one assault, firmly established himself in the field of Art as a radical iconoclast. Old reputations were shivered at a blow, new ones made in a breath, time-honoured systems overturned at the first bout." [17]

But what was it, exactly, that made Ruskin's realism so unsettlingly new? Clearly, the revolutionary novelty of *Modern Painters* did not lie in its call for truth in art, since aestheticians for centuries had been calling for some version of aesthetic truth. Nor did it lie in Ruskin's dedication to nature, since some degree of fidelity to the natural world was a mainstay of landscape theory. It was not truth or accuracy per se that made Ruskin's theory of art revolutionary. Rather, I want to suggest that Ruskin's novelty lay precisely in his insistence on the testing of representation.

There was no need for experimentation in eighteenth- and early-nineteenth-century aesthetics, which emphasized the general or "ideal" truths located in the mind rather than the world. An influential example can be found in Joshua Reynolds's *Discourses on Art* (1778), a text so authoritative, according to one of Ruskin's contemporaries, that artists were unwilling to entertain alternatives to Reynolds's ideas forty years after its publication.[18] For Reynolds, nature encompasses both the seeing subject and the world. "My notion of nature comprehends not only the forms which nature produces, but also the nature and internal fabrick and organization, as I may call it, of the human mind and imagination." In this paradigm, the forms of the world actually match the forms of the mind, and human consciousness and the valuable truths of external objects exist in perfect harmony: "Whatever pleases has in it what is analogous to the mind, and is therefore, in the highest and best sense of the word, natural." Indeed, at one point, Reynolds broadens his definition of truth so far that it comes to include all harmonious relations and correspondences: "The natural appetite or taste of the human mind is for *Truth;* whether that truth results from the real agreement or equality of original ideas among themselves; from the agreement of the representation of any object with the thing represented; or from the correspondence of the several parts of any arrangement with each other." Truth aims at the perfect fit—at composition, calibration, or conformity, at internal balance and satisfying correspondence. When it comes to mimesis, we take pleasure in seeing representation correspond with the world, and when we feel such satisfaction, we call it "truth." Thus harmony is itself truth, and humankind has a "taste" for harmonies that are not limited to mimesis alone but take various aesthetic shapes: "It is the very same taste which relishes a demonstration in geometry, that is pleased with the resemblance of a picture to an original, and touched with the harmony of musick."[19] Strongly favoring harmonious correspondences over the "deformities" of actual natural objects, Reynolds sees a set of idealized forms as the truths suitable for art.[20]

Kant's *Critique of Judgment* suggests a rather different context for Ruskinian realism. While radically unlike Reynolds in aim and method, Kant does assume that the appreciation of harmonious relations is always already in the mind and is not a recognition that needs to be learned or verified. Kantian "beauty" is not so much a relation between world and mind, as it is the apprehension of form, which excites all minds to the same agreeable sensations; beauty is therefore both subjective, in that it happens within the subject, and objectively universal, in that it is shared by all: "The excitement of both faculties (imagination and understanding) to indeterminate but yet, through the stimulus of the given sensation, harmonious activity, viz. that which belongs to cognition in general, is the sensation whose universal communicability is postulated by the judgment of taste."[21] There is no struggle here, no negotiation: the presence of a beautiful object spontaneously stimulates imagination and understanding into harmonious activity.

In the generations that lead up to Ruskin, in other words, the artist is urged to achieve a harmony, whether between the ideas of the mind and idealities of the world, as in Reynolds, or between faculties of the mind, as in Kant. This harmony is understood as the aim of truthful art. To be sure, the category of the sublime—so important in the eighteenth and early nineteenth centuries—is all about rupturing harmonies, but it is explicitly separated from discussions of representational "truth."[22] When it comes to truth in art, Ruskin offers us something radically new. In *Modern Painters,* we are so far from immediately apprehending the truths of the world that we cannot even see them when they are before our eyes, unless we labor to cast off the authoritative and misleading images we have inherited. Thus the arduous goal of the artist in *Modern Painters* is not to communicate general or ideal shapes but to recognize the overwhelming and *unfamiliar* particularity of the world.[23] In attending to the real, the viewer must learn to counteract conventional habits of mind, seeking out the minute truths that are in fact initially obscure to us, corrupted as we are by the deceitful surfaces of painting. Ruskin's "real" is radically *other* to the human mind, understood after self-denial rather than inner peace, grasped by strenuous, time-consuming labor rather than by immediate satisfaction.

If the mind in its immediacy can be fooled by falsehood, then there must be a radical disjuncture between mind and world. Indeed, it is my contention that Victorian realism begins with the premise that the truth is not self-evident. G. H. Lewes points to the inevitability of disputes over questions of truth and falsehood in representation:

> You may have a lively sense of the unreality with which a writer has conceived a character, or presented a situation, but it is by no means easy to make him see this, or make his admirers see it. In vain would you refer to certain details as inaccurate; he cannot recognise their inaccuracy. In vain would you point to the general air of unreality, the conventional tone of the language, the absence of those subtle, individual traits which give verisimilitude to a conception; he cannot see it; to him the conception does seem lifelike; he may perhaps assure you that it is taken from the life.[24]

As in Reynolds's *Discourses,* realist theory concerns the problem of correspondence—correspondence between mind and world and between reality and mimesis—but for Ruskin and his contemporaries, the world never simply reveals its consonance with the mind. And since mind and world are separate and incongruent, the work of mediation becomes absolutely crucial.

The surprise of Ruskinian realism, then, is its emphasis not on the visual accuracy of the painted image but on the experimental activity of both reader and artist when confronted with that image. Refusing to take any representation on faith, realism calls for a critical, mediating approach to the unfamiliar alterity of the world. Refusing to rest easy with the harmonious correspondences of conventional beauty, realism demands the difficult labor of experimentation. And Ruskin's insistence on testing points to the skeptical epistemology at the foundation of his new aesthetics: testing assumes a distance between mind and world and offers a complex process for contending with the distance that divides them. After all, the experiment is required only when the real is not immediately manifest. Thus Ruskin's realism might best be defined as the arduous method by which we struggle to apprehend the hidden truths of the world.

Ruskinian Socialism

If Ruskin insisted on the laborious effort of testing for both artists and viewers in *Modern Painters,* labor itself became his overwhelming concern in *The Stones of Venice.* It is true that Ruskin studiously avoided the use of the word "socialism" to describe his own political program and repudiated the socialists altogether in a footnote to "Unto This Last," first published in 1860 (*Works* 17: 107 n). Yet the importance of Ruskin's text to socialists such as F. J. Furnivall and William Morris and their followers suggests that its emphasis on a radical alternative to factory labor played a crucial role in the socialist aesthetics of the nineteenth century, whatever Ruskin's claims to the contrary.[25] In "How I Became a Socialist," Morris wrote: "It was through [Ruskin] that I learned to give form to my discontent."[26] One of Morris's disciples, John Bruce Glasier, later chairman of the Independent Labour Party, named Ruskin as one of the writers whose work was giving "fitful expression" to nascent socialist thought midcentury.[27] And a well-known 1906 report suggests that Ruskin was one of the most influential voices for radical politics at the turn of the century: a survey of the first large group of Labour Members of Parliament asked the fifty-one new members to name the authors who had most powerfully affected them. Seventeen of these named Ruskin—more than any other single author.[28]

Despite Ruskin's refusal of the title of socialism, then, his "discontent" with the condition and freedom of workers was seized, used, and disseminated by Victorian friends of socialism. In particular, the famous middle chapter of *The Stones of Venice,* called "The Nature of Gothic," circulated as a pamphlet for working-class readers.[29] It is Ruskin's call for a society based on free, creative labor—a resistance to the stupefying, dehumanizing redundancy of industrial work. The most deliberate target of attack is mechanical repetition. The modern demand for factory-perfect precision, Ruskin argues, means an enslavement of the worker because it makes "him" into nothing more than a machine, replicating patterns prescribed for him by others and prevented from using his own mind.[30] "Let [the worker] but begin to imagine, to think, to try to do anything worth doing; and the engine-turned precision is lost at once" (*Works* 10: 192). Mechanical duplication and perfection cancel out all possibility of thought. And if European societies continue to block laborers from enjoying thoughtful, imaginative work, then, according to Ruskin, will come the frustrated violence of revolution—and it will be an undialectical social upheaval that will ultimately lead nowhere: "It is verily the degradation of the operative into a machine, which, more than any other evil of the times, is leading the mass of nations everywhere into vain, incoherent, destructive struggling for a freedom of which they cannot explain the nature to themselves" (194). The more constructive solution to the violent degradation of mechanical slavery would be to introduce freedom of thought into the work of every laborer.

Architecture is typically the index of a whole culture for Ruskin, and he warns us not to mock the "ugly goblins and formless monsters, and stern statues" on Gothic cathedrals, "for they are signs of the life and liberty of every workman who struck the stone" (*Works* 10: 193–94). Ugliness, formlessness, and sternness: these are rough, eccentric qualities, if we take conventional aesthetics as our guide, but for Ruskin they are the proper antidote to the endless duplication of perfect, machine-made form. He sets the playful variation and rough vitality of Gothic art against the deadening repetition of the machine as the model of healthy work. The Gothic worker had the freedom to create objects that were the emerging, irregular, variegated products of his own thought. This freedom, Ruskin explains, is crucial to any just and strong society: "it is only by labor that thought can be made healthy, and only by thought that labor can be made happy" (201). With Gothic art, we find the ideal type of human work: it unites mind and body, intellectual and manual labor, individual freedom and the needs of the community.

This account of *Stones* will probably sound familiar, but according to the chronology of Ruskin's work, his attack on industrial labor in *The Stones of Venice* was both preceded *and* followed by his commitment to a laborious realism. This means that if we can articulate a clear link between the two projects, then Ruskin's influential realism will emerge as a revolutionary aesthetic. Indeed, given Ruskin's known influence on writers as crucial to conventional assessments of nineteenth-century realism as George Eliot, Charlotte Brontë, Henry James, and even Proust, the connections among Ruskin's volumes may recast Victorian realism as an altogether revolutionary project.[31]

Radical Realism

What do the ugly goblins and formless monsters of Gothic architecture have to do with "realism"? More, it seems to me, than we might at first imagine. In "The Nature of Gothic," Ruskin's political call for freedom comes intertwined with an extended discussion of what he calls "naturalism."[32] For example, the Gothic builder inherited conventionalized images of leaves and flowers from his predecessors but "saw there was no veracity in them, no knowledge, no vitality. Do what he would, he could not help liking the true leaves better; and cautiously, a little at a time, he put more of nature into his work, until at last it was all true" (*Works* 10: 232). The Gothic artist might be politically and intellectually free, but he was *also* committed to the truths of the natural world. So committed was he, in fact, that he began to ignore the other elements of his work, to celebrate his love of nature at the expense of other aesthetic demands.[33]

Of the six moral elements of Gothic (savageness, changefulness, naturalism, grotesqueness, rigidity, and redundance), Ruskin gives more attention to naturalism than to any of the others.[34] Recent criticism has resisted this fact of Ruskin's writing, overlooking his insistence on representational fidelity to nature in *Stones*. In a 1985 edition of *Unto This Last, and Other Essays,* editor Clive Wilmer calls Ruskin's discussion of naturalism in "The Nature of Gothic" a "digression": "much of it interesting but of more relevance to the argument of *Modern Painters* than to that of the book in hand."[35] Wilmer sees the shift to nature as out of place, having little to do with the central political problems of *Stones*. He simply cuts it out. But this is to miss the crucial union of socialism and realism. An emphasis on the truth of the natural world as a model for architecture runs throughout *The Stones of Venice,* finding its way into practically every chapter. And even the title of "The Nature of Gothic" hints at the crucial importance of natural life: it points us, after all, to the *nature* of Gothic.

In *The Stones of Venice,* truth to nature comes intertwined with the politics of humanizing work. Indeed, it appears that the artist's struggle to represent nature is the *same* as the free labor of thought. So: what is the link between representations of nature and liberating work?

We can frame an answer by turning back to *Modern Painters*. It was his fierce anti-conventionalism that most upset Ruskin's contemporaries, who saw *Modern Painters* as a radical attack on tradition. But there is more to Ruskin's realism than the rejection of the past. He repudiates traditional images not only because they are false and conventional, but because they fail to celebrate one particular fact, one truth, that nature offers. That fact is nature's boundless diversity. ✓

Throughout the five volumes of *Modern Painters* we encounter Ruskin's determined insistence on the infinite variety of the natural world. Of all of the unconventional aspects of nature, it is its endless variation that is hardest and most important for us to see: "there is a continual mystery caused throughout *all* spaces, caused by the absolute infinity of things" (*Works* 6: 75). When we perform our experiments, it is the infinite variety of the natural world that we always find at the end of our careful tests. Ruskin tells us over and over again in *Modern Painters* that this variety is the essential and unfamiliar truth that painters must labor to portray. Infinity even becomes the sine qua non of Ruskinian realism: "if we wish, without reference to beauty of composition, or any other interfering circumstances, to form a judgment of the truth of painting, perhaps the very first thing we should look for, whether in one thing or another—foliage, or clouds, or waves,—should be the expression of *infinity* always and everywhere, in all parts and divisions of parts" (*Works* 3: 387).

If the gap between world and mind is the crucial hallmark of Victorian realism, what makes the world *other* for Ruskin is its infinite variety. The "deep infinity of the thing itself" is what "separates" us from nature (*Works* 6: 103). In this context, it becomes clear why we have to labor to see nature. Traditional representations, with their emphasis on types, are hopelessly mechanical, doomed to reproduce formulas and patterns:

> Claude has given you the walls below in one dead void of uniform grey. There is nothing to be seen, or felt, or guessed at in it; it is grey paint or grey shade, whichever you may choose to call it, but it is nothing more. Nature would have let you see, nay, would have compelled you to see, thousands of spots and lines, not one to be absolutely understood or accounted for, but yet all characteristic and different from each other. . . . none, indeed, seen as such, none comprehensible or like themselves, but all visible; little shadows and sparkles, and scratches, making that whole space of colour a transparent, palpitating, various infinity. (*Works* 3: 331–32)

Claude's uniformity is false and "dead" by contrast to nature's extraordinary complexity and diversity—a variety here so overwhelming that it amounts even to unintelligibility. We take Claude's paintings as true and realistic because we are so accustomed to repetitive uniformity in painting that we do not recognize the infinite variety of the "real." Consequently, Ruskin demands that we go outside to look and test for ourselves. What we will see there, according to Ruskin, is "the old story over and over again—infinity" (454).

Only nature can offer us the experience of infinite variety. Indeed, Ruskin goes so far as to suggest that deadening, unnatural repetition is actually the fundamental quality of the human mind:

> it is impossible for mortal mind to compose an infinity of any kind for itself, or to form an idea of perpetual variation, and to avoid all repetition, merely by its own combining resources. The moment that we trust to ourselves, we repeat ourselves, and therefore the moment that we see in a work of any kind whatsoever the expression of infinity, we may be certain that the workman has gone to nature for it; while, on the other hand, the moment we see repetition, or want of infinity, we may be certain that the workman has *not* gone to nature for it. (*Works* 3: 387)

To put it simply, we have the infinite variety of nature on the one hand and the repetitive patterns of the human mind on the other. Indeed, our dangerous cultural inheritance is a set of repetitive conventions so deep that the human mind, when left to its own devices, opts for repetition rather than variety. Thus the *only* way to resist this repetition, according to Ruskin, is to go to nature.

At this point, we can return to the concerns of the *Stones of Venice,* with its insistence on the varied, irregular, free labor of thought in place of the slavish repetitions of mechanical labor. Ruskin seems to be telling us in *Modern Painters* that the *human mind itself is precisely like the machine:* it opts for redundant, mechanical patterns, just like the dehumanizing industry of the *Stones of Venice.*

If we bring together the logic of the two texts we find what might seem, at first, to be a paradox: in the "Nature of Gothic," thought is liberating and humanizing when compared to the machine, while in *Modern Painters,* mechanical repetition is the basic tendency of the human mind. In the socialist text, infinite variety is the proof of human thought, while in the realist text, infinity is a sign that the workman has suppressed his own inclinations and has been faithful to nature.

But I would like to suggest that these two texts are not contradictory. Ruskin says that variety is proof of human thought and that repetition marks the absence of thought, while he also argues that repetition is the natural inclination of the human mind. In other words, *thought is not our natural inclination*. We will fall into habits of repetition when left to ourselves, but this is not thinking. Thinking we do only when we suppress our own inclinations and attend carefully to the otherness of the world. Our tendency is to passivity, compliance, submissiveness to the repetitive machine, while thought disrupts these established patterns. Thought itself is alien to the human mind, and so it comes only with effort. We learn it, laboriously, by turning to that which is *not ourselves*—to nature. Thus the "real" of Ruskinian realism leads us to practice the anticonventional act of thinking, an act that both represents and fosters a resistance to the repetitions of the machine. Simply to see the truths of nature demands the laborious act of setting aside our habits of mind—centuries of received opinion, repetitive custom, and cultural passivity—in order to practice thinking, which leads us to active skepticism, infinite irregularity, and revolutionary freedom.

Always prone to the perilous descent into deathly convention, the human mind must counteract its own inclinations by a strict focus on the otherness of the natural world: "nature is so immeasurably superior to all that the human mind can conceive, that every departure from her is a fall beneath her" (*Works* 3: 137). The mind needs the real in order to think. And it is clear in *The Stones of Venice* that thought frees us to resist the duplication of the machine.[36] Or to put this another way, nature teaches us to resist industrial society. In the end, then, Ruskin's new "realism"— a careful, laborious attention to nature's infinite variety—is capable of triggering a social revolution.

2   Ruskin's Plots

Modern Painters and *The Moonstone*

By the 1840s, British writers had been quarreling for decades over the value of a national art gallery. Those in favor of a public collection argued that it would raise the standard of British art: the "Old Masters" would inspire and teach young artists. In 1836, John Eagles suggested an annual competition between the Old Masters and young British artists, since "The hope of a proud eminence would be a spur to very great efforts."[1] On the other side, William Hazlitt staunchly opposed a national gallery, claiming that the arts had declined in all countries that celebrated the art of the past. The academic study of art bred pedantry and unnecessary erudition, and it distracted artists from nature—which for Hazlitt was the only proper model for artists. Inferior painters like Carlo Maratti and Raphael Mengs, Hazlitt insisted, tried to "blend borrowed beauties." Great painters like Correggio perfected their craft only by looking at the world of nature.[2]

Into this long dispute entered the young Ruskin, with his bold and polemical *Modern Painters*. Ruskin opens this sprawling work with an argument for the superiority of modern British artists over the Old Masters and insists on the supreme value of nature as the model for all art. The perils of learning from painting loom in the very first pages of the first volume: "In no city of Europe where art is a subject of attention, are its prospects so hopeless, or its pursuits so resultless, as in Rome; because there, among all students, the authority of their predecessors in art is supreme and without appeal, and the mindless copyist studies Raffaelle, but not what Raffaelle studied" (*Works* 3: 83).

At first glance, Ruskin would seem to belong to Hazlitt's camp, on the side of those condemning studies of the "ancient masters" and praising the moderns for pursuing the truths of nature. But unexpectedly, Ruskin did not oppose a national collection of art. In a letter to the *Times* in 1847, Ruskin complained about the poor restoration of paintings in the National Gallery and hoped that England "having no high art of her own . . . would at least protect what she could not produce."[3] He went on to argue that the gallery should be reorganized so that the works of every artist would appear in chronological order, accompanied by studies and copies of those works. And despite his denunciation of most of the paintings—"of little value individually"—Ruskin contended that "their collective teaching is of irrefragable authority" (*Works* 12: 403).

Why was the young champion of nature's truths so concerned with the reorganization of the National Gallery? And why was it that the Old Masters, "of little value individually," became essential to the progress of the fine arts when taken *together*?

There seems to be something of a paradox here. Hazlitt, who admired the achievements of the Old Masters, did not want to see them patronized by the public galleries, whereas Ruskin, who despised the paintings of the past, was eager to see them displayed and protected. But what was at issue was not the quality of the Old Masters: it was the quality of public judgment. Hazlitt had little confidence in public taste, arguing that the "mob" might be sensible enough to choose their political leaders, but they could not distinguish good from bad in art and should therefore be shielded from their own poor taste.[4] Ruskin agreed with Hazlitt that the public lacked taste, but he went on to argue that "modern" readers could reach better judgment if they learned an appropriate method. The public, he said, were capable of "opinions formed on right grounds" (*Works* 3: 79). Indeed, the five-volume *Modern Painters* can be read as a sustained attempt to show the most ordinary readers how to reach judicious aesthetic opinions. *Modern Painters* pushed beyond Hazlitt's democratic politics to embrace a democratic criticism, one that would never be "borne down or affected by mere authority of great names" (84).

education from art AND nature

In a debate in which some favored nature and others art as the best education for artists, Ruskin favored both. Nature was the best paradigm for aspiring artists, but it could not be the only model because, Ruskin argued, the images that art provided simply could not be avoided. Art was always already in cultural circulation; there was no way to escape its formative effects on every viewer. Ruskin therefore urged his readers not to ignore painting, but rather to look carefully and skeptically at the duplicitous Old Masters in order to unsettle their authoritative hold on perception. "It is my purpose," he wrote, "to raise, as far as possible, the deceptive veil of imaginary light through which we are accustomed to gaze upon the patriarchal work" (*Works* 3: 83).

Far from trying to protect a gullible public from dangerously false and conventionalized images, he entreated readers to set these paintings against the world they depicted, to see whether or not the conventions of the painters and the verdicts of the critics really corresponded to their own perceptual experience. If Hazlitt sought to protect the public from its own poor judgment, while salvaging the splendor of the Old Masters for those few who could appreciate them, Ruskin wanted to teach the broader public how to judge the difference between truth and falsehood by promoting a method that would reveal the failures and deceptions of the Old Masters.

The method that Ruskin adopted was the scientific experiment. Rigorous experimentation would allow all readers—however ordinary they were—to test the authoritative judgments of the critics for themselves. It would be difficult to count the experiments Ruskin exhorts us to perform in the course of five volumes. To give one example, in *Modern Painters* 4 he urges the following test: "sitting about three yards from a bookcase (not your own, so that you may *know* none of the titles of the books) . . . try to draw the books accurately, with the titles on the backs, and patterns on the bindings, as you see them. You are not to stir from your place to look where they are" (*Works* 6: 79). If we follow these steps and compare our own experience to the images produced by the Old Masters, we will come to see that the most admired paintings have misled us in their reliance on minute detail. Indeed, Ruskin goes so far as to argue that all painting that depicts objects with clear and definite outlines is deceptive: "all *distinct* drawing must be *bad* drawing, and nothing can be right, till it is unintelligible" (79).[5] This is a surprising conclusion, perhaps, but if we test it we can see for ourselves whether or not it is true.

clear & definite outlines = deception

unintelligibility = right

Performing a series of empirical trials, we will come to throw off the clear and focused visions of nature produced by Old Master paintings, Ruskin says, and only then will we appreciate the startling, unorthodox, and often surprisingly impenetrable visual truths of lived experience.

The experiment, with its back-and-forth movement between art and the world, allows us to be exposed to art without being corrupted by it; and this has political consequences, since a public reliant on its own sound methods of judgment does not have to be sheltered from dangerous images by knowing authorities. Yet we readers, Ruskin laments, are not eager to take on such responsibility. Our inclination is lazily to accept the firm judgments passed on to us by convention and authority. For this reason, Ruskin sternly urges his audience into experimental activity again and again in *Modern Painters:*

> Go out some bright sunny day in winter, and look for a tree with a broad trunk, having rather delicate boughs hanging down on the sunny side, near the trunk. Stand four or five yards from it, with your back to the sun. You will find that the boughs between you and the trunk of the tree are very indistinct, that you confound them in places with the trunk itself, and cannot possibly trace one of them from its insertion to its extremity. (*Works* 3: 303)

Unsettlingly, the boughs do not look at all like Old Master paintings. Now we should be less sure of our convictions, aware thanks to Ruskin's questions that we have never looked carefully at trees in sunlight to understand the relations between light and shade. And if Ruskin's experiment is persuasive in this single instance, his skepticism about representation carries general implications. The next time we see a landscape painting we should recognize its potential for duplicity and should proceed to nature to check its claims to truth.

Such a story may sound simple enough, but the chronology of this exercise leads us to some surprising conclusions. It is only once we have looked at the world ourselves that we can assess the truth-value of the representation. Thus painting alone cannot communicate nature's truths. Indeed, since representations are more often than not a source of corruption, we must not trust them to offer us anything but falsehood.[6] This puts art in a strange position. If painting must represent the truth of

nature but cannot convey that truth unless its viewers already know it,
art would appear to become altogether purposeless.

Yet Ruskin complicates this conclusion. The truths that he encourages his readers to look for in nature are explicitly *painterly* truths. He repeatedly urges us to see nature in terms of chiaroscuro and perspective, line and brushstroke. And he often imagines nature as a practicing artist:

> It is the constant habit of nature to use both her highest lights and deepest shadows in exceedingly small quantity; always in points, never in masses. She will give a large mass of tender light in sky or water. . . . She will then fill up all the rest of her picture with middle tints and pale greys of some sort or another, and on this quiet and harmonious whole she will touch her high lights in spots. (*Works* 3: 310)

The truths of the world turn out, in other words, to be the truths of the world as they are *for painting*. This might seem an odd premise, given Ruskin's relentless critique of painting, which he is always faulting for its falsehoods. But if paintings are dangerous precisely because they precede us, shaping our capacity to see the natural world, then Ruskin's reliance on painting as a paradigm for nature begins to make sense: the images given to us by culture lay the problematic groundwork for all experience. We automatically see nature in painterly terms, as if access to the world could only ever begin from a foundation in representation. In short, Ruskin shows a shrewdness about the acculturation of perception: the seeing subject has itself been made by representation. Despite the apparent priority of the real, it is the image that always comes first in our own Ruskinian narrative of knowledge, preceding and even creating our experience of the world.

To put this another way: in the experiments of *Modern Painters,* the paintings perform as *hypotheses*. Art might not itself tell truths, but it has always already shaped our capacity to imagine what might be true. Only a vigilant back-and-forth movement between the image and the world permits us to become sound judges. In this light, it seems perfectly logical for Ruskin to want the Old Masters on show to the public, though he disliked their duplicity. He wanted to train the eyes of the public on the deceptions of pictures in order to goad us to look for truth, provoking us to desire the knowledge that only lived experience could offer. It is the ever-present potential of images to mislead us that stirs us to go out into the world to see for ourselves. Curiously, then, the works of the Old Masters, *by their very failures,* are crucial to a realist education. In themselves, they tell us nothing certain, but in their relentless potential for duplicity, they provoke us to desire more trusty truths. Their withholding of the truth, that is, generates suspense.

We have seen that what makes Ruskin's realism new is its insistence on testing the claims of representation. What concerns us in this chapter is the fact that this realist experimentation takes a specific *narrative* shape. The first moment in the story is the hypothesis, usually taken from some assumption or conventional image of the world. Then comes the pause, laden with doubt, as we labor to separate ourselves from our guesses, images, and habits of mind, suspending judgment—holding ourselves back—as we compel ourselves to ask whether our best hypothesis will succeed or fail. The third step is our attempt to cross the distance between mind and world, moving back and forth between the hypothesis and our experience of the real to detect their similarities and differences. Finally we confront the information fed back to us by the world, which all too often unsettles the hypothesis and points to a continuing obligation to speculate, suspend judgment, and test again.

Although suspense was not new in the nineteenth century, and Ruskin certainly did not invent its strategies, what entered the scene with the realist experiment was a wholly new seriousness—as the pleasures of suspense joined forces with a sober scientific epistemology. This chapter divides into three sections, each of which considers a different Victorian instance of the close relations between plotted suspense and experimental knowledge. The first example is the favorite plot of Victorian science, and the one that Ruskin borrowed—the scientific experiment itself. For contemporary scientific thinkers, the experiment imposed a necessary discipline on the desire to leap to familiar conclusions, and this discipline brought with it significant consequences for storytelling, even within scientific circles. The second plot is Wilkie Collins's novel of 1868, *The Moonstone,* which incorporates a scientific experiment into its highly suspenseful narrative structure. Although Collins was not typically considered a realist in the twentieth century, he was a serious reader of Ruskin, and this novel neatly exemplifies the subversive structures and strategies of Ruskin's realism. Thus I want to suggest that the sensational Collins was in fact an exemplary Victorian realist.[7] The last plot is the one that Ruskin expels from *Modern Painters* as pernicious and corrupt. Surprisingly for a self-proclaimed realist, he banishes from his aesthetic all painting that looks *too* real. Why? Because trompe l'oeil art encourages smug complacency instead of provoking the uneasy apprehensions of suspense. Ruskinian realism requires a mystery, and that is exactly what trompe l'oeil cannot provide.   *suspense here antithetical to ataraxia*

The Plots of Victorian Science

Ruskin's work took shape in an intellectual context where scientists and philosophers of science turned to the experimental method as the best model for the pursuit of knowledge.[8] With its pressure to restrain speculation and imagination, nineteenth-century scientific epistemology began to call for the very suspension of the self. In 1854, John Tyndall argued that good scientists must struggle to quell themselves in order to grasp the otherness of the world:

> The first condition of success [in science] is patient industry, an honest receptivity, and a willingness to abandon all preconceived notions, however cherished, if they be found to contradict the truth. Believe me, a self-renunciation which has something lofty in it, and of which the world never hears, is often enacted in the private experience of the true votary of science. And if a man be not capable of this self-renunciation—this loyal surrender of himself to Nature and to the facts, he lacks, in my opinion, the first mark of the philosopher.[9]

Tyndall praises the experimental method as the only way to accomplish this self-renunciation: "By its appeals to experiment, [science] constantly checks itself, and thus walks on a foundation of facts."[10]

With his focus on restraining the self, it is Tyndall who best reveals the consequences of the scientific method for narrative. In his biography of Faraday, he reveals a close alliance between skeptical experimentation and narrative suspense. Tyndall was a prominent scientist who had succeeded Faraday as professor of natural history at the Royal Institution. He became a popularizer of science and a defender of Darwin. In the 1860s he was an acquaintance of Ruskin's, and although they later quarreled over the methods of geology, they shared enough in the way of fundamental principles to engage in a lively debate.[11] In his admiring biography of Michael Faraday, "the greatest experimental philosopher the world has ever seen," Tyndall explained the scientist's need to wrestle with doubt, to hope, to guess, and to wait as he tested his imaginings against the world. His disappointments, Tyndall tells us, were many, but he remained committed to the rigors of experimentation. "Faraday always recommended the suspension of judgment in cases of doubt," Tyndall explains: "His mind was full of hopes and hypotheses, but he always brought them to an experimental test."[12]

In his quest to categorize different kinds of electricity, Faraday began to wonder whether his overarching concept of electricity was itself misleading. Suddenly he found himself forced to confront serious doubts about the foundation of his own knowledge. Tyndall writes:

> It was to him a discomfort to reason upon data which admitted of doubt. . . . He wished to know the reality of our nescience as well as of our science. "Be one thing or the other," he seemed to say to an unproved hypothesis; "come out as a solid truth, or disappear as a convicted lie." After making the great discovery which I have attempted to describe, a doubt seemed to beset him as regards the identity of electricities. "Is it right," he seemed to ask, "to call this agency which I have discovered electricity at all? Are there perfectly conclusive grounds for believing that the electricity of the machine, the pile, the gymnotus and torpedo, magneto-electricity and thermo-electricity, are merely different manifestations of one and the same agent?"[13]

Tormented by uncertainty, Faraday is propelled from one experiment to the next, each one pushing him to new discoveries—and new doubts. These hesitations are not only essential to his success as a scientist of integrity; they are also crucial to the narrative unfolding of scientific knowledge.[14]

To put this another way: Tyndall's biography of Faraday suggests that suspense is the very substance of experimental science. Experiments always hold out the possibility that the facts will prove the hypothesis wrong, or worse, that they will show nothing. Though we may crave a particular answer, the skepticism of the method demands that we must remain in doubt, waiting for the test to confirm or reject our hopes. The experimenter willingly tests hypotheses rather than taking them for granted, all the while acknowledging the possibility of failure.[15] In this context, a kinship between empirical science and narrative desire begins to emerge: both suspenseful narratives and scientific experiments assume a gap between initial suspicions and later revelations. Both demand a delay between the intriguing enigma and the eventual satisfactions of knowledge.

G. H. Lewes broadened the call for suspense to include all knowledge seeking: "in our eagerness for an explanation [we] readily accept conjectures as truths. The anticipating rush of thought prefigures qualities and foresees consequences; instead of pausing to ascertain whether our anticipations do or do not correspond with fact, we proceed to argue and to act on them as if this mental vision were final."[16] Like Tyndall and Ruskin, Lewes is eager to persuade us to counteract our own inclinations, to pause, suspending judgment. And like Ruskin, too, he is particularly concerned about the dominance of cultural assumptions, seeking to overturn the weight of established authority.

But Lewes's discipline also goes hand in hand with something far less solemn, far less earnest: the exciting pleasures of curiosity, held in abeyance by the possibility that the facts will surprise us. John Herschel celebrated the "delight" with which science "lays itself open to enquiry."[17] And in the twentieth century John Dewey brought together the pleasures of plot and the rigors of skepticism in his *Quest for Certainty:* "The scientific attitude may be defined as that which is capable of enjoying the doubtful."[18] To enjoy one's own doubt: surely this describes the experience of reading a novel of suspense just as well as it describes a questioning science. Perhaps the pleasures of suspense have always left an unsettlingly passionate trace on the diligent detachment of scientific inquiry. Gillian Beer likens the scientific experiment to narrative fiction in that both share the promise of an unpredictable future. And for her, too, both kinds of skeptical interrogation produce *pleasure:* "The element of surprise, including unforeseeable reorderings of known data, new information, formal boldness, are qualities valued in scientific enquiry as in fiction. One pleasure they both offer is enfranchisement: they release us from the loop of the foreknown, they enlarge possibility."[19]

Such pleasurable scope for the new, such enlargement of possibility, such "enfranchisement": these phrases fit well with Ruskin's radical resistance to the status quo, his desire to subvert authority and established relations. As Avital Ronell puts it: "The experimental spirit is . . . a vitality that disrupts sedimented concepts and social values."[20] To experiment one must be willing to suspend one's own judgment, to acknowledge the otherness of the world, and to imagine its possible resistance to convention. In this light, plotted suspense, scientific inquiry, and radical politics converge.

Plotting *The Moonstone*

The connection between realist narrative and empirical science is not in itself a new discovery. In his classic study of the eighteenth-century novel, Ian Watt connects the realism of the first British novels with the empiricism then being theorized by the philosophers. In his analysis, the elements of "philosophical realism" at first share some striking similarities with Ruskin's project: "critical, anti-traditional, and innovating; its method has been the study of the particulars of experience by the individual investigator, who, ideally, at least, is free from the body of past assumptions and traditional belief." But the empirical characteristics of the itinerant narratives of Defoe or Fielding turn out to be rather different from the suspenseful Victorian plot. For Watt, the empiricism of the eighteenth-century novel shows itself in its refusal to retell traditional stories from mythology or history, in its emphasis on the particularity of individual characters and events in place of symbolic types, a new, specific sense of time and space, marked by the "use of past experience as a cause of present action," and a new prose style that claimed authenticity and immediacy.[21] All of these factors were thoroughly familiar to readers by the early nineteenth century. New to the Victorian period were plots structured entirely around the activity of guessing and testing. Unlike the peripatetic *Robinson Crusoe* or the steadfast *Pamela,* Victorian novels repeatedly mobilized compelling enigmas, deliberately tantalizing readers by withholding knowledge.[22]

If literary critics have not been inclined to see suspenseful narrative as a radical form,[23] Ruskin's rebellious experiments should prompt us to take a second look at the political potential of plot. For Ruskin and the scientists, the results of the experiment, if they are in the least unconventional, expose narrowly conventional convictions as partial, misguided, and insufficient. But even when the results confirm and resettle conventions, the delay before that resettling leaves them pointedly up in the air. Indeed, the very pleasures of suspenseful narrative lie in the experience of anxiety, the uneasy sense that the world may not conform to predictable outcomes. To have an experience of suspenseful uncertainty is to acknowledge that there is more than one credible ending to the narrative, more than one potentially plausible solution to the mystery. In this context, closure does not so much dictate an arbitrary conclusion, as it compels us to recognize the *otherness* of the world, the ever-present possibility that the facts may refuse to validate our prejudices. Viewed in this light, suspense emerges as a profoundly subversive literary technique.

It is intriguing that in critical circles such subversions have remained largely invisible. Working from the assumption that the conclusions of Victorian narratives were always already formulaic and predictable, scholars have largely neglected the experience of nervous unease provoked by the narrative middle. Indeed, I want to suggest that literary critics have been inclined to forget what it is like to read Victorian novels *for the first time.*

Take, for example, *The Moonstone* (1868), where Wilkie Collins uses a scientific experiment to unveil the novel's central mystery. D. A. Miller, arguing against a tradition of criticism that has celebrated the perspectival instability of a novel told in multiple voices, makes a forceful case that *The Moonstone* is actually monological, "always speaking a master-voice that corrects, overrides, subordinates, or sublates all other voices it allows to speak."[24] Although the novel may seem to sustain a diversity of perspectives, Miller contends that every voice in the novel—whether willingly or no—actually confirms the complacent, shared, central perspective of Betteredge, Blake, and Bruff. Thus very little is actually truly mysterious in the novel:

> As early as the First Period, one could make an accurate guess at the thief simply by ranking the main suspects (Rachel, Rosanna, Blake, and Ablewhite) in the distance to which each stands outside of the collective cognition whose spokesman is Betteredge. . . . By the time Godfrey is associated with Miss Clack, and it is known that he has asked to see Lady Julia's will, there is little to learn except the logistics of the theft and the details of the secret life motivating it. Indeed, one might say that the remaining

actions in the novel—the discovery that Franklin Blake stole the diamond, its confirmation and disconfirmation—merely distract characters from the obvious epistemological gaps that identify Godfrey as the thief. In this sense, the revelation at the end is a fact that the community knew all along, but simply didn't know that it knew.[25]

Miller's reading works beautifully—with hindsight. But to make sense of the theft from the vantage point of the finished ideological whole is quite different from the readerly experience of doubt and uncertainty that attends the first reading of a compelling detective story like this one.[26] To use Miller's example: even if we are inclined to suspect Godfrey Ablewhite from the beginning, it is clear that plausible alternatives continue to compete for suspicion right to the end of the novel, generating the excited interest that provokes us to continue reading. Franklin Blake might make an early claim on our sympathies, but the narrative clearly invites us to wonder—and to fear—that he might in fact be the guilty party. Certainly contemporary reviewers of the novel did not expect readers readily to anticipate the conclusion. Geraldine Jewsbury, writing for the *Athenaeum,* compared readers on the point of finishing *The Moonstone* to "persons . . . in a state of ravenous hunger":

> Those readers who have followed the fortunes of the mysterious Moonstone for many weeks, as it has appeared in tantalizing portions, will of course throw themselves headlong upon the latter portion of the third volume, now that the end is really come, and devour it without rest or pause; to take any deliberate breathing-time is quite out of the question, and we promise them a surprise that will find the most experienced novel-reader unprepared.[27]

Jewsbury does go on to recommend a second reading of the novel to appreciate the construction of the whole, but she distinguishes the pleasure of this kind of contemplative rereading from the initial enjoyment of the puzzle.[28]

It is true, of course, that the novel's ending finally brings some of the comforts of a conservative conclusion. And since a great number of nineteenth-century fictions end happily ever after, critics of the Victorian novel have read its forward-looking plots as heading, willy-nilly, to safe, bourgeois resolutions.[29] But perhaps at midcentury the happy ending of the suspenseful plot was not quite as predictable as we like to assume. Indeed, we might think of the mid-Victorian novels that conclude with radical uncertainty: the deliberately suspended finish of *Villette,* for example, or the multiple endings of *Great Expectations,* which we will look at more closely in a later chapter. In these texts, suspended questions do not simply give way to soothing answers, advancing inexorably to definite, ideologically tidy conclusions. And a first-time reader of *The Moonstone,* having read some unnerving endings such as those of *Villette* and *Great Expectations,* might not be as secure of the guilt of Godfrey Ablewhite as perhaps it seems, in retrospect, we ought to have been.

To illustrate my point a little further, let me turn to the scientific experiment arranged by Ezra Jennings and Franklin Blake. We have heard Rachel Verinder's testimony that Blake has stolen the diamond before her eyes, but then we are presented with a hypothesis that might clear him: the possibility that he has taken the diamond unconsciously, under the influence of opium. Rachel herself claims to be thoroughly convinced by the hypothesis itself and to need no further proof than Jennings's explanation of it. As Jennings puts it: "She tells me, in the prettiest manner, that my letter has satisfied her of Mr. Blake's innocence, without the slightest need (so far as she is concerned) of putting my assertion to the proof" (449). We too, like the heroine, may need little persuading: perhaps we are convinced, as Miller suggests, that Blake has always been on the side of good and right, needing only an explanation to absolve him. Indeed, in order to strengthen the exoneration of Blake, Jennings puts forward a remarkably strong case for the influence of opium, complete with arguments culled from actual scientific sources.[30]

But why, if we are all so easily persuaded of Blake's innocence, does the text go to so much trouble—and cover so many pages—to perform the experiment that puts the hypothesis to the test? Far from being a mechanical exercise, the experiment is fraught with anxiety—since it invites both characters and readers to consider that the truth it reveals will not be the solution we desire. As Jennings reminds the eager Blake, the proof of his innocence "rests . . . on a mere assumption" (444). And Jennings himself worries uneasily about the evidence as the experiment proceeds: "Will the parallel still hold good, when the final test has been tried? The events of the night must decide" (463). When Blake suddenly stops short on his midnight walk, the suspense of the experiment reaches its height. Jennings writes: "There was a pause of some sort. A pause in the action of the opium? a pause in the action of the brain? Who could tell? Everything depended, now, on what he did next. . . . A horrible doubt crossed my mind" (477). The narrative pauses, laden with doubt, suspending us for dozens of pages between hypothesis and conclusion, between expectation and certainty. Despite the fact that we may all be thoroughly persuaded of Blake's innocence, such suspense works to throw our most cherished convictions into doubt—they rest, after all, on a mere assumption. The delay of the experiment compels us to admit that our beliefs—however much we are attached to them—do not necessarily correspond to the facts of the world.

Perhaps it is for this unsettling reason that the very idea of an experiment upsets a number of the most trustworthy characters in the novel—trustworthy, at least, according to D. A. Miller's schema. Betteredge and Bruff fiercely resist the experiment: not just its hypotheses or its conclusions, but the method itself. Betteredge starts by insisting that the very idea is a "delusion and a snare" (456). And in order to dissuade the experimental pair, Bruff tells Jennings that he has consulted a medical authority on the subject who has expressed doubt about the whole affair (452).

In order to emphasize these misgivings and hesitations, Collins gives us a scientist whom the world finds difficult to trust. His ambiguous racial identity and peculiar appearance—his "piebald" hair—make him suspicious to most of the novel's characters. Then, too, his past haunts him—a set of false accusations, so he says, that have followed him through life. Both Jennings's history and his appearance are "against him," according to Betteredge and almost everyone else who encounters him. It is partly for this reason that his hypothesis is not enough to persuade an authoritative audience. Jennings says: "these notes are of *my* making; there is nothing but *my* assertion to the contrary, to guarantee that they are not fabrications. Remember what I told you on the moor—and ask yourself what my assertion is worth. No! my notes have but one value, looking to the world outside" (438).

At the moment that the experiment begins, then, there are actually three prejudices at work: the readerly prejudice in favor of Franklin Blake and the conservative characters' presumptions against both the scientist and his method. The interval of the experiment suspends all three: readers must hold on to find out whether Blake is indeed innocent, just as conservative characters are shown to be waiting and watching, compelled to wonder whether there can be anything to Jennings's theory after all. The suspense of the experiment obliges even the most conventional, resistant audiences to suspend judgment.

The results of the experiment clear up the prejudices for the sympathetic Blake and against the suspicious Jennings, but perhaps more surprisingly, they manage to overturn the conservative pressure against the method itself. In part, as Jennings suggests, the experiment works because it provides *impersonal* evidence: testimony that is not attached to the strange person who has generated the hypothesis but appears to come from the world itself. Yet Collins hints at a more readerly possibility: the experiment persuades the skeptics to take it seriously—against their own inclinations—because of the *pleasurable interest* it excites in them. Both Bruff and Betteredge are carried along, in the end, simply by the desire to see whether the experiment will work. First Betteredge, at the start of the process, loses his prejudice to rapt attention: "the strong, dramatic interest which the experiment was now assuming, proved . . . to be too much for Betteredge's capacity of self-restraint" (473). Then the resistant Bruff, a moment later, drops the books he has been reading: "The suspended interest of the situation in which we were now placed, was slowly asserting its influence even on *his* unimaginative mind" (474). Just as science gives a serious epistemological value to plotted suspense, then, suspense lends power to the scientific experiment.

As if to underscore the dramatic excitement of nineteenth-century suspense as a new phenomenon, *The Moonstone* juxtaposes its own thrilling interest against the more composed narratives of eighteenth-century literature. Jennings checks the books in Blake's room before the experiment begins to make sure that the subject will not affect the test's results by inappropriate reading. Richardson's *Pamela* and Mackenzie's *Man of Feeling* are the novels on the shelves, which is a relief to Jennings, who claims that these "possess[ed] the one great merit of enchaining nobody's interest, and exciting nobody's brain" (470). Just as Collins's novel is doing its best to enchain the interest and excite the brains of Bruff, Betteredge, and the reader, it pokes fun at its eighteenth-century precursors for failing to do exactly that. In this light, Betteredge's comic reliance on *Robinson Crusoe* as a way to divine the future looks like a satire on the itinerant patterns of classic eighteenth-century fiction, which markedly fail to hint at the excitements of the future, unable or unwilling to use suspenseful enigmas to enchain the readers' interest in what is to come.

Indeed, I take my cue partly from Collins in suggesting that the unsettling pleasures of suspense—as they emerged in science, politics, and fiction—were new to the nineteenth century. Of course, fiction and drama had used suspenseful devices for centuries, and eighteenth-century Gothic fiction was famous for its chilling suspense. But Victorian suspense relied on the model of the scientific experiment, uniting its skeptical epistemology with anxious pleasure in order to teach readers to enjoy a new approach to the realities of the world that extended well beyond the popular fiction of the time. This vision of suspense was new precisely in its claims to widespread and serious significance.

Evidence that the mainstream press was slowly learning to take suspense seriously began to show in 1860, when Collins begged reviewers not to give away the plot of *The Woman in White*. Suspense might not itself have been a new invention, but reviewers, according to Collins, needed to learn to treat it in a new way:

> In the event of this book being reviewed, I venture to ask whether it is possible to praise the writer, or to blame him, without opening the proceedings by telling the story at second-hand? . . . if [the critic] tells [the story] at all, in any way whatever, is he doing a service to the reader, by destroying, beforehand, two main elements in the attraction of all stories—the interest of curiosity, and the excitement of surprise?[31]

The *Times* responded snidely that it was virtually impossible to say anything at all about *The Woman in White*, "lest we should let the cat out of the bag." Other periodicals—including the *Critic* and *Guardian*—underscored the novelty of Collins's request by responding to it explicitly and sarcastically.[32] But despite the reviewers' criticism of Collins's reliance on clever plot twists and their discomfort with the novelist's direct appeal to their discretion, all three of these reviewers quietly granted his request and, contrary to their usual practice, gave few of the plot's events away. Even the most recalcitrant of critics were learning a new respect for suspense, and with this respect, perhaps, a new and unsettling way of reading.

In both *The Woman in White* and *The Moonstone,* Collins hints that his suspenseful plots depart from earlier narrative patterns. It is perhaps no surprise, then, that Collins was a serious reader of Ruskin.[33] Indeed, it may be necessary to grant that the sensation novelist shared his methods not only with art critics and scientists but also with philosophers. At around the same time *The Moonstone* was differentiating its suspenseful plots from those of its forerunners, G. H. Lewes was exhorting skeptical readers to suspend judgment, and Cambridge philosopher Henry Sidgwick was congratulating his intellectual contemporaries on their newfound willingness to remain in suspense:

> We are growing more sceptical in the proper sense of the word: we suspend our judgment much more than our predecessors, and much more contentedly: we see that there are many sides to many questions: the opinions we do hold we hold if not more loosely, at least at arm's length: we can imagine how they appear to others, and can conceive ourselves not holding them. We are losing in faith and confidence: if we are not failing in hope, our hopes are at least more indefinite; and we are gaining in impartiality and comprehensiveness of sympathy.[34]

Sidgwick hails a new movement of skepticism, impartiality, and feeling for otherness, bringing these together under the rubric of suspending judgment—and he does so at virtually the same moment that the mystery of *The Moonstone* appears. In the 1860s, then, novelists and philosophers marked as new the unsettling union of scientific inquiry and the patterns of plotted suspense.

Complex historical links between Victorian literature and Victorian science have been emerging in scholarship for some time, but the connection between the scientific method and suspenseful plotting has not been among them. In *Darwin's Plots,* Gillian Beer argues that among the sciences, evolutionary theory carried particularly important implications for nineteenth-century plotting. "Because of its preoccupation with time and with change evolutionary theory has inherent affinities with the problems and processes of narrative." She observes, too, that the Victorian exploration of "experiment-based" science introduced a "new methodology" to nineteenth-century fiction writers. And for Beer, this new methodology has everything to do with novelistic plots:

> hypothesising, a reliance upon the future for confirmation, projecting possibilities rather than confirmed data; replotting observed relations of cause and effect or of possibility; observation; perceiving underlying patterns by means of analogy; a pleasure in boldness, a sense of the insufficiency of present understanding; the recognition of a world beyond the compass of our present knowledge.[35]

Beer's claim that fiction and science "have much in common" is both powerful and persuasive. But her own meticulous analysis of the impact of Darwin on fictional narrative, and vice versa, does not, in fact, make much of the work of experimentation. Evolutionary narrative provides two plots, neither of which calls for the pleasures of suspense: "At first evolutionism tended to offer a new authority to orderings of narrative which emphasised cause and effect, then, descent and kin. Later again, its eschewing of fore-ordained design (its dysteology) allowed chance to figure as the only sure determination."[36]

In fact, Darwin's own plots have little to do with suspense: his narrative of evolution, far from withholding particular elements of crucial knowledge, works on the logic of adaptation and adjustment.[37] Thus, although Darwin's startling narratives might well throw light on the concerns of the nineteenth-century novel, they fail to describe the new patterns of suspenseful plotting that were emerging in this moment.[38] And if the Victorian novel shares certain formal and epistemological properties with scientific experimentation, it certainly makes sense to turn to thinkers who appeared on the scene before Darwin, whose *Origin of Species,* first published in 1859, was by no means the first model of the scientific method. Surely we might sooner turn to *Modern Painters,* which burst on the scene almost two decades before *The Origin of Species* and brought the anti-conventional experiment to the arts.

Ruskin is an appropriate figure to bridge the gap between art and science, since his own immersion in scientific research is well documented.[39] In fact, his lifelong commitment to the study of geology is particularly compelling for our purposes, since at the time he became interested in the subject, scientists were engaged in a turbulent quarrel specifically over the legitimacy and value of the experimental method to the study of geology.[40] Chronologically, Ruskin's exposure to geological debate went hand in hand with his early interest in aesthetic judgment, and he clearly saw them as related concerns, bringing his scientific and artistic questions together on more than one occasion.[41] Indeed, for Ruskin scientific inquiry and artistic representation had the same objective—access to nature's truths. With his reliance on experimental suspense and his careful interrogation of representation, Ruskin seems to come closer to exploring the aims and foundations of the novel than Darwin's evolutionary theory.

Problem Plots: Ruskin's Dreaded Trompe l'Oeil

Ruskin may have shared epistemological concerns with scientists, philosophers, and novelists, but no doubt readers will object that it is implausible to see the text of *Modern Painters* as suspenseful. Written in a forceful didactic tone, Ruskin's own writing would seem to share more with sermons than with sensation fiction. But rather than claiming that *Modern Painters* provokes the same lingering anxiety as novelistic mysteries, I want to suggest that Ruskin's contribution to Victorian narrative form was to offer the clearest theoretical articulation of the epistemological seriousness of narrative suspense. He prescribes the experimental method in order to encourage his readers into a permanently suspenseful relationship to the world. The pause is crucial to Ruskinian realism. He writes: "when you have stood by this [waterfall] for half an hour, you will have discovered that there is something more in nature than has been given by Ruysdael" (*Works* 3: 530). The experimental method teaches us to wait—for half an hour, let us say—to see whether the world will meet or defy our expectations.

In his insistence on pausing and suspending judgment, Ruskin shows his clear departure from the realism of immediately legible appearances. Indeed, if we were ever tempted to think that perfect resemblance was the goal of Victorian realism, we are put right at the very beginning of *Modern Painters*. "Imitation," Ruskin writes, "is the destruction . . . of all art" (*Works* 3: 108). The reason for this, as we will see, has everything to do with narrative.

What Ruskin calls "imitation" we might call "trompe l'oeil"—an image that comes so close to the real that it temporarily fools the eye.

Ruskin describes imitative art as painting that seeks to hide the fact that it is a flat canvas, covered with paint, pretending to be an ordinary object in the world. Yet, while pretending to inhabit the real, this kind of art always has "some means of proving at the same moment that it *is* a deception" (*Works* 3: 100). Imitation spawns two conflicting experiences: initially, we mistake the picture for a three-dimensional object in the world; then we detect the artifice.[42] Indeed, Ruskin argues that the revelation of the artifice is necessary to the experience of trompe l'oeil. After all, if we never recognized the trick, we would continue to take the image as a reality—and would never grasp it as a representation at all.[43]

As we come to realize that the painted image is not the object it represents, we become conscious of its flat, material reality as canvas and oil paint. For Ruskin, it is in the moment of passage from one impression to the other that the spectator feels a *frisson*—"a kind of pleasurable surprise, an agreeable excitement of mind" (*Works* 3: 100). Thus trompe l'oeil entices the viewer into enjoying the feeling of exposing an artifice. Indeed, in the process of discovering the deception, we do not care what kind of object is represented: "The simple pleasure in the imitation would be precisely of the same degree (if the accuracy could be equal), if the subject of it were the hero or his horse" (101). We move back and forth between our initial perceptions and our knowing grasp of the trick, admiring the success of the illusion. The effect might be described as irony: the self-consciousness of art as art, playing back and forth between vision and knowledge, pretending to inhabit the real, while asserting at the same time that it is a skillful artifice.[44]

The more surprising conclusion of Ruskin's argument comes, however, when we recall that imitative painting is the consummate art of verisimilitude, looking to us much like the object it represents. It is a quintessentially mimetic project, yet, at the same time, it is also an art form that draws attention to the work of art as such, to the technique and materials of the artifice. And these two sides of trompe l'oeil are inextricably intertwined: the closer the image comes to the real, the greater will be our surprise and enjoyment at the discovery that it is, in fact, a trick; the greater our appreciation of the illusion, the less we will focus on the "content" of the representation, preferring to marvel at the difference between the illusion and the real.[45] Thus, the more conventionally "realistic" the image, the less the work of art will tell us about the object it portrays. In pretending to inhabit the real, painting—paradoxically—draws attention to itself as painting.[46]

In our own time, we have come to believe that any quest for an unreflexive mimesis is both misguided and unsophisticated, and realism has typically seemed to imply a naive inattention to the complexities of signification. Ruskin, apparently in keeping with this definition of realism, deliberately distinguishes his new aesthetic from the self-referential art of trickery. But what makes this complex and interesting is that trompe l'oeil is also remarkable for its capacity to picture the world, and it specifically allows Ruskin to differentiate his aesthetic from the attempt to achieve transparency in representation. Strikingly, then, the critique of trompe l'oeil permits Ruskin to reject *both* mimetic representation *and* reflexive artifice in the very same blow.

But if Ruskin rejects both illusion and reflexivity in representation, what project is left for the artist? The answer, he tells us, is the general category of "truthful art":[47]

> a marble figure does not look like what it is not: it looks like marble, and like the form of a man, but then it *is* marble, and it *is* the form of a man. It does not look like a man, which it is not, but like the form of a man, which it is. Form is form, *bonâ fide* and actual, whether in marble or in flesh—not an imitation or a resemblance of form, but real form. The chalk outline of the bough of a tree on paper, is not an imitation; it looks like chalk and paper—not like wood, and that which it suggests to the mind is not properly said to be *like* the form of a bough, it *is* the form of a bough. (*Works* 3: 101)

Truthful mimesis acts something like a road map: it is an accurate representation of the world, without reproducing the lived visual experience of a real object. Conventional maps document not impressions but relations, points of reference on a relational diagram.[48] If such maplike relations constitute truthful art for Ruskin, then, logically, flat, pictorial representation is successfully mimetic even when it looks entirely *different* from the object it represents, replicating proportions but not visual images. Indeed, Ruskin implicitly suggests that representation can be truthful as long as it works only within the confines of its own materials. A drawing can truthfully give us the line of real objects; a sculpture can replicate the shape of real things in the world; charcoal can replicate tonal variations. And these kinds of images allow us to attend to the truths of the world, rather than focusing our attention on the skill of the artist. As soon as the image begins to look too much like the real, it starts to draw attention to the skillful facility of the painter and to the confusion between art and life, rather than to truth as it is in the world.

Is Ruskin therefore banishing reflexive art in favor of the transparency of unmediated reference? Not quite: such a claim would miss the fact that Ruskin's truthful art is also, in its own way, a self-reflexive representational practice, self-conscious about the materials and conventions by which it is made: marble sculpture exposes the materials of its making from the outset, which then allow us to think beyond those materials to the world. It is not as if the viewer of such a statue is fooled into thinking that the sculpture gives her unmediated access to the real. "It does not look like a man, which it is not, but like the form of a man, which it is."

What is the real difference, then, between truth and imitation? The crucial distinction, I want to suggest, is best framed in narrative terms, by considering the viewer's *sequence of experience*. With truthful art, the spectator begins by recognizing the materials: instantly discerning chalk or marble, we then go on to think, at leisure, about the object it represents. Truthful art works "have no pretence, nor hypocrisy, nor legerdemain about them;—there is nothing to be found out, or sifted, or surprised in them;—they bear their message simply and clearly, and it is that message which the mind takes from them and dwells upon, regardless of the language in which it is delivered" (*Works* 3: 108). Truthful mimesis allows us to pass quickly by the obvious intrusion of the medium in order to focus on the world it seeks to portray.

When it comes to trompe l'oeil, it is quite literally a different story. We start by believing that we are confronting just an ordinary object in the world, and only then are we surprised to discover the materials of the art. Amazed by the deftness of the trick, our delight comes in having spotted the hoax. "[T]he mind, in receiving an idea of imitation, is *wholly occupied* in finding out that what has been suggested to it is not what it appears to be" (*Works* 3: 108; emphasis mine). With truthful art we begin by acknowledging the artifice and then shift to contemplate the world;

with imitation we begin with the world and then are startled *into* a focus on the making of the artwork. Thus the trompe l'oeil sequence is a narrative that concludes with the defamiliarization of art: it leads us, inescapably, to contemplate the artfulness of the artifice.[49]

It has become a critical commonplace, these days, that all art is reflexive. But Ruskin invites us to complicate this generalization by offering us two opposing *narratives of reflexivity*, one that begins by referring to the world and ends in a focus on the materials, and one that begins by attending to the materials and ends in a focus on the world. Perhaps, therefore, we should be telling two—or more—different stories about the experience of reflexivity.

In his preferred sequence, Ruskin wants spectators to pass quickly by their recognition of the medium in order to attend carefully to the content of the work of art. But what is it, exactly, that allows a spectator to ignore the medium? The most likely answer is a historically specific one. In the later nineteenth century, when artists began to want viewers to focus on art's materiality, they would use surprising new materials or apply old materials in unfamiliar ways. Turning this around, we might say that the way to invite an audience to disregard the medium is by using materials so *familiar* to them that they are, quite simply, uninteresting. Ruskin's examples of truthful art are works made out of chalk and marble and paint. Readers who ignore these materials are presumably those so accustomed to seeing representations made in these media that the materials themselves fail to draw their attention. For an early-twenty-first century audience, a color photograph is so ordinary that we are likely to attend more to the scene it represents than to the act of photographing. Our capacity to disregard the medium is contingent on the familiarity of that medium. Ruskin, favoring the familiar use of chalk and marble and paint, claims that our recognition of the making of the artwork is the first and least interesting moment in the story. Reflexivity is not the point of the exercise: the excitement of the mystery is still to come.

Thus Ruskin's distinction between imitation and truth could be recast as a distinction between surprise and suspense. Trompe l'oeil surprise denies the gap between the real and the representational altogether at first, only to spring it on us suddenly a moment later. It sets up our experience as if recognizing the difference between art and its objects were itself the startling revelation of art. By contrast, truthful mimesis begins with the separation between representation and the real and then invites us to bring them into relation. Recognizing representation's limitations pushes us, or provokes us, to learn about the otherness of the world. While imitation delights us with both its cleverness and our own, truthful art encourages a process of doubting and testing to arrive at a tentative understanding of the relationship between art and its objects. It invites us to enjoy our own curiosity.

Far from prizing the illusions of a perfect mimesis, Ruskin's realism relentlessly insists on the inadequacies of representation. And if we take Ruskin to be the earliest theorist of realism, then the very concept of realism in English comes into being with a denunciation of mimetic transparency. Indeed, mimesis, imitation, and representation had been synonymous before Ruskin, but "realism" came onto the scene by breaking them apart, claiming for itself a role distinct from that of the cleverly lifelike trick. It is thus with the critique of trompe l'oeil that Victorian realism is born.

Ruskin requires rigorous testing because his basic presumption is that visual representation is always playing us false. And I want to suggest that *Modern Painters* rejects imitation not only as a goal for painting but also for narrative. Indeed, the realist experiment—like the scientific experiment—never purports to describe the intrinsic emplotment of the real. What Ruskin's plot chronicles is a method. Suspense is the experience by which readers learn to doubt their own convictions and approach the mysteries of alterity. Suspenseful plotting, then, is not the form of the real; it is the form of the acquisition of knowledge—and specifically of a skeptical epistemology that insists on testing authoritative claims to truth.[50]

Protagonists in the Victorian novel, like Ruskin's readers, learn to doubt and test the conventional images that surround them, and wait, expectant, ready to come to a more unconventional knowledge of the world. And so Ruskin's experiments allow us to bring together the most notable innovations of nineteenth-century fiction: a self-conscious realism, the doubts and pleasures of suspenseful plotting, and the Bildungsroman—the plot of coming to knowledge. Although it may seem somewhat paradoxical for Ruskin's "realism" to insist relentlessly on the deficiencies of representation, it represents a paradox only if we put our emphasis on the artwork rather than on the process of looking and representing. The goal of Ruskinian realism is the creation of a responsible relationship between the viewer and the real *by way of* the art object. For Ruskin, representation is valuable because, whether it succeeds or fails, it teaches us a new relationship to the world.

PART II

The Serious Pleasures of Suspense Fiction: Brontë and Dickens

3 "Harmless Pleasure"

Gender, Suspense, and *Jane Eyre*

In 1850, Charlotte Brontë was still in mourning. Having lost both of her sisters at the end of the 1840s, she decided to honor them by publishing a new edition of their novels, *Wuthering Heights* and *Agnes Grey*. It was in her preface to this volume that she unveiled the Brontës' identity publicly for the first time. Given her lonely sorrow, the reason she gave for this revelation might come as a surprise. "The little mystery, which formerly yielded some harmless pleasure, has lost its interest."[1] The pseudonyms had become a bore.

The "little mystery" she so coyly invokes here was not so trivial in the eyes of the literary world. From the moment that *Jane Eyre* appeared, reviewers speculated wildly about the writer's identity. "The whole reading-world of London was in a ferment to discover the unknown author," wrote Elizabeth Gaskell.[2] When the names of the three sisters emerged, it was something of a shock to the London literati to discover that the writers of these "coarse" and "repulsive" novels were sheltered Yorkshire women who had seen little of the world.[3] Although the secret had been slowly coming out, it was in 1850 that Charlotte Brontë put the speculations to rest with her "Biographical Notice of Ellis and Acton Bell." The brothers Bell, she confessed, were actually the sisters Brontë.

This version of the story is familiar to most Brontë enthusiasts. And much has been made of the Brontës' shyness, their passionate desire for privacy and isolation from the world.[4] But perhaps we should stop and wonder at Charlotte's own version of the story, which puts only a mild stress on the impulse to retreat from the public eye. Indeed, Charlotte decides to uncover her little mystery, so she says, because it has ceased to offer her the "harmless pleasure" it had yielded before. *Pleasure*—surely an intriguing, playful motive for the keeping of a pseudonym.[5] Why, then, does Charlotte Brontë confess to taking pleasure in concealing her identity?

I propose an answer to this question through a reading of two mysteries: the public riddle of Currer Bell's identity and the narrative enigmas of *Jane Eyre*. Persistently provoking guesses and speculations, Brontë uses suspenseful stratagems to political ends, overturning widely held convictions about femininity. Suspense emerges as a powerfully subversive tool, and Brontë's "pleasure" in her games of delay and equivocation hints at her discovery of a new kind of political power. Indeed, Brontë carefully transforms the suspense she inherits from her Gothic precursors, putting narrative mysteries to newly unsettling ends. A comparison between Ann Radcliffe's *Mysteries of Udolpho* and Charlotte Brontë's mysteries of *Jane Eyre* uncovers this shift, as realist fiction reworks the Gothic.

Suggestive Pseudonyms

"Averse to personal publicity," Charlotte writes in 1850, "we veiled our names under those of Currer, Ellis, and Acton Bell; the ambiguous choice being dictated by a sort of conscientious scruple at assuming Christian names positively masculine."[6] The sisters were not lying; they were donning veils, maidenly and modest garments for virtuous women outside in the world.[7] But if the veil is proper and eminently feminine, it is also a tease: never concealing entirely, it always acknowledges that something lies behind it. And sure enough, the three unusual names of uncertain gender invited immediate curiosity and speculation. Thus the pseudonyms had everything to do with suspense: like veils, they offered some tantalizing hints about what they were hiding—like first initials and sibling relations—but kept back the fascinating truth.

Yet Charlotte insists that it was a "conscientious scruple" about lying that kept the sisters from taking plainer, more unequivocally masculine names. Indeed, at one point she even suggests that the pseudonyms suited the ambiguous gendering of their writing. Emily's poetry, for example, was so unlike conventional women's writing that Charlotte registers her shock: "I looked it over and more than surprise seized me—a deep conviction that these were not common effusions, nor at all like the poetry women generally write. I thought them condensed and terse, vigorous and genuine."[8] Emily's voice is, on the one hand, *unfeminine* and, on the other hand, *genuine*. Thus Charlotte implies that it may actually be more truthful to call her sister by an ambiguously gendered name.

After this subtle, if casuistic, justification of her honesty, Charlotte contradicts herself, offering a more conventional explanation of the pseudonyms. "We did not like to declare ourselves women," she writes, "because—without at that time suspecting that our mode of writing and thinking was not what is called 'feminine'—we had a vague impression that authoresses are liable to be looked on with prejudice."[9] Performing a sudden about-face, Charlotte wants us to see the sisters as knowing nothing about the relations between their own work and "what is called 'feminine.'" How strange, since only a few lines before, we have heard Charlotte state her "deep conviction" that Emily's poetry had never struck her as "at all like the poetry women generally write."

What is going on here? Either the sisters had noticed that their work was unfeminine and scrupulously decided to take male pseudonyms as true to their work, or they were innocent of the gendering of Victorian writing, subject to vague impressions, naive and guileless women who did not know the ways of the world. Apparently intent on having it both ways, Charlotte manages to defend herself and her late sisters against two contradictory charges of immodest behavior. In her capable hands, the Brontë sisters emerge as earnest, demure, and—most importantly— feminine.

But this decorous play of identity, you remember, has also been *pleasurable*. Modesty has had its thrills. And perhaps it is not hard to guess at those delights. The veil suggests but does not tell, provoking desire.[10] The pleasures of the veil are those of the erotic. Veiling is, as Roland Barthes would say, a "snare."[11] And snares are the stuff of suspense.

Charlotte Brontë was no innocent when it came to the workings of suspense, as any reader of *Jane Eyre* can attest. Take the end of volume 1, where the final scene represents the romantic equivalent of a cliff-hanger. Jane has just saved Rochester from the fire, and when he thanks her for saving his life, he has "strange energy" and "strange fire in his look" (187). However tempting it is to interpret, this "strangeness" is enticingly inconclusive. "He paused; gazed at me; words almost visible trembled on his lips—but his voice was checked" (187).[12] "Checking" his speech, the hero hints all too broadly that he has secrets he cannot tell. A few chapters later, after reproaching Jane for leaving the party too early, he suspends his words again: "'Good night, my—' He stopped, bit his lip, and abruptly left me" (226). Seductively, Rochester hints and halts, and both reader and character become increasingly invested in what Jane calls his "equivocal tokens" (201). D. A. Miller defines such equivocation as the very model of plotted suspense: "To flirt . . . means to cultivate suspense in relationships: to hesitate between meaning, and not meaning, the gestures to which flirtation gives rise. In its teasing approach to meaning and its avoidance of definitive nomination, flirtation is well qualified to motivate the moment of narratability."[13] Flirtation is the ideal vehicle for readerly desire, even for narratability itself. And flirtation is all about dodging the truth, about suggesting and withholding. It is, we might say, all about "veiling."

Suspense, withholding, equivocation—these are the private pleasures of Charlotte's "little mystery," just as they are the readerly pleasures of *Jane Eyre*. Reading the novel and the pseudonym together suggests that Charlotte Brontë was no shrinking violet, seeking the shade of privacy. Despite the fact that she goes to some lengths to have us believe in her demure, all too feminine, timidity, I want to suggest that teasing equivocation plays a rigorously critical role in Brontë's project.

Suspense and the Unsettling of Gender

The title page of the first edition of Charlotte Brontë's novel reads: "JANE EYRE. An Autobiography. EDITED BY CURRER BELL." Far from straightforwardly declaring the text's authorship, these words might well puzzle the reader not in on the "little mystery." At first glance, the text purports to be an autobiography. If this were true, then the author would be a woman—to be precise, a woman hitherto unknown to the literary world, by the name of Jane Eyre. But few of the novel's early readers were gullible enough to fall for that trick: by 1847, reading audiences understood the literary device of the fictional editor.[14] Thus many guessed that the *real* author was a man. Ambiguous but certainly not feminine, the name "Currer" was widely presumed to be masculine, and it would not have been unusual for a male novelist to pose as a female autobiographer in order to tell a story with a woman protagonist. Numerous readers therefore leapt to the conclusion that *Jane Eyre* was not an autobiography at all, but a novel by a man who was posing as a woman. The *People's Journal* took this for granted, noting that "Mr. Currer Bell is already slightly, but rather favourably known to the public, as one of the writers of a small volume of poems."[15] But then again, "Currer" was such an unfamiliar and suspiciously ambiguous name—"a mere *nom de guerre*—perhaps an anagram"—that it could easily be a pseudonym for a woman trying to conceal her identity.[16] Perhaps a woman had taken a masculine name in order to get away with the novel's "coarse" writing and immoral hero. Or perhaps, as G. H. Lewes insisted, any good fiction must "be built out of real experience," and thus *Jane Eyre*'s author must be female, like the protagonist.[17] If such were the case, then *Jane Eyre* was written not by a man, but *by a woman posing as a man posing as a woman.*

This last alternative is, of course, the oddly circuitous truth. On the title page of *Jane Eyre,* a woman, Charlotte Brontë, pretends to be a man, Currer Bell, who, in turn, pretends to be a woman, Jane Eyre. Given this entanglement of possibilities, it is not surprising that reviewers started to speculate wildly about the gender of the author. Presumably, the only fact that the enticingly indeterminate title page made clear to readers was that something peculiar was going on. Indeed, the conspicuous periphrasis of this opener was a perfect case of "veiling"—suggesting and withholding, drawing readerly attention directly to the mystery of the author's gender.

Yet why bother to craft such an elaborate gender game for the title page? We do not have to look any farther than *Jane Eyre* for an answer. There, Rochester plays his own gender game with Jane when he dresses up as an old gypsy woman and claims to be able to tell her fortune. Pretending to divine Jane's prospects, the disguised Rochester returns again and again to the topic of love and marriage. "Have you no present interest in any of the company who occupy the sofas and chairs before you?" he asks. "Is there not one face you study? One figure whose movements you follow with, at least, curiosity?" (248). If Rochester's furtive plan is enigmatic during the interview, his reasons for dressing up as an old woman are no mystery once he reveals his identity. Jane immediately accuses him: "I believe you have been trying to draw me out—or in: you have been talking nonsense to make me talk nonsense" (253). Or, as

Rosemarie Bodenheimer puts it: "The manipulative character of Rochester's power to move Jane to involuntary speech is underlined in his attempt to trick her into self-revelation by disguising himself."[18] Quite simply, Rochester takes on the trappings of femininity in order to prompt Jane to divulge her secrets.

We might begin to make sense of Charlotte Brontë's own cross-dressing in light of her hero's motives for veiling his identity. If the revelation of another's secrets is the point of playing gender games, then Brontë might well have had her own audience in mind when she published her tantalizingly ambiguous title page. Like Rochester, that is, she might have assumed an intriguing disguise in order to extract confessions from her readership.

Which is exactly what happened. The reviewers, when confronted with the ambiguous pseudonym, "Currer Bell," were tricked into self-revelation. In the course of their fervent speculations about the identity of the author of *Jane Eyre,* they disclosed their firm convictions—or, to be more accurate, their prejudices—about the capabilities and limitations of women writers. Take, for example, Elizabeth Rigby's famously scathing review, which offers clear evidence that the novel could not have been written by a woman:

> No woman—a lady friend, whom we are always happy to consult, assures us—makes mistakes in her own *métier*—no woman *trusses game* and garnishes dessert-dishes with the same hands, or talks of doing so in the same breath. Above all, no woman attires another in such fancy dresses as Jane's ladies assume—Miss Ingram coming down, irresistible, "in a *morning* robe of sky-blue crape, a gauze azure scarf twisted in her hair!!" No lady, we understand, when suddenly roused in the night, would think of hurrying on "*a frock.*" They have garments more convenient for such occasions, and more becoming too. This evidence seems incontrovertible. Even granting that these incongruities were purposely assumed, for the sake of disguising the female pen, there is nothing gained; for if we ascribe the book to a woman at all, we have no alternative but to ascribe it to one who has, for some sufficient reason, long forfeited the society of her own sex.[19]

Playing a bit of a gender game herself, Rigby pretends to be a man con-
sulting a lady friend. And clearly, she is canny about snares: acknowledging that the "incontrovertible" evidence of masculine authorship might
be a clever plant—a red herring—she concedes that *Jane Eyre* might
have been written by a female pen in disguise. But if this is the case, then
the author must be a fallen woman—one who has long lost the society
of other women.

On the other side, the *Christian Remembrancer* affirmed: "We, for our
part, cannot doubt that the book is written by a female, and, as certain
provincialisms indicate, one from the North of England. Who, indeed,
but a woman could have ventured, with the smallest prospect of success,
to fill three octavo volumes with the history of a woman's heart? . . .
Mr. Rochester, the hero of the story, is clearly the vision of a woman's
fancy, as the heroine is the image of a woman's heart."[20] With Elizabeth
Rigby on one side and the *Christian Remembrancer* on the other, Currer
Bell seems to have publicly achieved his—and her—emancipation from
the confining trappings of both genders.

Most engaging of all was the conclusion reached by Edwin Percy
Whipple. He decided that *Jane Eyre* was the collaborative work of three
siblings, two brothers and a sister:

> From the masculine tone of Jane Eyre, it might pass altogether
> as the composition of a man, were it not for some unconscious
> feminine peculiarities, which the strongest-minded woman that
> ever aspired after manhood cannot suppress. These peculiarities
> refer not only to elaborate descriptions of dress, and the minu-
> tiae of the sick-chamber, but to various superficial refinements
> of feeling in regard to the external relations of the sex. . . . The
> leading characteristic of the novel, however, and the secret of its
> charm, is the clear, distinct, decisive style of its representation of
> character, manners, and scenery; and this continually suggests
> a male mind. In the earlier chapters, there is little, perhaps, to
> break the impression that we are reading the autobiography of a
> powerful and peculiar female intellect; but when the admirable
> Mr. Rochester appears, and the profanity, brutality, and slang
> of the misanthropic profligate give their torpedo-shocks to the
> nervous system,—and especially when we are favored with more

than one scene given to the exhibition of mere animal appetite, and to courtship after the manner of kangaroos and the heroes of Dryden's plays,—we are gallant enough to detect the hand of a gentleman in the composition. There are also scenes of passion, so hot, emphatic, and condensed in expression, and so sternly masculine in feeling, that we are almost sure that we observe the mind of the author of Wuthering Heights at work in the text.[21]

Whipple presumes that a woman must have had a hand in the writing, given details of dress, the sick chamber, and certain feminine "refinements of feeling," but then clarity, decisiveness, profanity, brutality, heat, passion, animal appetite, and slang—these are clear hallmarks of masculine writing. In fact, these markers of the male intellect are so conspicuous that the novel must have been written, at least in part, by that indisputably masculine mind, the author of *Wuthering Heights*.

So much for speculation. When Charlotte revealed the Brontës' identity in 1850, she effectively discredited a whole array of assumptions about women's writing. Women, she proved, could write with the clarity and passion of men; they could represent fearful brutality and sensuality; and, pace Elizabeth Rigby, respectable women could write about highly irregular relationships without sacrificing their virtue. By veiling her own gender, Charlotte had successfully provoked the world to speculate and, in speculating, to venture strong opinions about masculine and feminine writing. Then, in unveiling herself as a decent Yorkshire woman, she proved a great many of these convictions simply and emphatically wrong. Such is the plot of her "little mystery."

Consider a final example, a review in the *Era,* which Charlotte later turned on its head:

Bulwer, James, D'Israeli, and all the serious novel writers of the day lose in comparison with Currer Bell, for we must presume the work to be his. It is no woman's writing. Although ladies have written histories, travels, and warlike novels, to say nothing of books upon the different arts and sciences, no woman *could have* penned "The Autobiography of Jane Eyre." It is all that one of the other sex might invent, and much more. . . . The tale is one of the heart, and the working out of a moral through the natural affections; it is the victory of mind over matter; the mastery of reason over feeling, without unnatural sacrifices. The writer dives deep into human life, and possesses the gift of being able to write as he thinks and feels. There is a vigour in all he says, a power which fixes the reader's attention, and a charm about his "style" and "diction" which fascinates while it edifies.[22]

Women are not capable of such intellectual, rational, powerful, and moral work—which means that no woman "could have" written the novel.

Charlotte Brontë wrote that this particular review, with its dismissals of feminine skill and its affirmations of masculine morality, gave her "much *pleasure*."[23] Perhaps, now, her pleasure begins to make sense. Like Rochester's, her veiled identity prompts her audience to divulge their innermost feelings, and being more skillful than her hero, Brontë's authorial strategy overwhelmingly succeeds. Her veiling provokes the literary world to reveal its complacent blunders and rigid misconceptions, and yields Brontë the opportunity, eventually, to put them all to shame. Emerging as a powerful critic of contemporary assumptions about men's and women's writing, Charlotte Brontë uses the techniques of suspenseful equivocation to make a significant political point.

At this juncture, we may return to the mysteries of *Jane Eyre*. It is here that we find our proof that Brontë was adept at the stratagems of suspense, and we might ask, in turn, whether her plotting in the public sphere throws light on the operations of her narrative. That is, if the veils of suspense serve a radical political purpose among the Victorian literati, might we say the same for the plotted mysteries of *Jane Eyre*?

If critics have been quick to condemn suspenseful narrative as complacently conservative—bemoaning its despotic withholding of the facts, its manipulation of readerly desire, its smug conclusions—Charlotte Brontë's uses of suspense, like Ruskin's, hint at a more unsettling possibility. After all, it is in the space between veiling and unveiling that *we reveal ourselves*. Mysteries offer us the opportunity for speculation, and in speculating, we necessarily overstep the bounds of the evidence, imposing our own preconceptions and desires on the world that we encounter. The mysteries that are so plentiful in the nineteenth-century novel, then, allow us to know our own impulses, our own longings, our own prejudices. And when the world checks or contradicts those presumptions, we may be compelled to give them up. Or so Brontë suggested to her critics.

But there is an important difference here between mystery and suspense. Brontë's complacent reviewers, when faced with a mystery, knew that something was being withheld from them but assumed that they knew the hidden truth. Blithely, they thought they could outsmart the world—and so leapt to their own favorite conclusions. By contrast, suspense demands a different and quite specific experience of the unknown; it is that mystery within a narrative context that cues a perception of the reader's own ignorance. Rather than encouraging us to jump to premature conclusions, suspenseful withholdings only work when they successfully stir up the anxiety that the world may not actually bear out our hypotheses. Even when the solution to the mystery ultimately substantiates our hopes and predilections, for there to have been suspense—for us to have remained absorbed, apprehensive, doubtful during the narrative—we must have been willing to entertain a range of credible resolutions. Thus suspenseful narrative does not so much reinforce a dominant value-system as it teaches us to hesitate in our convictions, to arrest the most urgent movements of desire and belief. Critics have claimed that suspense operates in the service of its conclusions, but we might say just as well that novelistic endings prove to us that we should always remain in suspense.

Not surprisingly, the text of *Jane Eyre* offers us a usefully illustrative example. After a series of seductive checks and equivocations relating to Jane, Rochester goes to visit the beautiful Blanche Ingram. As Jane waits, suspended, for his return, she seeks to convince herself that she has been wrong about his interest in her: desiring but not knowing, she resolves to put her faith in conventional wisdom, which tells her that "a dependent and a novice" could never be loved by "a gentleman of family, and a man of the world" (201); "It does good to no woman to be flattered by her superior, who cannot possibly intend to marry her" (201). These are examples of what Roland Barthes calls the "implicit proverbs" of the cultural code—"written in that obligative mode by which the discourse states a general will, the law of a society . . . a maxim, a postulate." [24] Like the insistence that respectable women *cannot* write with the vigor and charm of the male pen, the notion that a superior can never intend to marry a dependent is sweeping enough to include the world of the reader as well as the world of the text, purporting to swallow up all particular cases. And this idea is certainly the prevailing orthodoxy, as Jane here makes clear.

Jane's experience will invalidate this maxim, unsettling the universalizing statements of "common sense." In good realist fashion, that is, her narrative upsets conventional ways of seeing and puts forward a new and more unsettling method for approaching the real. We soon learn that a gentleman of family and man of the world can indeed intend to marry a dependent and a novice, which goes to prove that the social authorities—the general will—have got it wrong. After learning to suspend judgment, we are invited to revise our understanding accordingly. But no sooner have we come to believe in this gentleman's good intentions than we discover that Rochester does not, in fact, intend to *marry* Jane, at least technically speaking. And when, in fact, he does marry her, she is no longer a "dependent and a novice." In this double about-face, we return to our starting point, but in the process we have presumably been forced to admit, however unwillingly, that the very open-endedness— the pleasurable uncertainty—of the plot suggests the genuine plausibility of alternative endings. By the time the narrative has finally resettled Jane's "implicit proverb," it has effectively thrown all automatic faith in the dictates of common sense into question. On the most general level, Jane's lesson, like *Modern Painters,* invites us to nurture a skepticism about maxims and generalizing representations, to test sweeping principles against the evidence.

From Gothic to Realist Suspense

To claim that the skepticism of suspense and the skill of veiling belong particularly to Victorian realism may prompt an immediate objection. Ann Radcliffe and her Gothic contemporaries certainly knew how to withhold knowledge, piquing their readers' curiosity. The mysterious "black veil" in *The Mysteries of Udolpho* is one of the most famous of Gothic secrets.[25] And Brontë's own debt to Gothic—and particularly to Radcliffe—has been well established.[26] Yet I would like to suggest that the suspense of Radcliffe's wandering narratives offers a significantly different reading experience from the driving intrigues of *Jane Eyre.*

By way of a comparison, I want to suggest that both Gothic and realist texts work as narratives of education—but they are radically different educations. *The Mysteries of Udolpho* is no classic Bildungsroman, and yet Emily St. Aubert is carefully educated by her virtuous father at the beginning of the novel, and she recalls his lessons throughout the narrative. The aim of this education is to elevate her mind above the "vexations of the world," to buoy her up with "hope and confidence and resignation."[27] Always in danger of succumbing to her exquisite sensibility, Emily must learn to rise above her own emotional tumult with fortitude. After her father's death, she reminds herself that "the faculties of the mind strengthen by exertion, till they finally unnerve affliction, and triumph over it" (1: 122). The terrifying events of the novel therefore function as tests of Emily's psychological stamina: will she be able to resist the mysteries and threats she faces at Udolpho simply by exerting her tranquility of mind? Even in childhood, before Gothic terrors have come to haunt her, Emily's father deliberately introduces disappointments and struggles into her life in order to "acquire that steady dignity of mind that can alone counterbalance the passions, and bear us, as far as is compatible with our nature, above the reach of circumstances" (5). Terror is there to be overcome.

In *Gothic Fiction/Gothic Form,* George Haggerty argues that Radcliffe "wants to have it both ways: she cautions us against an overactive imagination while giving our own imaginations more than enough material to create the horrified response for ourselves."[28] Such a double message might seem to represent the hypocrisy of a sensationalist, moralizing about the dangers of indulging the imagination while offering that same imaginative faculty a series of seductive delights. But instead I suggest that we read Radcliffe's twofold message as an education for reader and protagonist alike. Virtue means refusing to succumb to the "weakness of superstition" (Radcliffe, *Mysteries of Udolpho* 2: 307). And so we are treated to vividly monstrous possibilities in order to test our powers of resistance. In the most famous example, Emily tears away the black veil to witness the horrifying image of "a human figure, of ghastly paleness, stretched at its length, and dressed in the habiliments of the grave" (334). Here, Radcliffe concedes that we are probably tempted to sympathize with her heroine's terror: "On such a subject it may readily be believed that no person could endure to look twice" (334). But even in this extreme circumstance, if we were to push panic aside, we would triumph over the tumult of our terror. "Had [Emily] dared to look again, her delusion and her fears would have vanished together, and she would have perceived that the figure before her was not human, but formed of wax" (334). A little coolness, a little faith, a little patience—and we would overcome the horror.

At the very end of the novel, Radcliffe writes of her own moral purpose:

> Oh! useful may it be to have shown, that though the vicious can sometimes pour affliction upon the good, their power is transient and their punishment certain; and that innocence, though oppressed by injustice, shall, supported by patience, finally triumph over misfortune!
>
> And if the weak hand that has recorded this tale, has by its scenes, beguiled the mourner of one hour of sorrow, or by its moral, taught him to sustain it—the effort, however humble, has not been in vain, nor is the writer unrewarded. (2: 344)

Goodness and justice ultimately prevail, making Radcliffe's plot a quintessentially Christian one. Doubt and fear are there to tempt us away from sustaining our faith, but the trials of suspense teach us to resist them.

For Radcliffe, the ending always brings justice, and the anxieties of the middle are the test of our virtue and the substance of our moral education. For Brontë, the middle of the story is similarly crucial for the education of both reader and protagonist. But far from prompting us to sustain prior certitudes, the bulk of the narrative is given to speculation, investigation, and active inquiry. From the outset, Jane seeks to understand the ways of the world by identifying mysteries and attempting to solve them. Her formal education begins with the puzzle of the stone tablet over the school door, which reads "Lowood Institution":

> I read these words over and over again: I felt that an explanation belonged to them, and was unable fully to penetrate their import. I was still pondering the signification of "Institution," and endeavouring to make out a connection between the first words and the verse of Scripture, when the sound of a cough close behind me made me turn my head. (55)

"Pondering," wanting to "penetrate," and trying to "make out connections," Jane at ten is already intent on solving the mysteries of her environment. But Helen Burns, like many of Jane's interlocutors in the text, refuses to divulge too much: "You ask rather too many questions. I have given you answers enough for the present" (57). If Jane produces an abundance of questions, she must face a marked withholding of the truth—an epistemological pattern that characterizes most of her experience.

In Brontë's text, the checks to knowledge only provoke a more fierce desire for the truth. Indeed, the impediments to knowledge become more and more demanding, as each new step brings with it new mysteries and new frustrations. Consider Jane's arrival at Thornfield, where her mistaken speculations follow in quick succession: she must first learn that Mrs. Fairfax is not the lady of the house, as she had thought, but merely the housekeeper; she must discover that her pupil is not Mrs. Fairfax's daughter but the child of a French dancer; and she must find out that there is a mysterious Mr. Rochester with a troubled but enigmatic relationship to Thornfield Hall. Soon, too, new mysteries emerge—a stranger on a horse, laughter in the attic, whispering servants—and new obstacles to knowledge appear at every turn. Without fail, Jane's experience involves finding her expectations thwarted, her assumptions flawed, and her companions unwilling or unable to divulge the crucial truths. But without fail, Jane generates new guesses, new speculations, and new questions.

The value of suspense has clearly changed from *Udolpho* to *Jane Eyre*. For Brontë, the doubts of suspense are not put forward only to be mastered and dismissed: doubting itself has become the central activity of the text. Perhaps Jane's willingness to guess and test is itself what makes her a compelling protagonist: disinclined to take her world on faith, she is a model of self-reliance, intelligence, and integrity. Her refusal to accept convention and her desire for knowledge always invite readerly collaboration and participation. Indeed, we might say that the realist novel encourages the reader to adopt a scientific epistemology as a method for ordinary life, and in this context Jane's intimate addresses to her readers can be read as invitations to join her in a new approach to the truths of the world.

If the lessons of suspense have changed from the eighteenth to the nineteenth centuries, so too have its formal qualities. Emily St. Aubert is so overwhelmed with curiosity that she removes the black veil to see what it hides, but she does so without speculating about its contents, and we do not discover what she finds until several hundred pages later, when the narrator simply interjects an explanation. Revelations in Radcliffe are sprung upon us suddenly—like the moment when Sister Agnes reveals that she has a miniature matching the one owned by Emily's father. Since the heroine has solemnly promised not to look into this mystery, the answer to it comes not from her own investigations but from happenstance—or providence. By contrast, the revelations of Brontë's narrative are typically tied to the questions Jane herself poses for us. What is going on upstairs in the third story? Will Rochester marry Blanche Ingram? We are carefully prepared to encounter answers to the questions the narrative asks by way of Brontë's suspenseful withholdings.

Thus the suspense of _Jane Eyre_ is what we might call recursive in its structure. The text poses a number of questions; it invites us to speculate about their answers; and then it returns us to these questions, often more than once, each time adding the experience of the narrative to attempt new solutions. In this way, the fiction conforms to the patterns of experimental science: a mystery, followed by a hypothesis, followed by a test, followed by an answer or a new obstacle to knowledge, which typically provokes a new test.

I would like to suggest that this recursive pattern challenges a critical assumption that is frequently made about suspense—namely, that suspenseful narratives can only sustain one reading. Edmund Wilson describes the obsessed reader of detective fiction this way:

> The addict reads not to find anything out but merely to get the mild stimulation of the succession of unexpected incidents and of the suspense itself of _looking forward_ to learning a sensational secret. That this secret is nothing at all and does not really account for the incidents does not matter to such a reader. . . . He does not think back and check the events, he simply shuts the book and starts another.[29]

Assuming that the excitement of suspense is all in the outcome, critics have insisted that we never need to read a suspenseful narrative twice. Thus Roland Barthes understands popular plotted fiction as part of a culture of rapid, uncritical consumption and waste: "rereading [is] an operation contrary to the commercial and ideological habits of our society, which would have us 'throw away' the story once it has been consumed ('devoured'), so that we can then move on to another story, buy another book."[30] But if we take _Jane Eyre_ as our model, then this critical tradition seems to have missed the fact that suspense *is itself all about rereading.* Victorian suspense returns us to our hunches and suspicions, inviting us to revise and amend them each time we encounter new evidence and new experience. Its structure is itself an invitation to read twice: to note the laughter in the attic and then to come back to it, again and again, until it has become intelligible.

But why does this matter? Why does the fact of rereading produce a new understanding of suspense as a narrative strategy? Let us return for a moment to an earlier example. Jane relies on common sense and conventional wisdom when she asserts that a gentleman cannot possibly intend to marry an impoverished dependent. But far from taking this for granted, Brontë uses suspense precisely to *estrange* this presumption, treating it not as knowledge but as a hypothesis to be tested rather than assumed. Thus, far from confidently reaffirming the dictates of common sense, the narrative of suspense models a readiness to open commonsensical notions to reading and rereading, a willingness to subject conventional wisdom to the process of active doubting and experimentation. Thus, if there is anything to be learned from Jane's experience, it is what we might call a skeptical attitude, or even a methodology: an invitation to mistrust inherited conventions, to see these as provisional speculation and tentative guesswork.

In this context, suspense emerges as a much more critical and even, in Barthes' sense, a much more *writerly* form than critics have typically imagined. Barthes famously opposed the conventional "readerly" pleasures of suspense fiction against the *jouissance* of the demanding "writerly" text, which "discomforts (perhaps to the point of a certain boredom), unsettles the reader's historical, cultural, psychological assumptions." [31] But Brontë's suspense makes it abundantly clear that suspenseful plotting, like the writerly text, also unsettles the reader's assumptions. The suspenseful middle of *Jane Eyre* is not an empty delay, a waiting game, but an active interpretive ground, where the reader enters into a critical relationship with ideological norms and conventions. Brontë expects her audience to generate conventional hypotheses when faced with a mystery but also to become aware that these are, in fact, *only* hypotheses—speculations, guesses, hopes, and desires. The middle of the story is actually intended to throw the operations of culture and convention into relief.

If the suspenseful mysteries of *Udolpho* are planted to test our faith that good will win out over evil, then doubt is there to tempt us away from conviction. The point is to hold fast to a faith that the vicissitudes of the world always threaten to upset. By stark contrast, the solutions to mysteries in Brontë quite deliberately ask us to lose faith, to overturn conviction, to revise our understanding of the ways of the world. They begin by setting out conventionally authoritative images, which are then cast into question and often permanently unsettled by experience. Radcliffe asks us to keep a tight grip on belief, whatever doubts should arise; Brontë asks us to put our beliefs to the test, to question whether they can withstand the trials of experience.

Jane Eyre models this education for us, learning, little by little, to question her own preconceptions. In so doing, she invokes the paradigm so crucial to nineteenth-century science—the experiment. For example, having lighted upon Grace Poole as the probable culprit for the fire in Rochester's bed, Jane tries to confirm her suspicions. The morning after the conflagration, she comes upon Grace sewing curtain rings:

> There she sat, staid and taciturn-looking, as usual, in her brown stuff gown, her check apron, white handkerchief, and cap. She was intent on her work, in which her whole thoughts seemed absorbed: on her hard forehead, and in her commonplace features, was nothing either of the paleness or desperation one would have expected to see marking the countenance of a woman who had attempted murder. . . . "I will put her to some test," thought I: "such absolute impenetrability is past comprehension." (192)

A murderer could not possibly look so ordinary, so "commonplace." The exceptional, Jane hypothesizes, must bear visible marks of its difference from the norm. But then, narrative suspense reminds us of what we know to be true: our images and expectations may well in fact conflict with realities. The proper response in such a case is, as we might have guessed, an experiment. "I will put her to some test," Jane decides.

Critics have typically imagined realism as an epistemological faith in the surfaces of things, but in Brontë as in Ruskin, it is the failure of the appearance to yield the truth that leads to the doubts, speculations, and experiments of suspense. And if we concede that Victorian texts incline surprisingly often to the stratagems of suspenseful plotting, then perhaps the nineteenth century did not imagine that the surfaces of things were so telling after all. Certainly Ruskin's realist experiments depend on the deceptions practiced daily on our eyes, misleading us to such an extent that we do not recognize the truth even when it is plainly before us. It is the impenetrability of appearances that generates Ruskinian realism, and it is the same impenetrability that provokes the pleasures of Victorian suspense.

And it is not just any pleasure—it is <u>politically unsettling pleasure.</u> Torn between conflicting solutions to the mysteries of her environment, Jane, like her author, disrupts orthodox conceptions of femininity. Wondering whether the enigma of Grace Poole involves a past sexual indiscretion, Jane considers the alternatives:

> Mrs Poole's square, flat figure, and uncomely, dry, even coarse face, recurred so distinctly to my mind's eye, that I thought, "No; impossible! my supposition cannot be correct. Yet," suggested the secret voice which talks to us in our own hearts, "*you* are not beautiful either, and perhaps Mr Rochester approves you: at any rate, you have often felt as if he did." (196)

If it is impossible for Rochester to have been in love with the square, dry Grace Poole, then it might be equally impossible that he loves the small, irregular Jane Eyre. Either he follows convention, in which case he cannot love either—or he is highly unusual, in which case he might well love both. Jane quells these anxieties, for the moment, by forcing a conventional conclusion: "I compared myself with her, and found we were different. Bessie Leaven had said I was quite a lady; and she spoke truth. . . . And now I looked much better than I did when Bessie saw me" (196). Jane, here, compares the two images and arrives at a comforting difference: she is prettier and of a higher class than Grace Poole. But, as if to make absolutely clear that all such conventions are up for grabs, it is immediately after this that the narrative introduces Blanche Ingram. If Rochester is interested in outward marks of class and beauty, then Blanche—not Jane—must be his chosen mate. If, however, he is attracted to the hidden and the exceptional, why not Grace Poole as easily as Jane Eyre? While we wait for the answers, the narrative casts significant doubt on the relationship between conventional marks of feminine attractiveness and their unsettlingly eccentric alternatives.

Skillfully deploying the open-endedness of suspense from beginning to end, Charlotte Brontë enforces strict lessons about gender. Much as we may bluster and swagger in our convictions, there is always the chance that the solution to the mystery may prove us wrong. In a world that confines and restricts women precisely by conceiving of women's potential as a limited, known quantity, Brontë's suspense teaches us to doubt, to experiment, to suspend judgment. When it comes to femininity, the veil teaches us to expect surprises. Which is not such a harmless pleasure after all.

4 Realism as Self-Forgetfulness

Gender, Ethics, and *Great Expectations*

In 1848, reviewer Edwin Percy Whipple asserted that *Jane Eyre* must have been partly penned by a man. His evidence was that it echoed the style of that decidedly masculine writer—the author of *Wuthering Heights*. Proved emphatically wrong by Charlotte Brontë's revelations of 1850, Whipple had learned his lesson by the time he came to review *Great Expectations* eleven years later. What he claimed to admire most in Dickens's new novel was the fact that the mystery had confounded him:

> In no other of his romances has the author succeeded so perfectly in at once stimulating and baffling the curiosity of his readers. He stirred the dullest minds to guess the secret of his mystery; but, so far as we have learned, the guesses of his most intelligent readers have been almost as wide of the mark as those of the least apprehensive. It has been all the more provoking to the former class, that each surprise was the result of art, and not of trick; for a rapid review of previous chapters has shown that the materials of a strictly logical development of the story were freely given.[1]

Whipple was not the only one to appreciate Dickens's skill in the art of plotting. The *Times* celebrated Dickens "as the greatest master of construction" of the era, the most expert at keeping "an exciting story within the bounds of probability." The *Athenaeum* praised him for his adroit sustaining of readerly interest: "Every week almost, as it came out, we were artfully stopped at some juncture which made Suspense count the days until the next number appeared." Even Margaret Oliphant, who dismissed *Great Expectations* as an absurd fantasy, understood that enthusiastic readers found the novel's incidents "strange, dangerous, and exciting."[2] Taken together, these nineteenth-century reviews suggest that suspense may have been the most alluring seduction of *Great Expectations* for the Victorian reader.

This chapter makes the case that Dickens not only thrilled his contemporaries by producing and sustaining a fascinating suspense plot, but he also articulated a clear ethical value for suspenseful plotting. Like *Jane Eyre, Great Expectations* brings together the exciting pleasures of suspense with its weighty significance. More surprisingly, perhaps, the novel suggests that in the context of Victorian culture, the gender of suspense was feminine. Dickens claims, as do Ruskin and Brontë, that we cannot unearth the hidden truths of the world without putting aside our most entrenched expectations; in order to know the world we must learn to suspend ourselves. And since Victorian culture insistently cast self-suspension as a quintessentially feminine virtue, women, it seemed, must be the most acute readers of the real. In this light, Biddy emerges as the epistemological ideal of *Great Expectations*.

Great Expectations also allows us to see how the skeptical epistemology of detective fiction moved beyond the literal inclusion of the detective. In order to make the claim that *Great Expectations* belongs in a tradition of detective fiction—quite as much as *Bleak House* or *The Mystery of Edwin Drood*—I start with a brief reading of Poe's "Purloined Letter," which, along with *The Moonstone,* is famous for having launched the genre. Poe shows us how central the suspension of the self is to the accumulation of hidden knowledge. If we read Poe alongside *Great Expectations,* we can see how the earliest detective fictions reveal a shared concern to disseminate a skeptical epistemology.

The Moonstone united the scientist and the detective, and Umberto Eco argues that such a combination is fitting, since they share a skeptical epistemology: they "suspect on principle that some elements, evident but not apparently important, may be evidence of something else that is not evident—and on this basis they elaborate a new hypothesis to be tested."[3] What science and detection have in common, in other words, is a thoroughgoing resistance to the assumption that the truths of world are readily apparent. Dickens broadens the scope of this method to suggest that the scientist's paradigm of suspicion is necessary to solving all mysteries—from formal detection to ordinary reading, including the most commonplace interpretive puzzles of everyday life. Like Brontë, then, Dickens uses the novel to disseminate the critical suspension of judgment and the epistemological project of testing.

The Ethics of Suspense: Poe's "Purloined Letter"

Critics have often claimed that suspenseful plots comfort socially discomfited readers with neat, safe endings. Clive Bloom writes that Edgar Allan Poe's orderly plots are responses to the "decentered and *disordered* society he found himself in." Thus "Poe's art is an antidote to contemporary social displacement on a wide scale." Similarly, Leo Bersani writes that "Realistic fiction serves nineteenth-century society by providing it with strategies for containing (and repressing) its disorder within significantly structured stories about itself."[4] Nineteenth-century novelists supposedly forced the real world to conform, through artful plotting, to historically conditioned conceptual paradigms and ideological oversimplifications.[5]

But this is to miss the lessons of suspenseful narrative. Charlotte Brontë, in her crafty equivocations, taught us to mistrust convention and the workings of our own desire in unearthing the secrets of the world. Before turning to Dickens, we can see the demand for self-suspension as the very first lesson of detective fiction. In "The Purloined Letter," Poe teaches us to recognize the dangers of relying on entrenched assumptions and desires.[6] The crucial error made by the Prefect and his officers, according to Poe's wise Dupin, is that "They consider only their own ideas of ingenuity; and, in searching for anything hidden, advert only to the modes in which they would have hidden it" (12). Like Reynolds and Kant, Ruskin's pre-realist predecessors, the detectives retreat into their own minds in pursuit of the truth. What they refuse to perceive, therefore, is the potential *otherness* of the real. As Jacques Lacan puts it, "the detectives have so immutable a notion of the real that they fail to notice that their search tends to transform it into its object."[7]

Dupin concedes one point to the Prefect and his men: "They are right in this much, that their own ingenuity is a faithful representative of that of the mass; but when the cunning of an individual felon is diverse in character from their own, the felon foils them, of course" (12). Relying on their own preconceptions, which exemplify *general* rules and ideas, the detectives fail to consider what Ruskin would call the "infinite variety" of the real. And this has consequences for method. Unwilling or unable to recognize the world's likely resistance to convention, the detectives never question their habits of detection. "They have no variation of principle in their investigations; at best, when urged by some unusual emergency, by some extraordinary reward, they extend or exaggerate their old modes of practice without touching their principles" (12). To put this another way, they never experiment, obdurately refusing to transform the hypothesis—the principle—even when it does not correspond with the evidence. The result, of course, is that the detectives cannot solve the mystery. Nor can the naive narrator, who is shocked at Dupin's willingness to overturn convention and exclaims: "You do not mean to set at naught the well-digested idea of centuries?" (13). Here, then, is realism in a nutshell: to know the world one must acknowledge its inaccessibility to traditional rules and conventions—and its basic, unyielding otherness.

It is this emphasis on alterity that leads me to argue that suspense not only offers a potentially subversive politics, as Brontë makes clear, but also disseminates an influential nineteenth-century ethics. Narrative mysteries in the Victorian period teach us to set aside self-interest and personal desire in order to attend to the surprising, unsettling world, a world that may well flout our prejudices and disappoint our expectations. From Poe to Dickens and beyond, the suspense of detective fiction unites ethics and epistemology in a skeptical method intended to teach us a new and more respectful relationship to the world.

Dickensian Suspense

Jaggers, in a perfect example of a plotted "snare," withholds a crucial piece of knowledge from Pip. "The name of the person who is your liberal benefactor remains a profound secret, until the person chooses to reveal it."[8] It is the checking of knowledge that leads directly to the production of Pip's mistaken expectations. And it is the failure to know the truth that gives rise to the desiring motors of the realist plot. We might even say that "great expectations" describes the experience of suspense so perfectly that Pip can only be a figure for the reader of the nineteenth-century novel.

But in fact, Pip and the reader have crucially different experiences of this particular mystery. For the reader, the withholding of the name of Pip's benefactor indicates quite unequivocally that a specific piece of knowledge is missing. By signaling the existence of a secret, Dickens forces us to recognize the fact of our ignorance and so piques a desire for further knowledge. Indeed, even if, as first-time readers, we suspect that it is Miss Havisham who is going to turn out to have been Pip's benefactor, the text offers us an inescapable sign that there is some reason for secrecy. We have to wait and wonder, to speculate and hypothesize, to know that there is something we do not know.

One of Pip's clearest failures in the novel is that he does not experience the moment of his inheritance as suspenseful: unlike the reader, he leaps to the conclusion that his benefactor is Miss Havisham, and he rushes to assume that this is all part of a plot to marry him to Estella. "[Miss Havisham] had adopted Estella, she had as good as adopted me, and *it could not fail to be her intention* to bring us together" (232; my emphasis). Pip, refusing to suspend judgment, sees the world as a reflection of his own hopes and expectations. The result is a drastic misreading. Harry Stone explains that Pip's "topsy-turvy vision" leads him to read the world in reverse.[9] And I would like to suggest that this topsy-turvy structure applies specifically to the text's *realism*. Pip exclaims: "My dream was out; my wild fancy was surpassed by sober reality; Miss Havisham was going to make my fortune on a grand scale" (137). Inverting the realist experiment, Pip rushes to assume that "sober reality" coincides with his representations. Thus he is in for a rude shock. He will never solve the mysteries of the world if, like Poe's inflexible detectives, he does not put his own methods and assumptions on trial.[10]

The trial—the testing of hypotheses in order to arrive at knowledge. Dickens shows us clearly why we find so many trials, both legal and scientific, in the nineteenth-century novel. Trials, whether in the courtroom or the laboratory, demand the suspension of judgment. Both scientific experiments and courtroom narratives, by their very structure, insist on a delay between initial appearance and more certain knowledge.[11] Both are perfect vehicles for narrative suspense. And perhaps most importantly, both involve plot's ethical imperative; the arresting of arbitrary desires and prejudices in the face of tested knowledge. In *Great Expectations,* Jaggers, the great figure of the law, sounds almost like a broken record in his reiteration of the importance of not leaping to capricious conclusions. Directly before introducing the mystery of Pip's expectations, he offers a disquisition on the legal presumption of innocence to the crowd at the Three Jolly Bargemen. "Do you know, or do you not know, that the law of England supposes every man to be innocent, until he is proved—proved—to be guilty?" (133). The double utterance of the need for proof, here, underscores the fact that the static, unchanging Jaggers will simply repeat the same lesson to Pip, over and over again. "Never mind what you have always longed for, Mr. Pip," Jaggers says, "keep to the record" (138).

Jaggers's instruction to the crowd at the Jolly Bargemen focuses on their leap to assume the guilt of the convict without the rigorous tests of the fair trial. "Are you aware, or are you not aware," asks Jaggers of Mr. Wopsle, "that none of these witnesses have yet been cross-examined?" (133). If to examine is to suspend judgment, then to cross-examine is to return to questions already asked and answers already given, to inspect, to question, and often to undermine the evidence. In its exacting methods, legal cross-examination outstrips other models of skeptical interrogation and takes its place as the consummately fair paradigm of knowledge seeking.

But Pip's upbringing has not prepared him for fair trials. The first appearance of the unjust Mrs. Joe reads like a cruel parody of a courtroom examination:

> "Who brought you up by hand?"
> "You did," said I.
> "And why did I do it, I should like to know!" exclaimed my sister.
> I whimpered, "I don't know."
> "*I* don't!" said my sister. "I'd never do it again. I know that."
> (9–10)

Assuming Pip's guilt and her own long-suffering goodness, Mrs. Joe's questions are hardly skeptical inquiries: she asks Pip to generate not knowledge but gratitude, not truths but justifications. This is capricious catechism rather than skeptical cross-examination.

In fact, Pip's childhood experience of the trial involves not only the presumption of his guilt and the willful disregarding of the facts, but the evil of questioning itself. "Drat that boy . . . what a questioner he is," Mrs. Joe says irritably, and adds: "Ask no questions, and you'll be told no lies" (14). Mrs. Joe claims to believe that questioning only invites falsehoods from the other. She therefore refuses to countenance inquiry altogether and considers questioning to represent a kind of guilt. "People are put in the Hulks because they murder, and because they rob, and forge, and do all sorts of bad; and they always begin by asking questions," she warns (14).[12] Pip seems to incorporate this lesson immediately, connecting his inquiry to his imminent crime: "I had begun by asking questions, and I was going to rob Mrs. Joe" (14).

On the one hand, Jaggers makes clear that the rigorous questioning of cross-examination is the sign of a fair trial; on the other hand, Mrs. Joe teaches Pip that to ask questions is to be guilty oneself. It is no mystery which of these two is in the right. Mrs. Joe does not even practice what she preaches: when Pip returns from Miss Havisham's, Dickens tells us pointedly that she asks "a number of questions" and shoves Pip's face against the wall for not answering the questions "at sufficient length" (66). She is rewarded with precisely the falsehoods she has claimed to expect when Pip invents a rich fantasy about the house he visits. Carried away with her own self-interest, she speculates greedily, enjoying her wonder about Pip's prospects. Criminalizing Pip's questions and violently insisting on answers to her own, however false, Mrs. Joe casts inquiry itself as a guilty, fruitless act, all the while enjoying it herself. Given this education in the failure of questions, is it any wonder, later, that Pip will not thoroughly interrogate his own "expectations"? He has not been educated in the fruitful patterns of plotted suspense, whether legal, or scientific, or novelistic. Dickens's readers will have the privilege of a different kind of education.

The Gender of Realism

If Jaggers in all his skeptical suspicion of the world is eminently, if impersonally, fair, while Pip's despotic sister criminalizes innocent inquiry, we can begin to draw a Dickensian link between skepticism and justice. Jaggers's presumption of innocence is a model of justice, and thus to be just one must begin by assuming that one does not know the truth, and in order to come to know the truth fairly one must conduct rigorous tests unprejudiced by personal preference and desire. Here is the quintessentially realist union of knowledge, ethics, and experimentation: the skeptical realist demands not so much the real itself, as a rigorously judicious relation to that real.

Yet, Jaggers is hardly the model of sympathetic humanity in *Great Expectations*. And despite his stated philosophy of presumed innocence, in the context of the courtroom Jaggers is not scrupulously fair but rather effectively partisan: it is a good thing when Jaggers is "for" one, no matter how guilty one is. Thus what he attempts to teach Pip is not his own practice but rather the impartial position of the law itself—the fairness of which demands the dual presumption of ignorance and skeptical inquiry. In theory, this ethical relationship to the world is all very well. But the impersonal logic of the law overlooks the force and experience of desire. However articulate a spokesman for abstract justice, the static Jaggers is missing the forward-looking pressures of aspiration and speculation, and so he is a poor model for Pip, whose desires make him all too susceptible to the joys of guesswork. Jaggers neglects the very impulses that motivate not only Pip but also the reader of suspenseful plots: the motors of keen preference and unfulfilled desire. It is easy enough to invoke the presumption of innocence; it is altogether another matter to quell conjecture, extinguish hope, and stifle inclination. The lawyer is not a good figure for the realist reader because, without desire, he does not have to work to set his desires aside; without prejudice, he does not have to labor to transform his prejudices into knowledge.

Unlike Jaggers, the realist text teaches us skepticism *in the face of* desire and prejudice. It is for this reason that realist experimentation is about self-denial, or as Pip calls it, "self-forgetfulness." The term "self-forgetfulness" actually appears in reference to Biddy, that consummate angel in the house, who repeatedly puts her own desires aside in order to attend to the needs of those around her.[13] At first, then, "self-forgetfulness" might seem a politically worrying description, attached as it is to the dangerously self-sacrificing model of Victorian womanhood. The familiar image of the self-denying woman would suggest that only one gender is required to "forget" its desires.[14] But to see Biddy as *only* an angel in the house is to miss her role as the text's most skillful reader, the novel's most expert interpreter of difficult and cryptic signs. In a text

packed with misreadings, Biddy's interpretations of the world are sensitive, astute, and just. Quick to spot Pip's bad faith and Joe's pride, she is
also adept at the technical skill of reading. Indeed, it is she who actually
teaches both Pip and Joe to read in the first place, and it is she who remains Pip's literary equal even without the benefit of his formal education. Pip is perplexed by her superiority to him in this respect: "'How
do you manage, Biddy,' said I, 'to learn everything that I learn, and always to keep up with me?'" (125). Biddy is intelligent, and above all, she
is an intelligent *reader*.

I would like to suggest that one minor incident in the novel uncovers the ethical-epistemological structure that drives the text as a whole,
and it puts Biddy's skill as an interpreter at its center. Mrs. Joe, after her
beating, has been communicating by tracing cryptic signs on a slate, including "a character that looked like a curious T." Pip at first interprets
it as an initial: "I had in vain tried everything producible that began with
a T, from tar to toast and tub." This strategy fails to offer up the truth,
and so, in good experimental fashion, he changes tactics, from reading
the sign as arbitrary linguistic signifier to reading it as a pictorial refer-
ent. Now he is on the right track: "At length it had come into my head
that the sign looked like a hammer," a hypothesis to which Pip's sister
expresses "a qualified assent" (122–23). We have seen Pip read this way
before—on the very first page of the novel he has read his parents' tomb-
stones as if the letters were images. Cannily, then, he shifts reading practices when faced with a mystery and moves a step closer to solving it. This
shift does not altogether solve the mystery, however, because Mrs. Joe is
not interested in the hammer itself when Pip presents her with it. Pip is
stumped. It is Biddy who comes to the rescue. More adept a reader than
Pip, she changes reading practices yet again, focusing on the hammer's
associations. Connecting the hammer with one who wields it in the forge,
Biddy presents Mrs. Joe with Orlick. Pip's sister nods vigorously, and
so the solution to the mystery is confirmed. The "T" is a metonymic
signifier, as well as an ideographic one. The process of discovering this
fact has entailed several radical shifts in hypothesis. Indeed, it has meant
not only identifying an array of possible solutions to the mystery but also
allowing variations in the practice of reading itself.

Consistently, Biddy emerges as the most skillful reader of the signs
Mrs. Joe communicates, understanding her confusing signals "as though

she had studied her from infancy" (122). It is this responsiveness that earns her a place as Mrs. Joe's caretaker. Thus what makes Biddy a sensitive reader is not only an experimental epistemology but also an ethical acuteness, which allows her to encounter the surprising alterity of the world on its own terms. Her quintessentially feminine labor as Mrs. Joe's nurse and interpreter involves both caring and knowing—both responding to the other and understanding that other. And unlike the abstractly fair Jaggers, Biddy's ethical-epistemological model is supple, *flexible:* she is not bound by written principles—the conventionalized letter of the law—but moves easily among paradigms of interpretation when confronted with the enigmas of the other.[15] Her letter can become metaphor or metonym, picture or arbitrary sign.[16] She can read the mysterious signs produced by Pip's sister because she can put aside her own presumptions to attend to the radical otherness of a mind unlike her own. This, then, is Biddy's "self-forgetfulness," just as it is the substance of experimental realism.[17]

If Biddy seems like a secondary character and her mysteries comparatively inconsequential, the text presents substantial evidence to suggest that her responses to the world should act as a model for both Pip and the reader. Pip, as we know, goes wrong when he does not follow Biddy's experimental example. When faced with the central mystery of his life, he does not test his hypotheses, and thus he imposes his mistaken guesses on the world. And it is Pip's self-absorption that makes him a poor reader: lacking humility, sure of his own judgment, he cannot put aside his own desires to ready himself for surprises. From the perspective of a scientific epistemology, Pip fails to know the hidden truth because he is incapable of what Tyndall calls "self-renunciation." Obviously consumed by self-interested desire, he reads into Jaggers's mystery just what he wants to understand—that Miss Havisham intends both her fortune and Estella for him—and therefore he misses the possibility that the world may not coincide with his expectations.

Biddy's skill at solving mysteries appears in the text directly—and suggestively—after Dickens has introduced a set of official detectives who fail to uncover Mrs. Joe's attacker. Much like Poe's Prefect, Dickens's detectives cannot solve the mystery because they rely entirely on their own ideas, refusing to discard hypotheses when these do not match the evidence. "They took up several obviously wrong people, and they ran their heads very hard against wrong ideas, and persisted in trying to fit the circumstances to the ideas, instead of trying to extract ideas from the circumstances" (121). Like Pip and Ruskin's Old Masters, they begin with the idea and assume that the important truths of the world will reflect the patterns of their minds. A better student of realism, Biddy solves her mysteries by knowing that she does not know, testing guess after guess against the evidence. Refusing rigid conventions and fixed principles, she comes both to know more and to act more compassionately than her novelistic counterparts.

And so, by uniting a sharp perceptiveness with a self-denying femininity, Dickens allows us to rethink the paradigm of the angel in the house. With Biddy as our model, it begins to look as though there might be a connection between Victorian femininity and Victorian science. Both demand a self-denying receptiveness to alterity. Both specifically call for the capacity to suspend desire and preconception in order to come to know the otherness of the world.[18] In this context, it is not surprising that Biddy is an unusually skilled reader in a world of perilously puzzling signs and willful misreadings—responding more skeptically and judiciously than any other character to the mysteries she encounters.[19] With "self-forgetfulness," Dickens is not simply offering us a limiting image of self-sacrificing femininity: Biddy, in responding to the otherness of the world on its own terms, is a model of reading for us readers. The thrusting, self-important hero would do well to learn the heroine's self-denying skepticism, both ethically and epistemologically. And if "self-forgetfulness" is both the foundation of realist knowledge and the ideal quality of Victorian womanhood, then the gender of realism is feminine.

The Lessons of Dickensian Suspense

Pip does finally recognize Biddy's wisdom as he sets off to marry her in the penultimate chapter of the novel, imagining that he will ask her to make him "a better man" (468). Indeed, though much has been made of the two endings of *Great Expectations,* we may say that there are really *three.* Before Pip encounters the lonely Estella in the last chapter, he deliberately and seriously plans to marry Biddy. We are treated to images of the happy home life with Biddy he forecasts for himself, "and of the change for the better that would come over my character when I had a guiding spirit at my side" (473). We are even given a verbatim account of the humble marriage proposal Pip has rehearsed, as if to underscore the earnestness of the plan. Then, the journey home is a suspenseful one: Dickens makes us wait as Pip gives full play to his expectations and finds them slowly disappointed, one by one. First his "hopeful notion of seeing [Biddy] busily engaged in her daily duties" is "defeated" (473); then "almost fearing," he finds the forge closed; and finally he discovers that he has arrived too late. Here, what Pip pointedly calls his "last baffled hope" (474) is not his marriage to Estella, but to Biddy.

Thus Pip fails to bring about the conventional end to the marriage plot—three times, and with two different women. Of the two candidates for marriage, Biddy is even a more credible companion for living happily ever after than Estella, as Dickens makes quite plain in Pip's rosy fantasies of their future together.[20] Furthermore, the suspense the novel builds up with Pip's "last baffled hope" is in direct contrast to the flat unexpectedness of the final meeting with Estella, at least in the first ending. Eleven years after his failed attempt to marry Biddy, Pip tells her that his "poor dream . . . has all gone by" (477), and then he simply happens upon Estella, without anticipation, without particular plans or desires. In the first ending, there is no prospect of a marriage. In this version of the novel, Biddy is indeed Pip's last *hope*—the last of his great expectations, the final object of suspense. Indeed, Dickens called the final meeting with Estella "the extra end . . . after Biddy and Joe are done with."[21] At the advice of his friend Bulwer-Lytton, Dickens then added suspense into his second ending, allowing expectation to sneak back into the text.

Why must Pip endure the suspense and disappointed hope of marrying Biddy and then undergo suspense again with Estella in the second edition of the novel? Why are we still encountering "expectations" in the final paragraphs of the novel?[22] Peter Brooks argues that none of these endings matters terribly much because the plot is effectively over with "the decisive moment" that is the death of Magwitch.[23] But this conclusion overlooks the text's careful teaching of the lessons of skeptical realism. Doubt is not over because the larger mystery of the novel is solved. The fundamental premise of realism is that the otherness of the world is *always* mysterious—always demanding tests, doubts, and guesswork. Thus the text of experimental realism emphatically refuses to let us forget suspense, because it must carry over into our own lives. It does not want to let us rest easy, satisfied with neat answers and conventional closures. We must learn the alterity of the real from these fictional plots and then transfer the practice of skeptical, anti-conventional doubt to the mysteries of our lives.

If the Victorian novel suggests that suspense demands the rigors of self-denial and the pains of self-annihilation, its extraordinary power lies in the fact that it is also *pleasurable*. Dickens focuses our attention on the intriguing seductions of suspense toward the end of the novel. Magwitch has come to stay, and Pip wants desperately to keep his existence a secret. The most important task for him, therefore, is to hide the convict from his domestic servants. Perfectly in keeping with the lessons of "The Purloined Letter," Pip decides that the best way to screen Magwitch is not to try to keep him out of sight, but to display him as something other than what he is:

> The impossibility of keeping him concealed in the chambers was self-evident. It could not be done, and the attempt to do it would inevitably engender suspicion. True, I had no Avenger in my service now, but I was looked after by an inflammatory old female, assisted by an animated rag-bag whom she called her niece, and to keep a room secret from them would be to invite curiosity and exaggeration. They both had weak eyes, which I had long attributed to their chronically looking in at keyholes, and they were always at hand when not wanted; indeed, that was their only reliable quality besides larceny. Not to get up a mystery with these people, I resolved to announce in the morning that my uncle had unexpectedly come from the country. (325)

To conceal is to "engender suspicion," and to keep a room secret is to "invite" curiosity. In other words, a mystery excites alert, skeptical attention. In this case, it is the attention of curious women that is "engendered," and perhaps it is no accident that the small male Avenger has been replaced by two daunting feminine investigators. Pip tries scornfully to divest these thieving domestics of their humanity—referring to them as an "inflammatory old female" and her "ragbag" niece—but one consequence of his scorn is that he narrows our knowledge of the servants to two basic facts: their femininity and their curiosity. Since Pip has markedly failed to indulge such curiosity himself, Dickens hints, once again, that the most canny readers are feminine readers, willing to acknowledge that the world may not match their expectations of it and enjoying the possibility that it might yield more than they know. If the elder servant and the person she "calls" her niece look through keyholes and try to grasp the hidden facts of the environment, Pip and the person he calls his uncle are their masculine others—the flip side of the epistemological coin, readers who fail to be interested in the mysteries around them, subjects of knowledge who do not enjoy the recognition that their desires may or may not match the world.

The female servants are strikingly like us, the readers of suspenseful fiction, and Pip, here, deliberately thwarts their excitement. Thus a knowing Dickens lays bare the structures of suspense: the excitement of interest in the not-self emerges from the knowledge that there is something we do not know. This withholding has a twofold effect: it compels the recognition that the world is other to us, and it acts as a spur to pleasurable, keen inquisitiveness. It is as if Pip, here, has not only learned the truth about his benefactor but also suddenly knows the truth about readerly desire: "to get up a mystery" is the surest way to stimulate the desire to solve that mystery, and, by contrast, to stifle the interest of cunning readers, one must know how to suppress and divert the enigmas of suspense. Pip masterfully disallows the pleasures of doubt—and thereby keeps himself safe from inquisitive reading.

By the time Pip comes to think of marrying either Biddy or Estella, he and the reader have, we hope, learned to doubt properly. We should have learned to enjoy our ignorance, not leaping to assume that our assumptions will be validated by events, not rushing to imagine that we know all of the answers. But just in case we have not learned our lesson, we are offered a coda of suspense, first with Biddy, later with Estella. We must not close the book thinking that there are no more questions, and so we are treated to a series of equally persuasive novelistic outcomes— all of which are plausible, and none quite realized. The conventional marriage plot is circumvented twice, only to reenter the text as an ambiguous, by no means certain, outcome in the second version.[24] If we are still reliant on conventional assumptions even after five hundred pages of suspense, then the multiple ending more or less inescapably leads us to doubt those assumptions. Willy-nilly, we must come to know that we do not know.

Competing endings are a fact of suspenseful plotting: for us readers to feel that there is interesting, unfinished business in the final pages of the novel, it must be plausible for Pip to marry or not to marry, to choose one woman or the other. By the end of *Great Expectations,* it may even be unclear whether it is Biddy or Estella who has all along been the most conventional mate for Pip, so plausible do both options appear. Dickens skillfully throws the conventional ending into question by explicitly including it while showing that it functions as only one alternative among several. Incorporating all manner of endings into the text proper, Dickens thus defamiliarizes suspense itself. We would not enjoy doubts about the narrative's course if it were not possible for it to end in a number of different ways.[25] Thus even conventional closure always takes its place among alternative outcomes, contending with less stable, less neat, less happy conclusions. The anxiety stirred up by suspense proves that we are not so sure that the happy ending is the necessary one. In fact, Dickens suggests that the ending hardly matters at all. Suspense is there to teach us to face the fact that time's unfolding might not offer us what we expect.

PART III
George Eliot Investigates

5 The Gender of Realism Reconsidered in *Adam Bede*

If Ruskin established a radical realism, it was a realism crucially concerned with alterity. The real in *Modern Painters* is that which is not ourselves, and Ruskin asks how we may do justice to its surprising and varied otherness. The solution—provisional though it must always be—is the experiment: that movement back and forth between conjecture and self-suppressing doubt that holds our judgment in suspense. Victorian novelists appropriated both the structure and the goal of this experimental realism: for Brontë as for Dickens, suspense teaches us that we are too readily inclined to rely on ourselves at the expense of the alterity of the world, and suspenseful plotting models the pause of the experiment as both the most ethical and the most successful method of gathering knowledge.

Specifically, *Jane Eyre* and *Great Expectations* move Ruskin's model into the social world, where both texts make clear that the realist experiment is closely intertwined with the question of gender. The mysteries of *Jane Eyre* lead us to conclude that our narrow conceptions of femininity might not fit the facts, and in *Great Expectations,* the shrewdest reader of the world is not the thrusting man but the self-sacrificing woman, the only character who knows how to suspend her own desires in the face of otherness. In *Jane Eyre,* suspense teaches us unsettling lessons about feminine skill and potential; in *Great Expectations,* realist knowledge seeking is itself a quintessentially feminine activity. Thus we might be tempted to conclude that femininity provides both the content and the form of Victorian realism.

Despite their common interest in the gender of realism, however, these two texts actually hint at dramatically different political conclusions. Brontë teaches us to doubt our assumptions about women's limitations, while Dickens associates the very process of doubting and testing with traditionally feminine self-sacrifice. Suddenly, the form and the content of realist narrative appear strangely at odds: on the one hand, the realist experiment pushes us to doubt convention—including the conventions of gender—while, on the other, it reinforces the conservative paradigm of the angel in the house, the figure who always acts well and wisely because she never permits her own longings to intrude. Perhaps, in this context, Ruskin's own maddening mixture of revolutionary socialism and domestic conservatism begins to make sense. In *Modern Painters* and *The Stones of Venice* he calls for the denial of the self and an appreciation of the otherness of nature as necessary to the construction of a better social world, and then, in *Sesame and Lilies,* it seems clear to him that women are the ones who are best fitted to practice this revolutionary self-denial.[1] In other words, if self-suppression is our best access to nature's variety—the variety that will free laborers from the machine—it is treacherous and destructive for women to reject their special capacity for self-suppression; it is one of society's most precious political assets.

By linking realism's demand for self-denial to an oppressive paradigm of femininity, Dickens and Ruskin might coax us to conclude that the gender politics of the realist experiment are always and necessarily conservative, but Brontë's own realist experiment challenges that conclusion, signaling the instability that haunts any settled sense of the method's conservatism. Reading *Jane Eyre* alongside *Great Expectations,* we can see that the thoroughgoing skepticism of the experimental method might be turned back on itself, used to unsettle even the powerful gender ideology that seems to support its workings.

Any contradiction between the form and the content of realism has been implicit up to this point, but I want to suggest that George Eliot brings this tension into focus in her early fiction—and thereby transforms the history of realism. In *Adam Bede, The Lifted Veil,* and *Romola,* she uses the skepticism of realism to unsettle its own unspoken presumptions, exposing and critiquing the conventions at work in the supposedly anti-conventional realist experiment.

Though George Eliot could not have read *Great Expectations* (1861) or *Sesame and Lilies* (1865) when she came to write *Adam Bede* in 1859, the celebrated paradigm of feminine self-forgetfulness was certainly in full circulation at the time.[2] Eliot's own Dinah explains that her aunt had "a loving, self-forgetting nature" (66), and Dinah is inclined to lose her bearings: "it's my besetment to forget where I am and everything about me and lose myself in thoughts that I could give no account of" (78). But Dinah's capacity for self-renunciation, far from acting as the paradigm of proper femininity, is actually the object of George Eliot's critique in *Adam Bede.* "Self-forgetfulness" prevents Dinah from becoming a mature and marriageable adult—a feminine self capable of loving an erotic other. Thus self-forgetfulness, and particularly *feminine* self-forgetfulness, is impracticable and ultimately undesirable. It becomes clear in the novel that Eliot rejects the Ruskinian model of self-suppression in favor of a balanced, equal, mutual recognition of self and other.

Eliot's apprehensions about the consequences of Ruskinian self-suppression for women prompt her to experiment not only with a new ethics but with the form of her own fiction writing: retaining crucial elements of Ruskin's realism, she pointedly rejects the familiar strategies of suspenseful plotting we have encountered so far, offering what I argue is a feminist critique of suspense fiction. Thus *Adam Bede* works as both a formal and a political reply to the model of self-denying femininity put forward by Dickens, Ruskin, and their contemporaries.

If the critique of Victorian femininity has implications for suspense, it also carries consequences for realism. George Eliot's famous theory of ethical realism, articulated in chapter 17 of *Adam Bede,* is fully integrated with her critique of feminine self-denial. Beauty and sympathy are set at odds in the famous essay on aesthetics, and this very same opposition shapes the plots of the two central women characters. In chapter 17, exquisite Italian Madonnas teach us to harden our hearts against our neighbors, while homely Dutch images lead us to love the other. In the narrative proper, Hetty's constant admiration of her own visual beauty allows her no room for an ethical appreciation for the other, while Dinah's "self-forgetfulness" prompts her to give to others at the expense of herself.

Dinah shares the same ethical stance as realist art, and it follows that

Dinah's plot is crucial to Eliot's rethinking of realism. But what exactly is the link between Dinah's femininity and Dutch painting? Looking first at the novel's articulation of a new aesthetics, and second at its critique of conventional femininity, I bring them together, here, to argue that in *Adam Bede,* realism and femininity come to share the same new standard, and it is a pointed departure from Ruskin's model. Neither aesthetics nor femininity can wholly depend on the model of "self-forgetfulness," since a recognition of the self is crucial to a proper relation to alterity in *Adam Bede.* Both realism and femininity alike must strive to achieve the delicate equilibrium of self-consciousness and other-consciousness—the balance of self and other.

Suspensions

Chapter 17 of *Adam Bede* is routinely quoted and excerpted as the locus classicus of Victorian realism.[3] We might expect realist texts to try not to break the frame of the fictional world, and thus it seems particularly odd for the quintessential realist novel to introduce a self-reflexive interlude.[4] But perhaps it is not so surprising, after all, that the most famous contemporary essay on realism interrupts a story line. In a moment "in which the story pauses a little," Eliot's prose essay enforces a delay, stopping both the reader and Arthur Donnithorne from rushing headlong into the future. That is to say, it only enacts the narrative suspending that is so much the staple of the realist experiment.

But is chapter 17 really analogous to the suspenseful enigmas of *Jane Eyre* or *Great Expectations*? My first aim is to suggest that it both is and is not: *Adam Bede* invites all the concerns we have seen in Ruskinian realism but carefully refuses the pleasures of suspense in favor of suspensions—gaps and pauses that do not stimulate the forward-looking impulses of desire. These suspensions replace the enigmas of suspense to encourage a new readerly relationship to alterity.

Dutch paintings invite us to focus sympathetically on the life around us, on "real breathing men and women" (151). By contrast, Italian images of the lofty and the sublime teach us to feel intolerant, indifferent toward our "everyday fellow-men" (153). It seems that we learn to love our neighbors by looking at certain pictures and disregarding others. As usual, then, the ethical work of Victorian realism involves forging a new and responsible approach to the world by way of the art object. But if Eliot's

Non Narrative Suspension

ethics sounds similar to Ruskin's, the images she proffers as ethical models are suspended moments that are distinctly nonnarrative, quite clearly disconnected from the context of narrative time: "an old woman bending over her flower-pot, or eating her solitary dinner, while the noonday light, softened, perhaps, by a screen of leaves, falls on her mob-cap, and just touches the rim of her spinning-wheel, and her stone jug, and all those cheap, common things which are the necessaries of life to her" (151). Caught *in medias res,* this is the still suspension of static painting, but it is not suspenseful. Similarly, Eliot's disquisition on realism, as it describes Dutch painting, functions as a still moment, discrete from the story but poised between events. Thus the twin suspensions of Eliot's ethical education—Dutch painting and her own prose essay on realism—are sandwiched inside a story.

In these moments of nonnarrative suspension, the text invites us to consider the links between visual beauty and ethical action, a problem that also haunts the text as a whole. Indeed, looking is an activity that reappears with startling persistence in *Adam Bede,* from the anonymous stranger in the opening pages, whose only role is to gaze, to Hetty's fixation with mirrors. The vision of the beloved is particularly problematic, if not downright dangerous. Adam looks at Hetty and is perilously misled by her loveliness; Hetty looks only at herself and meets with a catastrophic end; Dinah stares at apparitions and absent faces but becomes suddenly responsive to romantic love when she knows herself to be keenly observed by Adam Bede. All of this suggests that this text—"undoubtedly the most scopophilic of George Eliot's novels"[5]—is busily posing the same question in a number of ways: namely, what is the proper link between vision and ethics, between looking at the world and feeling love?

At times, the novel suggests that the two are actually indistinguishable. In one example, Dinah misunderstands Hetty's expression of discontent, and the narrator likens her ethical mistake to visual activity:

> It is our habit to say that while the lower nature can never understand the higher, the higher nature commands a complete view of the lower. But I think the higher nature has to learn this comprehension, *as we learn the art of vision,* by a good deal of hard experience, often with bruises and gashes incurred in

taking things up by the wrong end, and fancying our space wider than it is. (138; emphasis mine)

Desiring a "complete view" of the other, even the best of us are bound to fail. Vision is no immediate faculty: it is learned, turbulently, with mistakes and misinterpretations riddling the path to knowledge. Sounding remarkably like Ruskin, George Eliot suggests that understanding the other, like seeing the world, is an activity fraught with the errors our minds bring to bear, corrupting our best efforts to grasp the truth.

If vision comes so close to ethics that the two seem to merge, in chapter 17 the narrator hints that ethics is even a species of visual aesthetics: "All honor and reverence to the divine beauty of form! Let us cultivate it to the utmost in men, women, and children—in our gardens and in our houses; but let us love that other beauty, too, which lies in no secret of proportion, but in the secret of deep human sympathy" (152). Capable of being read in two ways, the "other beauty" of human sympathy is both an alternative to the beauty of form—*another kind of beauty*—and an aesthetic of alterity, an attention to *the beauty of the other*.

In *Adam Bede* the problem of the visual absorbs the project of acting ethically, and there may be no more important lesson in the novel than the task of seeing well. Indeed, the text repeatedly reminds us that even the best, most generous characters see badly: Dinah's failure to "see" Hetty warns us that learning to see is a difficult and challenging process, destined to run into trouble. But then, this conclusion troubles the lessons that Dutch painting seemed to teach us earlier: since the static frames of realist art are themselves visual objects, perhaps we must learn to see them too, and they cannot by themselves teach us a new relationship to the real. Activity may not belong to the painting at all, but to the viewer, who will always be tempted to "tak[e] things up by the wrong end." Indeed, the narrator invents an "idealistic friend" who simply dismisses Dutch painting for its "vulgar details" and "clumsy, ugly people" (151). The pictures clearly fail to lead him to a new ethical consciousness. Thus the realm of visual appearance in *Adam Bede*—as in *Modern Painters*—teaches us nothing that we do not already know.

But if this sounds like the skeptical realist relation to visual appearance we have met before, it departs from Ruskin, Brontë, and Dickens in one crucial way: George Eliot refrains from setting up the failures of the *failure ≠ suspenseful enigmas*

visual as suspenseful enigmas. The problem of reading visual appearance does arise in the novel proper, and Eliot invites us to witness the mistakes of her characters when they impose their flawed assumptions on the world. Mrs. Irwine says, "If I don't like a man's looks, depend upon it I shall never like *him*" (56). As if in protest against the lessons of chapter 17, she refuses to give her love to the homely and the ordinary. Following a similar logic, Adam and Arthur are captivated by Hetty's beauty, reading her graceful appearance as the mark of moral goodness. And this, Eliot suggests—with no little irony—is a commonplace view:

> Ah! what a prize a man gets who wins a sweet bride like Hetty. How the men envy him who come to the wedding breakfast, and see her hanging on his arm in her white lace and orange blossoms. The dear, young, round, soft, flexible thing! Her heart must be just as soft, her temper just as free from angles, her character just as pliant. If any thing ever goes wrong, it must be the husband's fault there: he can make her what he likes, that is plain. . . . Every man under such circumstances is conscious of being a great physiognomist. Nature, he knows, has a language of her own, which she uses with strict veracity, and he considers himself an adept in the language. Nature has written out his bride's character for him in those exquisite lines of cheek and lip and chin, in those eyelids delicate as petals, in those long lashes curled like the stamen of a flower, in the dark liquid depths of those wonderful eyes. How she will dote on her children! (130–31)

Such a conventional faith in the legibility of feminine features must be put to the test: Adam will find that Hetty fails to "dote on her children" in the most violent of ways. Thus Eliot assembles the familiar ingredients of the realist experiment for her plot: conventional belief, set up to be tested by experience. Adam imposes his own desires on the other, and Eliot generalizes this impulse to include all of us: "We look at the one little woman's face we love, as we look at the face of our mother earth, and see all sorts of answers to our own yearnings" (177). Clearly, we must all strive to suspend judgment, since "It is so very rarely that facts hit that nice medium required by our own enlightened opinions and refined taste!" (150).

But although Hetty's beautiful face misleads Arthur and Adam, it offers no mystery to the *reader.* Indeed, rather than tempting our curiosity about Hetty's character by suggesting and withholding the truth, the narrator simply tells us outright early on that she is beautiful but hardhearted—"as unsympathetic as butterflies sipping nectar" (87). In other words, in *Adam Bede,* the reader encounters the very same patterns of presumption and error we have seen in the novels of Brontë and Dickens—without ourselves being carried along by plotted suspense.

Why come so close to suspense only to reject it? By way of an answer, I want to suggest that Eliot resists suspense for the same reason that Ruskin, Brontë, and Dickens insisted on it: in order to teach her readers a new relationship to the otherness of the world. Specifically, she takes the ethical project a step further than her predecessors, supplanting narrative enigmas with nonnarrative suspensions in order to emphasize the difficult labor of grasping alterity. In chapter 17, she stresses that realism always involves arduous work: "Falsehood is so easy, truth so difficult," she writes, opposing the "marvellous facility" of fanciful imagination to the difficult labor of producing "real unexaggerated" truths. She exhorts the reader to reserve our highest praise for those "men ready to give the loving pains of a life to the faithful representing of commonplace things" (152–53).

If ethical realism demands painful, arduous work, then perhaps it calls for a form more laborious than the readerly pleasures of suspense. Endowed from the start with a knowledge that is hidden from Adam and Dinah, readers of *Adam Bede* are not invited to indulge the speculations of conjecture and hypothesis. But we are expected to consider characters who guess and assume and fail, often tragically, to understand their world. What this means is that the characters remain *other,* unlike ourselves. Eliot deliberately prevents us from identifying too closely. Critical theorist Diana Fuss argues that the concept of identification always evokes a set of contradictory aspirations and anxieties, since on the one hand it seems to allow one to cross the boundaries of alterity to understand the other, but at the same time it may involve "annihilating the other *as other*" and thus carries with it the perils of "mastery and possession." The resulting paradox is a troubling one: "if we are true to the Other with whom we identify, then we must respect the Other as Other and stop identifying."[6] Similarly, if realism's most urgent aim is to teach us to build responsible relationships with the alterity of the world, then surely we readers should not learn to assume a perfect identity between our own felt experience and that of the characters we encounter. Rather, we must keep our distance so that we may fashion a relationship of forgiveness and understanding across the gap that necessarily divides us from the other. It is no wonder, then, that George Eliot sets her novel in a time remote from that of her readers: we must remain vigilantly conscious of the distance between ourselves and the represented world.

Similarly, chapter 17 may be read as an example of Eliot's insistence on the other *as other*. The text inserts a "pause" in the narrative in which we are invited to reflect on the workings, construction, and purpose of visual representation. But by using visual art instead of novels as its paradigm, the theory remains "other" to the narrative, not folded into the events but blatantly disconnected from them. The intrusion into the narrative of a remarkably independent essay on aesthetics would seem to invite a contemplation of the story and characters in terms of those aesthetics, yet the narrative is irreducible to the terms put forward in the essay—since static painting, suspended, is crucially different from narrative time. Indeed, although the theory might well find echoes and resonances in the lives of the novel's characters, a look at the critics will prove that there has been no consensus about the ways in which the theory may be mapped onto the storyline.[7] Thus we might say that the relationship between the visual image and the complex context of narrative time is precisely one of incommensurability. To put this another way: we cannot simply impose the theory on the text because it does not "fit," and so, like Ruskin's unreliable Old Masters, it calls for some work from us. *Adam Bede* preserves a separation between the story and its ruminations on aesthetics—so that we may forge the links ourselves.

And so we come back, once again, to Dutch painting. The picture, on its own, fails to teach its viewers a new and more ethical relationship to the world. But perhaps alterity is not required to lead us to an understanding of it. It may be, instead, that it is up to us to decide to seek it out. Dutch painting does not lead us unerringly to ethical action, but it does offer us the opportunity to work toward an "other" aesthetic. The task of the ethical subject is to choose to negotiate the complex space between self and other. What the suspenseful plots of the realist experiment have been missing, therefore, is the labor of approaching otherness. *Jane*

Eyre and *Great Expectations* made the difficult lessons of the world seem easy. Work reenters the scene with the suspended moments of *Adam Bede,* where we must take "loving pains" to cross the gap that divides us from the other. The suspended scene of Dutch painting and the suspended interruption of the novel alike can help us to a new sympathy for the ordinariness of the life around us, but it is up to us to use the painting and the essay to bridge the gap between self and other.

Links

Painting is not the only suspended moment in *Adam Bede.* At numerous points, the narrator pauses to anticipate shocked and judgmental responses on the part of an imagined reader. For example, the narrator asks: "Are you inclined to ask whether this can be the same Arthur who, two months ago, had that freshness of feeling . . . which shrinks from wounding even a sentiment, and does not contemplate any more positive offence as possible for it?" (264). A little later, the narrator pauses to remark: "Possibly you think that Adam was not at all sagacious in his interpretations, and that it was altogether extremely unbecoming in a sensible man to behave as he did—falling in love with a girl who really had nothing more than her beauty to recommend her" (297). And chapter 17 opens this way: "'This Rector of Broxton is little better than a pagan!' I hear one of my readers exclaim. 'How much more edifying it would have been if you had made him give Arthur some truly spiritual advice!'" (149). In all three examples, the imagined reader is expected to judge harshly, to want to amend the text to suit a more unyielding moral assessment than the one the narrator favors. Though often ironic in tone, these addresses to the reader nonetheless suggest that our judgments may be radically at variance with those of the narrator.

At this point, George Eliot's resistance to suspense in *Adam Bede* may become even plainer. The suspenseful withholdings of *Jane Eyre* and *Great Expectations* invited us to recognize our assumptions and to rein them in by enjoying the act of doubting. George Eliot adds another step to the process. Whatever the world offers us, however unsightly and irresponsible and anti-conventional, we should work to love *as other.* And unlike the texts of suspense, the structure of the novel refrains from *compelling* us to experience this position of laborious compassion. The text is at pains—even "loving pains"—to persuade us to love and forgive the

prosaic ordinariness of the world, but its confrontational language reinforces our detachment and certainly does not require that we go along.
By suspending the narrative with vigorous reflections on ethics rather
than titillating mysteries, George Eliot frees us to choose whether or not
we will embrace the "other beauty" of human sympathy. Paradoxically,
then, Eliot's novel seems didactic precisely because her narrative does not
oblige us to take her side.

   But this freedom is not quite the end of the story. Indeed, it is quite
literally the middle of the story, since up to this point we have considered
the narrative's pauses—its lulls, gaps, and interruptions. But what happens to this lesson in the context of the plot? When Hetty sets out on her
long journey, we hear, first, that "Bright February days have a stronger
charm of hope about them than any other days in the year. One likes to
pause in the mild rays of the sun" (305). But then, Hetty, we learn, is not
hopeful at all: "She hardly knows that the sun is shining; and for weeks,
now, when she has hoped at all, it is for something at which she herself
trembles and shudders" (306). If at first we readers are embraced by the
text—included in its generous, general "one"—we soon discover that
we are disconnected from the character, detached from her particular
experience. Thus "one" is not so general after all, and Eliot implies a certain irony about her own sweeping proclamations. Yet it would clearly
be misleading to suggest that Eliot is interested only in irony, separation,
and detachment. Difference need not mean total disconnection, since,
if Dutch painting is anything to go by, we ought to remain "mindful" of
the other. And although the narrator distances us from the text, "he" also
regularly invites us to connect ourselves to the represented world.[8] For
instance, lest the erring Arthur seem too unlike ourselves, the narrator
warns: "There is a terrible coercion in our deeds which may at first turn
the honest man into a deceiver, and then reconcile him to the change"
(264). Including the world of the reader as well as the world of the text,
this sweeping statement implicates even "the honest man" in Arthur's fall.

   Throughout the novel, general statements about the world alter-
nate with the specific experiences of individual characters. George Eliot
therefore seems to swing rapidly between a Ruskinian desire to get at the
infinite particularity of the world and the large, sweeping generalities of
convention. Indeed, she suggests a close—even a *systematic*—relationship between these two poles. Moving between generals and particulars,

the narrator repeatedly urges us to make "links"—that crucial term in *Adam Bede*[9]—to consider similarities and differences between characters and between our own lives and the ones represented in the text. The particular is there to challenge the general, and the general is there to allow us to understand the particular. The play between the two permits us an appropriate relationship to otherness—which is neither radically divorced from the self nor entirely collapsed into it, neither entirely like nor entirely unlike ourselves.

To put it simply, Eliot is deeply interested in identification—"the play of difference and similitude in self-other relations."[10] Within the novel proper, Adam and Dinah fall into error when they identify Hetty as too much like themselves and miss the radical difference that divides her responses from their own. Adam falls into error when he sees too little of himself in Arthur and his father, neglecting fellow feeling in favor of harsh judgments. These particular examples imply that however "good" we may be, we cannot avoid the imposition of the self on the world. Ironically, when Dinah misreads some of her own impulses reflected in Hetty, we see that even self-denial can intrude itself on a reading of the other.[11] To put this another way: if identification is "the detour through the other that defines the self,"[12] *the self cannot be effectively suspended.* What this means is that the scientific model of self-renunciation—and "feminine" model of self-forgetfulness—are either crude or simply untenable: they call for a total overlooking of personal inclination, knowledge, and desire in the face of the other, and thus fail to acknowledge the obdurate, ineradicable imposition of the self on the world.

Feminine Selves

Dinah Morris is George Eliot's response to the paradigm of self-denying femininity, a woman who must learn to recognize the crucial role of the self in self-other relations. Scholars in recent years have not been inclined to read *Adam Bede* as a feminist text. Judith Mitchell has written that the novel "basically endorses the idealization of feminine beauty," while Nancy Paxton reports that "Eliot's treatment of Hetty's narcissistic sexuality . . . has often been read as an expression of her neurotic envy of the female beauty she did not personally possess."[13] But these diametrically opposed readings have neglected to take account of the potentially polemical force of Eliot's two antithetical examples of femininity in

Adam Bede. Neither the unself-conscious Dinah nor the excessively self-conscious Hetty, taken alone, can stand for Eliot's normative view of femininity. Critical of both examples, Eliot suggests that women, on display, must learn to negotiate their femininity through their roles as both subjects and objects of vision. Ethics and the aesthetics of feminine beauty emerge as significantly related concerns: how can women, so much the beautiful objects of vision, become active, seeing, *ethical* subjects, capable of the kind of vision implied by Dutch painting?

When they have attended to feminine beauty, critics have largely focused on Hetty, hardly noticing that Dinah is also a spectacle. From the beginning, however, the woman preacher is looked at, unrelentingly and with real interest—a kind of visual curiosity. For all the talk, though, Dinah remains unruffled by the crowd of gazes that surrounds her. Her self-forgetfulness is one of her most marked characteristics, and one that surprises the many who gaze at her. Surely she knows how much attention she attracts? As Reverend Irwine asks: "And you never feel any embarrassment from the sense . . . that you are a lovely young woman on whom men's eyes are fixed?" (79). Dinah responds firmly in the negative: "No, I've no room for such feelings, and I don't believe the people ever take notice about that" (79).

But of course they do. Dinah is innocently wrong about how much notice is being taken of her. Everyone, from Arthur Donnithorne to Wiry Ben, has something to say about Dinah's appearance.[14] Importantly, too, it is not only her beauty but specifically her unself-consciousness that is apparent to all, perceptible even to those who have never seen her before. "The stranger was struck with surprise as he saw [Dinah] approach and mount the cart—surprise, not so much at the feminine delicacy of her appearance, as at the total absence of self-consciousness in her demeanor" (19). Dinah's principal visual impact on a stranger is not her feminine delicacy: it is that she seems not to know that she is being looked at.

Adam Bede is likewise unaware of his appearance, but this is not marked for us as surprising: the text implies that unself-consciousness is perfectly in keeping with a healthy masculinity.[15] Indeed, such unawareness of the self may be a quintessentially masculine characteristic, since at two moments in the text Dinah's unself-consciousness actually renders her *boyish.* "Dinah . . . seemed as unconscious of her outward appearance as a little boy; there was no blush, no tremulousness, which said 'I know you think me a pretty woman, too young to preach'" (19). The second example registers in Dinah's voice, which affects the listener "as a melody strikes us with a new feeling when we hear it sung by the pure voice of a boyish chorister" (24).

Eliot's references to boys here are as perplexing as they are suggestive. It is not clear, in 1859, that boys are the budding archetypes of hardy, intrepid, and vigorous masculinity that they will become by the end of the century. In fact, it is precisely around this time that the gendering of children begins to take shape with social force, manifested in a growing institutional emphasis on the distinction between boys and girls.[16]

On the other hand, there is no question that Eliot is deliberate about her use of the figure of the boy for Dinah. And we can draw from clear evidence in *The Mill on the Floss,* published just a year after *Adam Bede,* that Eliot was interested in the gendering of children. Tom Tulliver seems uncannily patterned on *Tom Brown's Schooldays* (1857), widely cited as the first example of the boys' fiction that would become standard by the end of the century.[17] In the section of the novel called "Boy and Girl," Eliot's Tom comes home from school in good Tom Brown fashion, filled with ideals of fair play ("I hate a cheat"), physical prowess ("I gave Spouncer a black eye, I know—that's what he got for wanting to leather *me*"), and honor ("Tom Tulliver was a lad of honour"), and entirely confident about the distinction between boys and girls: "all girls were silly—they couldn't throw a stone so as to hit anything, couldn't do anything with a pocket knife, and were frightened at frogs."[18] These boyhood traits, of course, are in tune with Tom's rigid and exacting punishments of Maggie, which will last into adulthood, and *The Mill on the Floss* might even be read as a critique of the principled, manly boyhood represented in *Tom Brown's Schooldays.*

To return to *Adam Bede,* we can begin to contextualize Eliot's curious choice of a boyish model for Dinah. It is between the publication of *Tom Brown's Schooldays* in 1857 and the passage of the 1870 Education Act that boys become closely associated with a masculine ideal, and thus *Adam Bede* is published at a transitional moment. But since we know that Eliot will be concerned with this question by the time she writes *The Mill on the Floss* in 1860, and since Dinah, in her unself-consciousness, is likened neither to women nor to girls, it seems clear that at the very least,

Eliot is dissociating Dinah from conventional femininity and implying that she blurs or crosses gender boundaries.

It is in the context of her unconsciousness of self that Dinah becomes like a boy. Thus Eliot seems most concerned to detach femininity from "self-forgetfulness." Indeed, in these early chapters of the novel, she pays particular attention to the relationship between self-forgetfulness and feminine *sexuality*. For example, Dinah's obliviousness informs Seth Bede that she is not in love with him. He looks for signs of reciprocated affection, only to find Dinah entirely unconscious of herself and of his presence: hers "was an expression of unconscious placid gravity—of absorption in thoughts that had no connection with the present moment or with her own personality: an expression that is most of all discouraging to a lover" (28–29). It would seem that lovers and women are self-conscious, while boys—and Dinah—are not.

At this point, we might come to a couple of eccentric conclusions. First, we might say that Dinah, here, is too much like a boy to accept Seth Bede's love. Read thus, Eliot's text can be seen to reinforce a heteronormative model in which love exists only between a man and a woman, and the woman must become sufficiently feminine for this love to emerge. Second, if Dinah is boyish because she is unself-conscious, then in order to shift from boyishness to mature womanhood she will have to become aware of her own appearance. Far from upholding the model of feminine self-forgetfulness, Eliot suggests that womanhood itself is contingent on a recollection of the self. And since such self-consciousness is also the stuff of love, Dinah will have to become aware of herself if she is to become a candidate for romance.

This is, of course, precisely what happens. Our conclusions about gender and self-consciousness lead us directly to the end of the narrative, where Dinah reaches adequate self-consciousness—and falls in love Adam Bede. Blushing furiously, Dinah reaches the end of the novel in a state dramatically different from her early self-forgetfulness. Blushing, as Margaret Homans has pointed out, is not just any signifier: in *Adam Bede* it is the telling marker of sexuality.[19] It certainly works as a revealing contrast between Hetty and Dinah. Blushing is precisely what Hetty does with perfect complacency, and what she fails to do when she thinks of Adam; but it is Dinah's sole sign of sexuality, appearing only when she feels herself to be seen by Adam.[20] Indeed, the blush functions as the very first signal to the reader of a possibility of romantic love between these two, coming as a total surprise to Dinah when Adam first looks at her:

> Dinah, for the first time in her life, felt a painful self-conscious-ness; there was something in the dark penetrating glance of this strong man so different from the mildness and timidity of his brother Seth. A faint blush came, which deepened as she won-dered at it. This blush recalled Adam from his forgetfulness. (100)

The erotic suggestion of this passage would be hard to overlook, but it is important to recognize the place of the eye in the gendering of this scene: Adam's way of looking, marked as strong and penetrating, is clearly more masculine than that of his brother and literally transforms Dinah from her boyish unself-consciousness into a self-conscious femi-ninity. The male gaze, we might conclude, is crucial to the construction of a feminine sexuality.

But then Adam, too, blushes with self-consciousness. When he is first introduced to the idea that Dinah may be in love with him, "The blood rushed to Adam's face, and for a few moments he was not quite conscious where he was; his mother and the kitchen had vanished for him, and he saw nothing but Dinah's face turned up towards his" (420). Whether masculine or feminine, it would seem, consciousness and self-consciousness are bound up in the mutual look of romantic love. For Eliot, a reciprocal gaze is apparently fundamental to a mature sexuality in men and women alike.[21]

By contrast, Adam's love for Hetty remains remarkably unself-conscious and entirely unreciprocated, in both ways unlike his blushing love for Dinah:

> For my own part . . . I think the deep love [Adam] had for that sweet, rounded, blossom-like, dark-eyed Hetty, of whose inward self he was really very ignorant, came out of the very strength of his nature, and not out of any inconsistent weakness. Is it any weakness, pray, to be wrought on by exquisite music? to feel its wondrous harmonies searching the subtlest windings of your soul, the delicate fibres of life where no memory can penetrate. . . . The noblest nature sees the most of this *impersonal* expression in beauty . . . and for this reason, the noblest nature

is the most often blinded to the character of the one woman's
soul that the beauty clothes. (298; emphasis in text)

"Blinded" by the impersonal nature of the aesthetic experience, Adam's
noble nature fails to "see" anything in Hetty but beauty itself, a beauty
as contentless and disinterested as a love of music. The separation of
Hetty's impersonal beauty from her consciousness is clearly a serious obstacle to reciprocation. Adam's love, it would seem, is entirely the affair
of the spectator, gazing at the impersonal object of his vision. Adam's sentiment may be noble, perhaps, and even aesthetically pure, but it is not
the stuff of true love and fruitful marriage. Or so the end of the narrative, with its rather different love, would have us believe.

Given Eliot's immersion in German philosophy, it is tempting to argue that Adam's love for Hetty is Kantian, his love for Dinah Hegelian.
Kant's theorization of the experience of the beautiful is that it is always
impersonal, requiring no particular self-interest, no particular embodiment. It is a disinterested experience, occurring spontaneously within
every human subject and focused on the beauty of form. Kant writes:
"The *beautiful* is that which pleases universally." [22] For Hegel, by contrast,
the self is absolutely incapable of ethical judgment, community, or
knowledge without a recognition of and by the other. This mutual acknowledgment is an absolute precondition of culture, political community, and ethical action. "Self-consciousness exists in and for itself
when, and by the fact that, it so exists for another; that is, it exists only
in being acknowledged." [23] From Kantian aesthetics to Hegelian self-
consciousness: this movement could be said to describe the trajectory of
Adam's *Bildung,* as he shifts from the love of Hetty's impersonal beauty
to the reciprocal acknowledgment that comes with Dinah's love. Both
are framed in terms of the visual: Kantian aesthetics "blinds" Adam, rendering him incapable of seeing Hetty's character and meeting Dinah's
gaze. Indeed, if we think again of chapter 17, the shift from aesthetics
to ethics in the novel is entirely framed under the larger rubric of aesthetics. Vision is clearly a metaphor for a more general problem of consciousness: seeing means illuminating, clarifying, comprehending the
real. But it is not just any metaphor: it is the organizing problematic of this
text. Under the aegis of visual aesthetics we find gender, love, sexuality,
ethics—in short, the many prominent thematic strands of this narrative.

If the end of the story is anything to go by, Eliot falls firmly on the side of a Hegelian self-consciousness; proper love is distinguished by the reciprocal acknowledgment of self and other. In keeping with the novel's insistence on the visual, this self-consciousness is represented by a shared *gaze,* in which each party is both subject and object of vision, conscious of the other and conscious of the self through the eyes of the other. By stark contrast, the admiring sight of Hetty's "impersonal" beauty causes ethical blindness, blocking a real consciousness of the other and, consequently, of the self.

With Adam and Dinah as our paragons of love, then, we begin to see that Eliot favors a love governed by a reciprocal self-consciousness, in which masculine and feminine, self and other, come to recognition through the gaze of the other. Thus love is impossible between Dinah and Seth, since she is oblivious to his presence, and between Hetty and Adam, since he recognizes only her impersonal beauty and without reciprocation. But what is wrong with the love between Arthur and Hetty? Unlike Dinah, Hetty is self-conscious indeed. And she and Arthur are even given to reciprocal blushing when face to face.[24] Moreover, Hetty is clearly made more self-conscious by Arthur's attention, just as Dinah is by Adam's.[25]

The obvious obstacle to true love between Hetty and Arthur is class. But theirs is not a love story destined to tragedy only by the differences in their social standing: such a tale would make *Adam Bede* a more radical text than it is.[26] Rather, the narrator insistently implies, Hetty is so self-conscious that she is incapable of reciprocated love and certainly of compassion. "Hetty would have been glad to hear that she should never see a child again; they were worse than the nasty little lambs that the shepherd was always bringing in . . . for the lambs *were* got rid of sooner or later" (133). She rejects tenderness, sympathy, affection—all emotions focused on the other. Indeed, her imagination is filled almost exclusively with visual images of herself. The narrator says: "of every [imaginary] picture she is the central figure, in fine clothes" (132). Even when she thinks of Arthur, she sees herself through his eyes: "Captain Donnithorne couldn't like her to go on doing work; he would like to see her in nice clothes" (129). Concerned entirely with the reflected image of her own appearance, Hetty sees herself in precisely the same way that Adam and Arthur see her—as an "impersonal" object of visual beauty. And Eliot is careful to point out that Hetty's beauty appeals not only to the masculine eye, but to everyone: "there is one order of beauty which seems to turn the heads, not only of men, but of all intelligent mammals, even of women. . . . Hetty Sorrel's was that sort of beauty" (72). Even Mrs. Poyser is transfixed: "continually gaz[ing] at Hetty's charms by the sly, fascinated in spite of her self" (72). Hetty's beauty, in good Kantian fashion, is universally pleasing, appealing regardless of the particular interests and character of the spectator. Her image appeals not to particular eyes, but to the eye in general—including even her own gaze, directed at herself. Consequently, she is incapable of seeing outward—toward the other— and equally incapable of recognizing herself as a seeing subject, able to look out on the world.

In this context, it will not be surprising that the mirror appears as Hetty's closest companion, mentioned even the first time we encounter her, part of the description of Mrs. Poyser's immaculate house:

> Hetty Sorrel often took the opportunity, when her aunt's back was turned, of looking at the pleasing reflection of herself in those polished surfaces, for the oak table was usually turned up like a screen, and was more for ornament than for use; and she could see herself sometimes in the great round pewter dishes that were ranged on the shelves above the long deal dinner-table, or in the hobs of the grate, which always shone like jasper. (63)

The contrast between Dinah's boyish unself-consciousness and Hetty's love of mirrors is set up, of course, as an experience of vision: while Hetty loves her mirror, Dinah loves her window.[27]

The mirror is Hetty's opportunity to gaze admiringly at her own beauty, but it also reveals her total identification with her own visual image. When we first encounter her before her bedroom mirror, she is admiring her own prettiness, consumed with the joy of self-regard. But later, when Arthur Donnithorne writes to tell her that their affair is over, the image is transformed: "there was the reflection of a blanched face in the old dim glass. . . . Hetty did not see the face—she saw nothing— she only felt that she was cold and sick and trembling" (280). A moment later, "she caught sight of her face in the glass: it was reddened now, and wet with tears; it was almost like a companion that she might complain to—that would pity her" (281). Thus Hetty's mirror image is, first, a delightful picture; second, total blankness, reflecting her virtual annihilation by Arthur; and finally, a second self, a sympathetic other. We might say that the visual image produced by the mirror allows the self to relate to the self *as other.* This is Dutch painting turned upside-down: the visual image, which was suspended before us in order to command love of the other, commands instead love of the self. Thus the "play of difference" so crucial to identification reaches its lowest point, allowing as little room as possible for alterity.

An excess of self-consciousness, clearly, turns out to be no better than a deficit. We are faced with two striking extremes: Dinah, filled with ethical love from the outset, is not capable of romantic, sexual love until she sees herself through the eyes of Adam Bede; Hetty, self-conscious and demonstrative of a coquettish sexuality from the beginning, fails to feel love for any of those who surround her. It is a revealing contrast: Dinah must become self-conscious in order to fall in love, marry, and multiply, whereas Hetty's self-consciousness seems to make her incapable of loving anyone—Adam, Arthur, her child. Dinah is too boyishly unself-conscious for romantic love; Hetty is so focused on the image of her own appearance that her only concern with others is her reflection through their eyes. If Dinah is too boyish, then Hetty, perhaps, is too feminine.

The trajectory of the narrative brings us to a normative middle ground, where Dinah manages to reach the perfect combination of ungendered sympathy and feminine self-consciousness. But how, precisely, do these two reach their happy fusion? I want to suggest that the crucial difference between Hetty's awareness of herself and Dinah's blush under Adam's keen stare is that Hetty responds to a *generalized* gaze, whereas Dinah answers to a specific pair of eyes. Adam, remember, is the only one who can make Dinah self-conscious. The same is not the case for Hetty. It is true that she blushes when beheld by Arthur, but he is not the only one whose eyes matter: "those other people didn't know how he loved her, and she was not satisfied to appear shabby and insignificant in their eyes even for a short space" (213). Hetty is so dependent on a universal gaze of admiration that she sees the world only as that gaze, reflecting her back to herself. If self-consciousness gestures to a proper, mature femininity in Dinah, it is only, it seems, because Dinah responds in this way *to a single gaze,* whereas Hetty is given to a kind of promiscuous self-consciousness, an internalization of the impersonal gaze of all others.

In the end, Eliot's paradigm turns out to be a bourgeois model par excellence, embracing the notion that a proper feminine sexuality appears only in the context of a single heterosexual couple: the woman is feminized when faced with the dark, penetrating gaze of a particular man. Her foil, the woman who internalizes the generalized gaze of admiration, seeing herself as she is reflected in the eyes of all who look at her, meets only with catastrophe. George Eliot's ethical-visual ideal is clear enough: the woman can be compassionate if she looks outward, but she can be maturely erotic only if she exchanges looks with one particular man. Hetty's ethical failure is therefore an excess of visual self-consciousness, just as Dinah's is a deficit, and for both it is a failure to exchange looks—which means, of course, that women are not there just to be looked at: they must also look back.

A Balance of Self and Other

Our look at looking brings us to a series of conclusions, all having to do with the significance of vision and reciprocation in *Adam Bede*. First, feminine fortunes are contingent on the ways that women respond to their roles as seeing subjects and visual spectacles. Second, the universal admiration of perfect beauty detracts from an ethical appreciation of the imperfect reality of the other. And third, both aesthetics and ethics are framed in terms of visual beauty—the one formal, ideal, and universally pleasing, and the other, well, simply *other*.

Taken together, these conclusions suggest a profound suspicion of formalist aesthetics and its accompanying detached eye. It is my contention, therefore, that Eliot is launching a critique of what is known to us as the "gaze." I am referring not to the explicitly gendered "male gaze" but rather to the term as it is employed by Norman Bryson, who defines it as a denial of "the locus of utterance": "*the disavowal of deictic reference . . . the disappearance of the body as the site of the image.*"[28] This definition concerns the impersonal, generalized eye, the model of vision that forms the object of George Eliot's attack in *Adam Bede*. When it is the basis of feminine sexuality, the gaze constructs a limited, self-absorbed, catastrophic consciousness; when it is the basis of art, the impersonal admiration of beauty directs attention away from the world in which we live. This aesthetic diversion of our sympathies has tangible consequences: "you," the reader, may choose to learn from idealist, impersonal representations to "turn a harder, colder eye" on "real breathing men and women, who can be chilled by your indifference or injured by your prejudice; who can be cheered and helped onward by your fellow-feeling, your forbearance, your outspoken, brave justice" (151). If Dutch painting cannot force "you" to love your neighbor, idealist Kantian aesthetics will try to persuade you that it is not even worth the attempt.

It might seem odd that Eliot frames her ethics very deliberately as a species of the beautiful, to be understood as an alternative aesthetic, set against the formalist beauties of harmony and proportion. But read polemically, Eliot's visual model offers a calculated critique of Kantian aesthetics: the *impersonal* beauty of form prompts the spectator to be blind to the reality of character, while ethical realism, focused on the reality of the other, is all about an exchange between *persons*. Thus a Kantian aesthetic allows women to be perceived not as persons but as forms—indeed, it blinds the spectator to their personhood—whereas a Hegelian ethics invites men and women alike to look and be looked at in full recognition of self and other. Eliot displaces formalism as an *unethical* aesthetic and pointedly supplants it with a radically *unaesthetic* aesthetic, the "rough," "stupid," "squat," and "ill-shapen" *beauty of the other* (152).

Both aesthetics and femininity must depend on a love of difference and a balanced, mutual recognition of self and other. But then, what exactly is the parallel between Dinah's self-conscious maturity and the novel's own realism? Clearly, the novel puts itself on the side of Dutch homeliness rather than Italian idealism in chapter 17, and yet, as I have argued, it maintains a distance between narrative and painting. Eliot also renounces suspense where the others might have used it—educating her readers in a rather more laborious and argumentative fashion, setting up a deliberate distance between narrator and reader. Indeed, even if we happened always to agree with the narrator's perspective, "his" quarrelsome tone would repeatedly invite us to confront the fact that another's judgment might well conflict with our own, partial position. Like the mature Dinah, therefore, we readers of realism are thrown back upon a recognition of ourselves as separate from the other.

Similarly, Eliot's minute descriptive language—perhaps the most familiar hallmark of realism[29]—resists the impersonality of formalist aesthetics in favor of a recognition of the partiality of the narrator. Again, we return to the visual—that crucial metaphor for consciousness in

Adam Bede. Throughout the narrative, it is striking that Eliot is absolutely scrupulous about locating vision in persons. Visual impressions are not presented from the perspective of the impersonal gaze but are embodied, located in time and space. This point is best demonstrated by the voice of the narrator, who draws attention even to the specificity of "his" own perspective.[30] "He" presents opinions as if they belonged to a specific character: "For my own part . . . I think . . . " (298). Descriptions of the novel's scenes come from a precise location in time and space: "We will enter very softly, and stand still in the open doorway, without awaking the glossy-brown setter who is stretched across the hearth, with her two puppies beside her" (47). In another example, the description of the Poysers' dairy is first presented as if from a neutral standpoint. The chapter begins: "The dairy was certainly worth looking at: it was a scene to sicken for . . . in hot and dusty streets" (71). This voice then switches to speak for Arthur, who has just come on the scene: "But one gets only a confused notion of these details when they surround a distractingly pretty girl of seventeen" (71). Thus Eliot constantly affirms that it matters who is looking, and from what standpoint. The real is not grasped by a detached, objective consciousness; it is in the domain of seeing persons, of embodied subjects whose vision is both partial and limited.

In the context of this careful embodiment of vision, it might seem peculiar that the text, like Hetty herself, is closely allied with the figure of the mirror. As if presenting realism as a pure and impersonal reflection of the world, the novel first poses as a mirror of the world it portrays: "With a single drop of ink for a mirror, the Egyptian sorcerer undertakes to reveal to any chance comer far-reaching visions of the past. This is what I undertake to do for you, reader" (5). But what kind of a mirror is it? In one of the best-known passages in the novel, the narrator claims "to give no more than a faithful account of men and things as they have mirrored themselves in my mind" (150). And this mirror is "doubtless defective; the outlines will sometimes be disturbed; the reflection faint or confused" (150). This is indeed a curious realism, relying as it does on the mind of the subject and refusing to promise either clarity or accuracy. But the reader will remember that Hetty's mirror, too, reflected the particularity of her own mind rather than a perfect, flawless reflection. It gave her back an image of her own absorbed self-consciousness. Thus the apparently incongruous parallel between Hetty's unethical self-consciousness and the ethical realism of the narrative is ultimately a good one: both attest to the limited particularity of the spectator, refusing to claim universal, neutral, or *impersonal* status.

In fact, the difference between Hetty's mirror of self-absorption and the narrator's mirror of realist alterity is instructive. While Hetty sees and admires herself, the narrator reflects the other—"men and things." Notably, the novel's mirror also reflects the world *for the other,* in the interests of instructing us to see the world differently, with human sympathy. If Hetty's admiration of herself is circular, showing her to herself, the narrative's reflection traces a far more circuitous, productive, and *social* path: it travels from "men and things" to the mind of the narrator; from the narrator to the reader; and—with any luck—from the reader back to the world, with sympathy.

Presenting vision as the single figure that links realism, ethics, and femininity, Eliot rejects the impersonal eye in favor of the embodied, mutual look, indicating the consciousness of both self and other. She urges us to refuse the disappearance of the self in three contexts: the denial of the self in the gaze, the suppression of the self in suspenseful narrative, and the renunciation of the self in love. We must pay close attention to the particular embodiment of the spectator, located in time and space; we must remember the distance that divides narrator, reader, and character; and we must accept the desirable return of self-consciousness in erotic femininity. Thus ethics, art, and femininity remain incommensurable but mutually revealing, all, we might say, caught up in the complexities of mutual identification.

In George Eliot's world it is worth noting that it is idealism—not realism—that joins with suspense and feminine self-forgetfulness as a suppression of the self. And all three of these—idealist art, suspenseful narrative, and conventional femininity—must be supplanted by a new balance, or exchange, between self-consciousness and other-consciousness. In Ruskin's realism, the real was inexorably separate from the self, and only arduous labor would allow us to recognize it in all of its surprising splendor. Much the same holds true for George Eliot—the same imposition of the self on the world, the same separation between self and other, the same need for labor. Yet Eliot's ethical realism moves beyond self-suppression in order to render an otherness that comes into being only in relation to the perceiving self. Ruskin offers a model of self-other relations perfectly in keeping with a feminine self-denial. In retrieving the self, Eliot both subverts the gender of realism and resists the seductions of suspense.

Realism Domesticated

And yet, to see aesthetics, ethics, and epistemology all in terms of the marriageable feminine subject may be to close down the disruptive political force of Ruskin's realism. Femininity is itself limited in *Adam Bede,* becoming principally a matter of the erotic. Dinah's attention is thrown back on herself at the very moment that Adam's look penetrates her, and it is then that she loses her boyish unself-consciousness. Gender and sexuality virtually merge into one, as femininity comes to mean feminine sexuality—desire.

What does it mean for Eliot to bring femininity and sexual desire so close together? Desire has arisen a number of times before in our look at realism. Suspense simultaneously provokes and checks desire—at once stimulating a longing to know the other and preserving a clear ignorance of that other. So far, so good: George Eliot's model of desire likewise emphasizes the separateness of the other and the longings of the self. But with Dinah, Eliot casts desire as eros rather than epistemology. It is not to know Adam that Dinah becomes painfully self-conscious. In fact, the novel strongly implies that it is impossible to know the other successfully, since even the best, most ethical characters fall into the trap of imposing themselves on the otherness of the world. The best we can hope for is a constant awareness that the other is separate from the self—which means that there can be no revelatory closure, no gratifying solution to the mystery. In this context, it begins to make sense for eros to take the place of epistemology as the novel's paradigm of desire: a consciousness of the self and a desire for the other must remain in steady equilibrium. Otherness and desire must persist, in conjunction, never to be resolved into knowledge.

The novel's paradigm of erotic desire, with its balance of masculine and feminine, is a perfect model for the respectful realist relation between self and world we have seen before—indeed, it may simply out-Ruskin Ruskin. The mature woman knows that she is different from the other and yet also desires that other, just as Ruskin's reader recognizes a separation from the world and yet longs to grasp that world. Surely, then, gender is an obvious model for the double stance of difference and desire. And of course, it is for this reason that gender and sexuality fuse in *Adam Bede:* femininity is not only in opposition to masculinity; it is an opposition structured according to desire. Realism and conventional, heterosexual desire therefore share uncannily comparable structures: the distance that divides masculine from feminine is a synecdochal image of the more generalized realist distance that divides self from not-self.

George Eliot's realism proves itself both more and less radical, in the end, than Ruskin's. In taking on his model of self-suppression, implicitly allied with the feminine, she undoes the self-denying model of femininity and replaces it with a more erotic alternative. She also takes his skepticism about knowledge a step further, suggesting that even hard-won knowledge might never begin to close the gap between self and world, and that the self remains, even in the face of the other. Yet, by putting the self back into self-forgetful realism, she drastically individualizes her model of the relations between self and other. In insisting on visual reciprocity, she imagines *exchange*—that most capitalist of paradigms—as the model for gender equality. And in using heterosexual desire and marriage as the archetype for relations between self and other, she reinstates some of the most familiar social conventions of gender and sexuality. Thus Ruskin's revolutionary realism is strangely converted, in *Adam Bede,* into a picture of domestic bliss.

6 Realist Narrative in Doubt

The Lifted Veil

Uneasy about the implications of suspenseful plotting for ethics and feminine subjectivity, George Eliot refused suspenseful hypotheses altogether in *Adam Bede*. But the problem of suspenseful narrative continued to trouble her, revisiting her fiction like an unanswered question. A strange short story about supernatural power was the first of her texts to follow *Adam Bede*. It came as a disappointment to her publishers, who saw it as an improper successor to the images of pastoral life that had made her famous. But if *The Lifted Veil* is not realistic in the classic sense, it takes the seductions of suspense as its central problem. The story concerns a character whose clairvoyance frees him from the activity of guessing at the future and at the inner thoughts of others. Such foreknowledge turns out to be a curse, because suspense, so the protagonist says, is the stuff of human life:

> So absolute is our soul's need of something hidden and uncertain
> for the maintenance of that doubt and hope and effort which are
> the breath of life, that if the whole future were laid bare to us
> beyond to-day, the interest of all mankind would be bent on the
> hours that lie between; we should pant after the uncertainties of
> our one morning and our one afternoon; we should rush fiercely

to the Exchange for our last possibility of speculation, of success, of disappointment; we should have a glut of political prophets foretelling a crisis or a no-crisis within the only twenty-four hours left open to prophecy. Conceive the condition of the human mind if all propositions whatsoever were self-evident except one, which was to become self-evident at the close of the summer's day, but in the meantime might be the subject of question, of hypothesis, of debate. Art and philosophy, literature and science, would fasten like bees on that one proposition which had the honey of probability in it, and be the more eager because their enjoyment would end with sunset. (43–44)

Ignorance seems to generate all of the pleasures of the mind, including art and philosophy, literature and science. And not just any ignorance: Latimer, the narrator, refers to precisely the kind of ignorance familiar to readers of plotted suspense—the unanswered question, the untested hypothesis, the unsettled debate. This is the ignorance of those who know the question and eagerly await an answer they know is forthcoming. All of human desire seems to emerge from this kind of circumscribed uncertainty—and it is from this desire that Latimer is unhappily excluded.

Mostly—but not entirely. In fact, the clairvoyant's only passion centers on the one woman whose mind he cannot read. He develops "a passion enormously stimulated, if not produced, by that ignorance. She was my oasis of mystery in the dreary desert of knowledge" (26). Seduced by sheer mystery, Latimer is carried away by his fascination:

> She was the only exception, among all the human beings about me, to my unhappy gift of insight. About Bertha I was always in a state of uncertainty: I could watch the expression of her face, and speculate on its meaning; I could ask for her opinion with the real interest of ignorance; I could listen for her words and watch for her smile with hope and fear: she had for me the fascination of an unravelled destiny. (21)

Speculation and uncertainty, hope and fear—together, these create infatuation, sexual desire. Doubt *about* the other and desire *for* the other thus come dangerously close together. Ignorance equals longing. This seductive combination, so much the staple of the suspense plot, produces a treacherous attraction that the narrator of Eliot's story knows he should resist. As Kate Flint puts it: "George Eliot's story is, among other things, a dramatization of the folly of pursuing Woman on the grounds that she represents a mysterious Other."[1]

On the one hand, then, suspense is the basic motivating force behind all intellectual and social life, but on the other hand, it endangers the responsible relationship between self and other, tempting the protagonist to pursue the "fascinating secret" of otherness at all costs, despite his better judgment (31). And as if it were not enough that the question of suspense emerges as central to knowledge, economics, sexual desire, and ethics, the narrator adds that the doubts of suspense are "the only form in which a fearful spirit knows the solace of hope" (33). To assess the value of suspense in this context begins to look difficult indeed, since it generates at once the patterns of desire, the dangers of mystification, and the comforts of hope.

But if suspense is so important to the narrator's assessment of human interaction, how does it operate in the narrative itself? Critics who have discussed *The Lifted Veil* have worried most about the moral dimensions of Latimer's strange condition, condemning him for his moral deficiencies rather than investigating George Eliot's formal project. Few have connected Latimer's obsessive interest in suspense with George Eliot's own narrative practice.[3] This chapter makes the case that *The Lifted Veil* offers a critique of the ethics of suspense, and it does so by commenting ironically and self-reflexively on its own suspenseful form.

The story begins with the most decisive of endings—the narrator's death, "For I foresee when I shall die, and everything that will happen in my last moments" (1). Latimer describes the event in detail, down to the precise time of death and the servants' failure to come to his aid in his last moments. The narrative then ends with the fulfillment of this vision. "It is the 20th of September 1850. I know these figures I have just written, as if they were a long familiar inscription. I have seen them on this page in my desk unnumbered times, when the scene of my dying struggle has opened upon me . . . " (67; ellipsis in text). Running in a dizzying circle, the story returns us to a beginning that is also an ending. And if the written narrative simply repeats an image of itself as already written, then the time of writing disappears into a kind of *mise-en-abîme*.

This circularity calls to mind some familiar twentieth-century anxieties about realism. Does the realist image strive simply to repeat a reality that precedes it? Does representation necessarily gesture backward in time? In *Modern Painters,* exact copies turn out not to be the aim of Ruskinian "realism." The near-perfect illusions of trompe l'oeil flaunt the skill of the artist at the expense of the object represented and invite the pleasures of self-reflexive irony. Thus Ruskinian realism labors to preserve the distance between representation and its objects. In *Modern Painters,* even nature itself goes out of its way to avoid the perfect doubling of trompe l'oeil. Water reflects other objects, but it never duplicates them perfectly: "the surface of water is not a mockery, but a new view of what is above it" (*Works* 3: 542). Ruskin, insistently progressive, denies that representation should ever try simply to repeat the world. And relying on the doubts and speculations of the experiment, he urges us to be ready to encounter discrepancies between the world and our images of it.

In this context, George Eliot's narrator looks something like Ruskin's ironic and pernicious trompe l'oeil artist. Barred from producing the new, and shut out from the hopes and doubts of suspense, the clairvoyant's life merely *doubles* his visions, producing perfect copies of the images in his mind. This is imitation turned almost literally upside-down: the world comes to match the mind so perfectly that the narrator's life effectively repeats his own representations. His first experience of clairvoyance, an image of Prague, is a "wonderfully distinct vision—minute in its distinctness down to a patch of rainbow light on the pavement, transmitted through a coloured lamp in the shape of a star" (12). Later, when he arrives in Prague, "There it was—the patch of rainbow light on the pavement transmitted through a lamp in the shape of a star" (34). The repetition of the words suggests sheer duplication, implying that the vision and the visual experience entirely correspond.

When the first vision of Prague comes to him, the narrator does not yet know that he is clairvoyant, and he imagines that the image is a product of his own poetic inspiration: "was it—the thought was full of tremulous exultation—was it the poet's nature in me, hitherto only a troubled yearning sensibility, now manifesting itself suddenly as spontaneous creation?" (13). Filled with hope that his illness has "wrought some happy change" in his constitution and turned him into a poet, Latimer decides that he will "test" his new condition. "Suppose I were to fix my mind

on some other place—Venice, for example, which was far more familiar
to my imagination than Prague: perhaps the same sort of result would
follow" (14). Like a good experimenter, Latimer sets up the hypothesis
against a new sample to see what will happen. The result is disappointment. "I could see no accident of form or shadow without conscious
labour after the necessary conditions. It was all prosaic effort, not rapt
passivity, such as I had experienced half an hour before" (14). If at first
he believes that he has been granted the gift of divine inspiration—the
same, he imagines, that came to Homer, Dante, and Milton (13)—when
he tries to make a picture of Venice by his own efforts, the result is failure. Thus the problem is explicitly one of *labor*. Latimer's perfect images
come to him through no exertion of his own, but rather in "rapt passivity." He tries to use his own exertions to create artistic images but cannot. This inability to work at creative labor, Eliot makes clear, is an in-
dication that our narrator is no artist. He soon gives up the "brief hope"
that he is an inspired genius: "I saw in my face now nothing but the
stamp of a morbid organisation framed for passive suffering—too feeble
for the sublime resistance of poetic production" (20).

Whether he works at it or not, the narrator's image of Prague is
clearly not a work of art by any usual definition. Prevision is something
given, something ready-made, a ghostly rather than an artistic image.
The eerie perfection of the representation takes it out of the realm of art.
To put this another way: the vision is not creative precisely because it
turns out to have been a flawless reproduction of experience. The visionary only replicates, in advance, what he will later see. And Eliot implies
that Latimer fails to become an artist precisely because art is not repetition but creation, not rapt passivity but imaginative labor.

Strange, given that a now-conventional definition of realism would
hold that the artist should strive to produce a perfect doubling of the
world. George Eliot, at the center of a Victorian dialogue about realism,
seems to set mimesis *against* art. And indeed, Latimer's visions, remarkably like Ruskin's trompe l'oeil, close the gap between mind and world.
His words simply repeat; his expectations and the evidence of experience
turn out to be identical. The narrative moves in a circle because there is
no difference between hypothesis and confirmation, between image and
reality. Expectations match the world so absolutely that they simply mirror one another: the closing scene echoes the opening one; the narrator's

experience of Prague duplicates his prophecy; the first visionary image of Bertha is immediately followed by the reality; Latimer hears the words of his companions before they speak them; and his forecast of Bertha's hatred for him is certainly confirmed by later events. Repetition forms the basic structure of this circular narrative. In the terms of the scientific experiment, Latimer is like a scientist whose hypotheses always and necessarily fit the evidence.

Yet the narrative does lay claim to its own share of suspense. As in an experiment, Latimer repeatedly waits with bated breath to see whether his experience will match his prevision. In one example, he draws out the space between his prediction of Prague and the later lived experience, eventually putting an end to "the suspense I had been wishing to protract" (34). To put it simply, Latimer is a clairvoyant who does not know that his visions will come true—and so he is compelled to test them. Even on the first page, when he foretells his death, he insists on an element of doubt: "If it were to be otherwise—if I were to live on to the age most men desire and provide for—I should for once have known whether the miseries of delusive expectation can outweigh the miseries of true prevision" (1). Unlike a scientist, of course, Latimer desperately hopes that the hypothesis and the evidence will prove *different*. He does not want to validate his initial visions because he urgently longs to hold onto the anxieties and doubts of ignorance. If, in the end, he sees exactly what he is afraid to see, along the way we readers do not know for sure whether his experience will validate his forecast, and we must wait, as in any suspense plot, to see what happens.

Lest we seem to be straying rather far from the realist experiment, we might remember that there is a scientific experiment within the narrative proper. Latimer's old friend, Charles Meunier, asks if he may perform a blood transfusion to resuscitate Bertha's maid.[4] The narrator has told us that there is a secret antagonism between Bertha and her maid; we do not know what it is, and our only hope of knowledge lies in the scientist's attempt to bring the maid back to life. By this time Latimer's clairvoyance has largely left him, and he too wonders, "What secret was there between Bertha and this woman?" (63). Thus there are two suspense plots working within the single experiment: the scientist wonders whether he can bring the woman back to life by transfusing blood, while the narrator and we readers are keen to discover Bertha's secret.

But there is a sleight-of-hand at work here. The retrospective first-person narrator does know, *as he narrates the story,* how it will all come out. Told in the past tense, the narration comes after the fact, comfortably knowledgeable about a future that we have not yet reached. In other words, the narrative's techniques of suspense are clearly there not to mirror the world but to intrigue and persuade the *reader.* This is not surprising, of course, since plotted narrative is intrinsically a prescient form, told from the perspective of the end. It is for this reason that suspense has typically been seen as manipulative and controlling, setting up the reader for prearranged conclusions. If nineteenth-century suspense comes into being as a stratagem to teach readers how to doubt their conventionalized assumptions about the world, it is because the texts of realism have craftily set these assumptions up to be tested. But unlike the plots we have encountered so far, George Eliot's story does not orchestrate new and unsettling conclusions—or even old and familiar ones. Rather, it repeats its own forecasts, validates its own hypotheses, as hermetic and isolated as its narrator. Unlike the experimental narratives of Brontë, Poe, and Dickens, the suspense of *The Lifted Veil* does not test common generalizations about the world, setting up conventional rules or principles to be tried out against the evidence of experience. Instead, the story predicts its own scenes, which then appear as doubles of their prediction. Far from unsettling our conservative expectations with new and surprising outcomes, Latimer's visions just repeat themselves, each one twice over.

George Eliot seems to suggest, then, that the *form* of suspense is always covertly circular, moving us both backward and forward in time. If a narrative signals that it is withholding a particular piece of knowledge from us in order to pique our interest in it, then we read on, but our later discovery is necessarily tied to our earlier uncertainty. Thus suspense has the potential to generate not new knowledge but repetition, to train us not into a progressive and skeptical posture in relation to the world but rather into endless reduplication. If we know that Eliot's Latimer produces the deathly, eerie repetitions of clairvoyance in his own life, then perhaps his mode of storytelling, too, might begin to look suspect. Is the narrative of suspense really a self-confirming form, returning only to corroborate its own predetermined hypotheses?

As U. C. Knoepflmacher explains, Latimer is only imperfectly clairvoyant: "capable of foreseeing some events, he fails to foresee others; free to see depravity, he is denied the opportunity to see altruism and love. This arbitrariness is deliberate: his negative conclusions must be founded on a partial vision of reality."[5] It is true that the narrator does not foresee his brother's death, saying emphatically of Alfred, "There was no evil in store for *him*" (38). He wonders, after the fact, whether he would have felt more sympathy if he had been granted foreknowledge of Alfred's tragic end:

> In after-days I thought with bitter regret that if . . . I could have had a foreshadowing of that moment when I looked on my brother's face for the last time, some softening influence would have been shed over my feeling towards him: pride and hatred would surely have been subdued into pity, and the record of those hidden sins would have been shortened. But this is one of the vain thoughts with which we men flatter ourselves. We try to believe that the egoism within us would have easily been melted, and that it was only the narrowness of our knowledge which hemmed in our generosity, our awe, our human piety. (32)

Would Latimer have behaved more generously if his foresight had included his brother's death? This is not a question that the events of the story will answer. Our narrator changes his mind about the proper response, alternating between hypotheses: perhaps the right images would generate pity and love—as the narrator in *Adam Bede* hopes—or perhaps a fuller picture of the future would do nothing to make us act more ethically. In *The Lifted Veil,* this is a question that is not framed suspensefully, the answer carefully withheld and delayed until later. Rather, the question is asked "in after-days," a counter-factual speculation that cannot write over the narrative that has already been written. And it is the question that has most concerned twentieth-century critics, who have wondered, along with Latimer, what would connect him more intimately and tenderly to his fellow human beings. Kate Flint asks: "If we could foresee the consequences of our actions, would we act differently? If sympathy towards others is a desirable thing, is it only possible when we do not know as much as it would be possible to know about the other person?" And Jennifer Uglow writes: "George Eliot pauses and asks, 'But *is* it really just a question of accurate vision? What would happen to individual choice if people could actually see into the future? Would it change their actions? Would it be a blessing, a curse, or a mere irrelevancy? And could there ever be such a thing as perfect insight or would it always be somehow coloured by the medium of perception—the individual personality?"[6] The critics have echoed, rather than answering, the central question posed by the text. And all of this ethical uncertainty suggests that Eliot has succeeded in suspending our judgments, in forestalling firm conclusions. But she does not achieve this suspension by means of narrative suspense: she prompts our doubts about the narrator's conclusions by making him seem an unreliable authority about his own life, a poor judge, a poor *reader*.

Significantly, if the narrative does not provide an answer to Latimer's question about his response to Alfred's death, it carefully inserts it into the text several pages *before* we readers hear the narrative of Alfred's death. By the time that Latimer tells us he believed that there "was no evil in store" for his brother, we know better. That is, the reader actually has a "foreshadowing" of Alfred's death in the context of the narrative. Indeed, if we had been reading the original serialized version, we would have had to wait a full month between the prediction and the event. Thus Latimer wonders whether he would have behaved more compassionately if he had predicted what he does, in fact, predict *for us*. On the one hand, then, George Eliot's character, denied suspense in all areas of his life but one, withholds fragments of knowledge in order to tell us a suspenseful story. But on the other hand, the reader is offered previsions of events that are refused to the seer.

At this point, it becomes uncannily apparent that the reader of suspenseful fiction is partially clairvoyant, just like the narrator. We are granted foresight when it comes to some events, denied it when it comes to others. Hardly creative ourselves, we do not make these visions—they simply happen to us—and we are left entirely dependent on forces external to our conscious efforts. In short, the reader of suspenseful plots is in *precisely the same position* as our "strange" narrator. Similarly passive, similarly subject to what is given to us, we are arbitrarily enlightened about some of the events that are to come and forced to wait for others. We have access to the internal lives of others in brief moments of illumination, and we have insights into some of the events that are to come.

Curiously, then, Latimer—who suffers from total isolation and an inability to have meaningful relations with others—turns into a figure for the reader of suspenseful narrative.

The consequences of this similarity turn out to be rather disturbing. We have a narrator who is not an artist but a duplicator of visions, a narrator who is neither omniscient nor entirely wrapped up within the first person. And he is much like ourselves. This is hardly a flattering likeness. Latimer is isolated, mean-spirited, and unforgiving toward others. Suspense, if Ruskin, Brontë, and Dickens are right, should generate a humble desire to know the truth along with a loving respect for alterity. But for Latimer, suspense about Bertha brings sexual desire, a perilous mystification of her, and a set of delusive hopes. At the same time, his partial knowledge—his insight and foresight—bring contempt for those around him, loneliness, and an increasing self-absorption. If Brontë and Dickens delayed a knowledge of the other in order to emphasize the gap between mind and world, George Eliot suggests that such stimulation might simply incite a more ferocious desire to impose ourselves on the other. And if Brontë and Dickens intended a knowledge of the otherness of the other to bring about an unsettling of the self, the difference might instead reinforce a sense of superiority and detachment. The veil produces not humility but obsessive desire; the lifted veil generates not love but scorn.

The Lifted Veil tempts us into a skepticism about the realism we have encountered so far. What Latimer learns over the course of time is what he always already expects. Though he seems to be knowledgeable about the world outside of himself, he cannot move beyond the circular reach of his own fears, desires, and absorptions. In short, he cannot suspend himself. And though Latimer's clairvoyance might seem to give us access to the internal lives of others, those lives are never individually characterized for us: we learn that Latimer's companions reveal "all the intermediate frivolities, all the suppressed egoism, all the struggling chaos, puerilities, meanness, vague capricious memories, and indolent makeshift thoughts, from which human words and deeds emerge like leaflets covering a fermenting heap" (19–20). But as for specific thoughts, fears, and hopes, we learn only about the narrator's own. Thus a knowing access to alterity is no guarantee of ethical acuteness; knowledge of the not-self does not generate selflessness. If, in suspenseful fiction, we read on to

discover what lies behind the veil, and then, ideally, we revise our atti-
tudes according to the new knowledge of the world we gather, in *The
Lifted Veil* we encounter a character who knows what lies behind the veil
and yet remains wedded to his own inclinations, yearnings, and terrors.
And thus George Eliot makes it clear that knowledge is not the same as
goodness.

As in *Adam Bede,* the concerns of *The Lifted Veil* are ultimately not
far removed from the aesthetic project of *Modern Painters.* When it comes
to aesthetics, Eliot, like Ruskin, seems to condemn repetitive passivity in
favor of imaginative labor. Like Ruskin, too, she insists that art should
signal and preserve the distance between mind and world. Moreover, her
apprehensions about a responsible relationship to alterity echo Ruskin's
interest in building an appropriate appreciation of the otherness of the
natural world. But *The Lifted Veil* reveals anxieties about the suspenseful
plot as a vehicle for approaching alterity. George Eliot's narrator, though
he sees more of the real and therefore knows more than his fellow human beings, offers moral judgments that waver between bitter cynicism
and fellow feeling, never coming to rest in affirmative conclusions.[7] Suspended rather than suspenseful, the ethical questions of the text linger on
unanswered. Thus Latimer's special knowledge does not make him a
wise judge or a reliable interpreter of the world. And if Latimer is like
us—the reader of suspenseful fiction—then perhaps we are not so wise
ourselves.

7   The Prophetic Fallacy

Romola

On first reading, *Romola* might appear to be the most Ruskinian of George Eliot's narratives. The novel is crowded with tests, trials, and experiments. The protagonist tries to live by a sequence of authorities—her father, husband, brother, uncle, and spiritual father—only to discover, on examination, that they all misrepresent the reality of her experience. Little by little, she comes to be skeptical of all authority but her own, until, in her most subversive moment, she realizes that "The law was sacred . . . but the rebellion might be sacred too" (552).

The form of Romola's *Bildung* is therefore familiar enough: it follows the pattern of empirical science, the skeptical testing of hypotheses against the evidence of experience. As her narrative progresses, Romola is increasingly prepared to create her own unconventional models. In good realist fashion, the plot of the novel throws gender orthodoxies into question. By the time we reach the epilogue, Romola has rejected all paternal authority and radically revises conventional relations between wife and mistress, adopting her husband's lover as her own partner in housekeeping and child rearing. Affirming a startling independence, the women run the household together, free from the demands and sanctions of men.[1] Thus the ending of *Romola* reveals its heroine obeying only the tutelage of her own experience, casting off all conventions and authorities that do not accord with her hard-won understanding of the realities of the world.

But a closer look at the novel suggests a less serenely Ruskinian conclusion. On the one hand, *Romola* does seem to embrace the realist experiment, repeatedly dismissing the power of visions, symbols, and prophecies in favor of tested, empirical knowledge. The protagonist staunchly refuses to listen to the "phantoms and disjointed whispers" of the prophets, preferring what the narrator calls "the large music of reasonable speech, and the warm grasp of living hands" (328). Rational discourse and human connection explicitly take the place of a faith in dreams and visions. Yet critics have largely ignored this rationalist strain in *Romola,* finding ample interpretive interest in the novel's dreams, symbols, and religious revelations—the very nonrational abundance of George Eliot's elaborate text. Felicia Bonaparte writes that *Romola* is "a symbolic narrative in which every character, every event, every detail—every word, in fact—is an image in an intricate symbolic pattern."[2] Mary Wilson Carpenter reads the whole novel as a text that employs a prophetic "method."[3] And Julian Corner argues that the "stalemate" ending of *The Mill on the Floss* prompted Eliot, in *Romola,* "to abandon the conscious mind as the exclusive medium of her quest for coherence, and to explore the possibility of reconciliation in the unconscious."[4]

Is *Romola* the quintessentially rationalist text, insisting on reason as the mainstay of healthy human communities and adopting empirical trials as the most reliable method for understanding experience? Or does the novel invite us rather to uphold the striking power of figure, dream, and allegory, unconscious desire and irrational belief? Perhaps, rather than choosing between these two—as critics in the past have done—we might imagine that George Eliot mobilizes both the rationality of the test and the nonrationality of the dream *as alternative modes of representing the world.* Indeed, I propose to read the novel as an interrogation of two conflicting ways of reading the real—one the realist experiment, the other the anti-realist model of prophecy. *Romola* is a narrative that asks how and whether we might establish one as more valid than the other.

The formal concerns of *The Lifted Veil* suggested that prophetic suspense depended on a kind of deadening circularity, and *Romola,* no less clairvoyant than its precursor, critiques prophecy as arbitrary, empty, and circular. But, as I argue here, it is in *Romola's* attempts to dismiss the voices of prophecy that this text reveals the hidden unreason of the narrative of suspense. Prophecy is explicitly rejected in *Romola*—criticized for its seductive and misleading authority. But despite unmistakable arguments against it, the visionary and the symbolic are never effectively shaken or disproved by narrative experience. And this is no accident: *Romola* cannot successfully contradict prophetic voices because prophecy is too much like plotted narrative. Narrative and prophetic meanings alike take shape only when we look back from the perspective of the future to read significance in the past. Unsettlingly, then, the formal similarities between narrative knowledge and prophetic persuasion mean that when suspenseful narrative actively discredits prophecy it also calls its own methods of persuasion into radical question.

Visual Mysteries and Narrative Knowledge

Appearances are misleading in *Romola,* and it is for this reason that treachery flourishes in fifteenth-century Florence. The young Greek stranger, Tito Melema, is impossible to decipher on the basis of visual clues alone.[5] The narrator explains:

> there was no brand of duplicity on his brow; neither was there any stamp of candour: it was simply a finely formed, square, smooth young brow. And the slow absent glance he cast round at the upper windows of the houses had neither more dissimulation in it, nor more ingenuousness, than belongs to a youthful well-opened eyelid with its unwearied breadth of gaze. . . . Was it that Tito's face attracted or repelled according to the mental attitude of the observer? Was it a cipher with more than one key? (102)

Given Tito's "negative" expression (102), anyone who tries to make sense of him on the basis of sight alone generates only prejudices and preconceptions. Romola immediately imposes herself on the other, imagining Tito to be compassionate and generous like herself. Indeed, she universalizes this confidence: "It seems to me beauty is part of the finished language by which goodness speaks" (195). With this "implicit proverb," George Eliot suggests that general statements about the world of the reader fall within the novel's evaluative scope. Thus when the text comes to prove Romola wrong—as it will—it also discredits a whole way of seeing the world. Indeed, we might say that this example follows the familiar pattern of the realist Bildungsroman: the text proposes a hypothesis—one that encompasses the reader's world as well as the world represented—and then rejects that hypothesis, replacing it with a new and more surprising way of seeing.

Early in the novel when we know very little about the anonymous stranger, Piero di Cosimo, the painter, asks Tito to pose as a model for Sinon, a classical traitor. Nello the barber immediately objects and, like Romola, universalizes this response: "I shall never look at such an outside as that without taking it as a sign of a loveable nature" (44). But the painter argues that it is precisely the beauty of Tito's face that would allow the Greek to act the traitor successfully:

> A perfect traitor should have a face which vice can write no marks on—lips that will lie with a dimpled smile—eyes of such agate-like brightness and depth that no infamy can dull them— cheeks that will rise from a murder and not look haggard. I say not this young man is a traitor: I mean, he has a face that would make him the more perfect traitor if he had the heart of one, which is saying neither more nor less than that he has a beautiful face. (42)

Piero, like Nello and Romola, suggests a generalization about visual clues: a successful deceiver is one who appears unmarked by deception. But this statement will hold true only if people are credulous, ready to believe that appearances are a reliable index of character. And so Piero implies a familiar realist lesson: if we learn to be skeptical about visual impressions, we will not be betrayed.

The novel puts these competing hypotheses to the test. Sure enough, good-natured Romola and Nello are wrong in their assumptions about the other, while Piero's skepticism proves itself perfectly justified. And lest we overlook this lesson, Piero and Nello return to their dispute over Tito's face a number of chapters later to remind us of it. By this time the reader knows that Piero's theory is right. Tito is suddenly distracted by fears that his guilty secrets will be publicly disclosed. Nello feels sure, however, that Tito is "absorbed in anxiety about Romola" and throws "a challenging look at Piero di Cosimo, whom he had never forgiven for his refusal to see any prognostics of character in his favourite's handsome face" (169).

In good suspenseful fashion, the first debate about Tito's face offers us a hypothesis, and then, when it is mentioned for the second time, we reread it from the more knowing present and have no trouble deciding which hypothesis was right. We have been educated. Such suspenseful foreshadowing highlights the temporal complexity of narrative plotting: we look backward from the perspective of the future to see that in the past a mysterious moment actually pointed toward unknown future events, which were then later realized. But the first debate serves an important purpose within realist narrative: Piero's suspicions about Tito may be without epistemological *value,* but they are about prompting an epistemological *desire,* provoking us to want to know whether or not Tito will become a traitor.

In *Romola,* as in other texts of the realist experiment, visual impressions work as hypotheses rather than illustrations—provoking doubt and speculation rather than offering us clear images of the world. Indeed, in their repeated failures to tell the truth, visual images excite a readerly interest in narrative unfolding. The image tells us nothing in the present, and we must wait to see what the tests of time will show. Thus the failures of the visual persuade us to put our faith in the epistemological fruits of narrative.[6]

The Problem with Prophecy

This narrative impulse toward tested truth is all very well, but Florence in 1492 is brimming with prophetic voices and superstitions. And a number of prophecies are actually confirmed by the unfolding of narrative events. Romola's visionary brother prophesies that her marriage will bring disaster, and he is later proven right. But Romola forcefully rejects the dream even once it has come true:

> What had the words of that vision to do with her real sorrows? That fitting of certain words was a mere chance; the rest was all vague—nay, those words themselves were vague. . . . What reasonable warrant could she have had for believing in such a vision and acting on it? None. True as the voice of foreboding had

proved, Romola saw with unshaken conviction that to have re-
nounced Tito in obedience to a warning like that, would have
been meagre-hearted folly. Her trust had been delusive, but she
would have chosen over again to have acted on it rather than be
a creature led by phantoms and disjointed whispers in a world
where there was the large music of reasonable speech, and the
warm grasp of living hands. (328)

From Romola's perspective, prophecy clearly fails to offer a valuable
knowledge of the real, but it fails on curious grounds. As Romola says, her
brother's prophecy does correspond to events, but only by *chance.* The
other models that Romola comes to reject—the correlation between
beauty and goodness, for example—collapse when they do not correspond to the real. Prophecy fits the real—and is dismissed nonetheless.

Characters in the novel offer three explicit reasons to distrust the
prophets. First, conflicts among prophetic visions prove that they cannot all be justified, and there is no way to tell which of the prophetic
voices is sound until events happen that correspond to one rather than
another. As Nello puts it: "With San Domenico roaring *è vero* in one ear,
and San Francisco screaming *è falso* in the other, what is a poor barber to
do?" (19).

The second interpretive doubt that haunts and unsettles the persuasive force of religious predictions involves misgivings about the validity
of prophecies that seem to have come true. Nello claims that religious visions are always self-justifying:

There is as wonderful a power of stretching in the meaning of
visions as in Dido's bull's hide. It seems to me a dream may mean
whatever comes after it. As our Franco Sachetti says, a woman
dreams over night of a serpent biting her, breaks a drinking-cup
the next day, and cries out, "Look you, I thought something
would happen—it's plain now what the serpent meant." (266)

Perhaps the event will always be capable of confirming the prophetic
voice, since both are vague enough to be stretched to fit the other. The
passage of time might validate any hypothesis if the audience is willing
simply to wait indefinitely and to "stretch" predictions to fit subsequent
phenomena.

In this particular scene, Nello is responding to Camilla Rucellai's prediction that the scholar Pico della Mirandola "would die in the time of lilies." When he dies in November—"not at all the time of lilies"— Camilla appears to have been discredited (265). But she replies with the assertion that her vision should be interpreted metaphorically: "it is the lilies of France I meant, and it seems to me they are close enough under your nostrils" (265). The "fitting" of words to events is rendered radically suspect by Camilla's metaphorical interpretation, which carefully upholds her own prophetic authority.

Third, the prophet may offer more than one future alternative: Savonarola, for example, threatens a scourge if Florence does not purify itself, and glory if it does. But if there are two possible outcomes to a prophecy, we are faced with a serious ex post facto epistemological problem: if we manage to prevent the realization of a particular outcome, we will never know whether the imaged future would have come true if we had not done as we were directed. Dino's dream is also an example of this kind of prophecy. Romola claims that she would not act on her brother's warning if she had the choice again, despite the fact that his prediction has come true. After all, if she had acted on the basis of the dream, she would never have learned the crucial lessons of her own experience—the collapse of the marriage tie and its eventual displacement by a more fitting moral law. Indeed, according to the paradoxical logic of warnings, if Romola had in fact averted the disastrous marriage predicted by her brother, she would never have known whether or not the warning itself was justified. Prophecies therefore frustrate the task of *Bildung*. Visions fail to draw connections between "experience" and interpretation, between cause and effect—leaving their listeners dependent on the prophets.

With prophecy, we face either an epistemological problem or a hermeneutic one: we do not know for sure whether a prophecy has "really" been fulfilled, and we have no firm, convincing way, even once time has passed, of distinguishing valid prophecy from vague assertions made after the fact. Thus Nello and Romola reject the prophets and assert a skeptical paradigm: the fitting of present experience to cloudy, dreamlike premonitions in the past is always potentially a process of distortion, tailored to establish the very validity of the premonitions.

But if the "fitting of certain words" can be "a mere chance," and if meanings are infinitely stretchable, how might we ever establish reliable links between guesses and certain knowledge? If Dino's vision is an accidental, inauthentic correspondence between words and the world, then what is the proper, grounded way of seeing? These questions are particularly important, presumably, in a historical novel, which elucidates real events from a historical past. How can we know if the temporal links offered by historical texts are convincing? If there are "chance" conjunctions of words and meanings, are there also legitimate and true correlations between words and meanings? And how might we tell one from the other?

The Laws of the World

At several points in the novel, George Eliot suggests a more grounded alternative to the arbitrary voices of prophecy: the duplicable, empirical laws of ordinary causality. Romola dismisses her brother's vision because she is "too keenly alive to the constant relations of things to have any morbid craving after the exceptional" (162). Setting the routine of "constant relations" against the strangeness of the "exceptional," the narrator implies that prophetic visions are worthless precisely because they do not describe *repeatable* links. According to Wendell Harris's definition of "empiricism," this emphasis on recurrent correlations makes Romola into a perfect Victorian empiricist, with a faith that "the discovery of truth depends on the analysis of relations between those things which make up our experience."[7]

Eliot is not the first to oppose the empirical to the miraculous. Her text takes its place in a tradition of nineteenth-century religious skepticism, including the works of Ludwig Feuerbach and David Friedrich Strauss, which Eliot herself translated. Strauss rejects the truth-value of the Gospels wherever the texts are marked by miraculous interventions that interrupt the laws of nature, because "the absolute cause never disturbs the chain of secondary causes by single arbitrary acts of interposition, but rather manifests itself in the production of the aggregate of finite causalities, and of their reciprocal action."[8] Assuming that God would never hinder the usual course of events because the laws of nature are his own work, Strauss, like Romola, dismisses the "exceptional" in favor of the "constant relations of things."

The empirical laws *Romola* affirms are laws of the social, rather than the natural, world. If the prophets believe in the dictates of a divine purpose, the text favors the principle of human agency. "Tito was experiencing that inexorable law of human souls, that we prepare ourselves for sudden deeds by the reiterated choice of good or evil which gradually determines character" (224). Eliot here implies not only a model of causality but a model of subjectivity: a chronological history of choices that comes to define an increasingly coherent self. Felicia Bonaparte argues that Eliot consistently replaces the conventional essentialist self, untouched by its actions and circumstances, with a selfhood that is coterminous with its actions. Thus there is no ontological distinction between the choices a character makes and character itself.[9] This may be a fact of narrative, as Shlomith Rimmon-Kenan suggests: "The repetition of the same behaviour 'invites' labeling it as a character-trait."[10]

Romola repeatedly confirms this "law" of repeated choices: Tito and Romola can be identified and differentiated on the basis of the ways they come to their conclusions about appropriate action. Tito's first treacherous acts precipitate events that call for further choices, and once he has begun to deceive, he becomes more and more wedded to his treachery. As the narrator puts it: "Our lives make a moral tradition for our individual selves, as the life of mankind makes a moral tradition for the race" (353).

If the self comes into being through a series of choices, then a character in the process of formation must be able to become a range of different selves. At the beginning of the novel, Tito has not yet decided to sacrifice his adopted father for the sake of his own comforts, and yet he has a strong preference for avoiding suffering and enjoying pleasure and, as the narrator tells us, "an innate love of reticence" (94). He has characteristics in place that will lead to his eventual treachery and duplicity, but the "innate" is no fixed trait: it is a desire, an "impulse," an inclination. And importantly, throughout Romola we find Tito caught in a moment of indecision, weighing the arguments for and against a particular action.

Character, then, involves not compulsion but self-persuasion, and there is always more than one real and plausible alternative in the choices that constitute the self. What Dino's prophecy most importantly disregards, in this empirical context, is that what actually brings about the disastrous marriage between Tito and Romola is not divine providence but a conflict between two ways of making choices that intensify as the narrative unfolds—a conflict between Tito's repeated pursuit of pleasure and the increasingly scrupulous choices of his more duty-bound wife.

This developmental "law" of character leads directly to the production of narrative suspense. For example, Tito at one point deliberates over whether or not to tell Tessa that their marriage is a sham. The tension of the moment before he settles on a single choice reveals his character in the process of formation, and it is pointedly suspenseful: "Tito felt the necessity of speaking now; and, in the rapid thought prompted by that necessity, he saw that by undeceiving Tessa he should be robbing himself of some at least of that pretty trustfulness which might, by and by, be his only haven from contempt" (153). In this moment of "rapid thought" we recognize Tito's desire to bury the past and secure the future, which has been with him from the outset. But this is also a character in the act of becoming: indecisive for this instant, he seems to be capable of choosing another course. And thanks to the central place of self-persuasion in the act of decision making, Tito's choice does not appear, even in retrospect, to have been the only possible outcome. It is in these moments of individual deliberation that the narrative produces a sense of openness and indeterminacy. Or, as Gillian Beer puts it: "The idea of a future foregrounds the insufficiency of determinism."[11] The novel clearly needs its sense of an open future in order to keep its readers' interest, relying on the workings of suspense. On a more ideological level, though, these moments reveal that character is not fixed, since humans are free to choose one of many possible moral "traditions." In other words, the empirical law of human agency requires narrative suspense.

In this context, we can return to Piero's reading of Tito as a traitor. This hypothesis is predictive in the sense that the painter can foresee a probable moral path for a face like Tito's, and it is also true in the sense that Tito does indeed pursue that course. But Piero's interpretation is valid in a more crucial way as well: it is right about Tito's *potential* for treachery, whether or not the character ever comes to realize that potential. In other words, Piero's theory does tell the truth in the present, because the only available truth about the developing self is its promise, its possibility. In effect, there is no "truth" of character in the present: character is molded by action; it is a history of choices rather than a fixed entity. Thus it is not only that we come to knowledge through plotted narrative, but that *valuable knowledge is itself narrative in form.* Visual images can never tell the truth about character: static visual clues necessarily fail to reveal the unsettled nature of emergent selfhood.

If George Eliot uses suspense to reveal the narrative workings of the world, her work marks a sharp shift in the realist experiment. *Romola* emphasizes hidden transformations, rather than hidden facts. What we want to know at the outset is not a secret truth that has been suggested but concealed. Rather, what is "concealed" from us at the beginning is something that is simply not yet in existence. If we want to know the truth behind Tito's features, then we want to know a history that will unfold in the future rather than a set of qualities already fixed in the past. Plotted desire depends in *Romola* on the principle of moral freedom.[12] And if the truths of narrative are truths that can only be told in narrative—if they are themselves temporal unfoldings—then the form and the content of the text come so close together that they become effectively indivisible. Here, then, is the crucial transformation in the realist experiment: suspenseful narrative is no longer conceived as a method for approaching the real but has instead become a mimetic image of the real. While *Jane Eyre* and *Great Expectations* used the strategies of suspense to teach readers to hold our own assumptions at bay while we waited for the truth to emerge, *Romola* teaches us that the world unfolds like a narrative—and, consequently, that narrative form itself reflects the truths of the world.

Set against the arbitrary voices of the prophets, firm, reliable narrative knowledge comes about in two ways in *Romola:* first is the knowledge that follows *empirical questions*—as in the debate about Tito's features; and second are the moments of *individual deliberation*—as when Tito tries to decide whether or not to enlighten Tessa about their marriage. It is my contention, however, that these two kinds of suspense are in fact two sides of the same epistemological coin: to know the truth of character lying behind Tito's features is to know what choices he will make. The suspense prompted by visual mysteries and the suspense surrounding the act of decision making alert us to precisely the same question: namely, what will Tito become? In two ways, then, suspense, the prompting of epistemological desire, leads directly to the knowledge of individual moral responsibility.

The Logic of Plotting

The plot of skeptical realism in *Romola* has brought us to a knowledge of bourgeois morality—which suggests that it might not be so skeptical after all. Indeed, if we return yet again to our first example of suspense in the novel—the representation of Tito as Sinon the traitor—we can begin to unravel the logic of plotting in *Romola*. In this scene, the terms of the debate are clear: either beautiful faces are always signs of lovable souls, or beautiful faces can come to hide traitors. If we read two alternative ways of seeing and return to reread the scene with the knowledge that only one of those alternatives fits the evidence provided by the novel, we have presumably learned a tested, empirical lesson.

But have we? After all, the temporal relationship among these interpretive moments in a narrative might be more complex than the model of experimental testing might suggest. In all plotted narratives, "the future is covertly converted into retrospect. The future we are about to read has already been inscribed by the author and experienced by the characters." [13] Thanks to the logic of narrative, we know that the discussion between the painter and the barber has been selected for us as worthy of notice from the perspective of the future, the implied time of writing rather than the actual time of the debate. Any narrative mystery hints at a truth that is unavailable to the reader in the present, and we must simply commit to memory cryptic signs whose later plenitude of meaning we simply take on faith. Peter Brooks calls this process of reading the "anticipation of retrospection": "If the past is to be read as present, it is a curious present that we know to be past in relation to a future we know to be already in place, already in wait for us to reach it." [14]

Expectant, we are dependent on narrative time to confirm or deny our misgivings, but since plotted narratives are always told from the perspective of the future, our dawning suspicions are, ironically, themselves prompted only by the events to come, the present actually prompted by the future. As Christopher Norris explains:

> "Causes" in the novel are brought into play by the need for some solution or (apparently) antecedent fact which explains and unravels a complicated plot. In this sense causes are really *effects,* since they spring from a given complex of events which creates

them, as it were, in pursuit of its own coherence. Effects are likewise transformed into causes by the same curious twist of logic.[15]

Perhaps any causal narrative, anticipating retrospection, has to reach its conclusions before it can take on meaning. And although it sounds topsy-turvy, we can say that Piero posits an intriguing, generalized way of reading beautiful faces in the world precisely *because* this view will later be validated by the novel's events.

Narrative, like the prophets it spurns, already knows the future in the present. And if prophecy and plot share a certain formal structure, then surely it is appropriate to turn the novel's critique of prophecy back onto its own form. Let us return to Dino's prophecy and compare it to the debate over Tito's features. On the one hand, the logic of narrative time validates the prophecy just as it validates Piero's hypothesis: the marriage between Romola and Tito is a disaster, as Dino has forewarned, as we readers expect, and as Romola recognizes. Yet unlike the lesson she has learned about beauty and treachery, Romola denies the significance of Dino's dream, even once it has been confirmed. The prophecy functions just like examples of epistemological suspense—a possible outcome to be tested, which in fact later comes true—but the novel then reads the correlation between proposition and event as worthless and empty.

What does it mean for the novel to suggest that its own details are meaningless? To raise suspicions and confirm them, only to deny the validity of some of these narrative messages? If narrative knowledge depends on the links we expect to make between suspenseful withholdings and later revelations, then surely George Eliot begins to render that knowledge radically suspect when she undertakes her careful critique of prophetic persuasion.

More unsettling still, the truths of *Romola,* as we have seen, are themselves narrative in form. Ruskin and his novelistic successors saw narrative merely as a means of coming to know the hidden truths of the real, but Eliot takes truth to be intrinsically narrative in *Romola.* Paradoxically, then, just as the novel approaches this new claim to mimetic perfection, it also incorporates a critique of narrative form, invalidating its own lessons and challenging its own structure.

As if to underscore the strong bond between the novel's form and its content, the character Romola makes it clear that it is impossible to deny the hold that the past claims upon the present. Indeed, our two major characters represent two antithetical ways of linking past to future: Tito tries constantly to bury the past or to conceal it, while Romola attempts both to make sense of the past and to value her initial ties. Unwilling to remember, Tito is also conspicuously unable to learn, whereas Romola, faithful to her promises and vows, learns both to understand and to work through the past. Moral ties and narrative time are thus one and the same. Immediately after the betrothal, Romola tells Tito that she remains frightened by her memories of Dino's dream. In response to this reborn memory, Tito locks Dino's crucifix into the casket painted with the glorious images of Tito as Bacchus and Romola as Ariadne, telling her that he has "locked all the sadness away" (204). But Romola remains unconvinced: "it is still there—it is only hidden," she murmurs (204). Tito still urges her to forget: "See! they are all gone now! . . . My Ariadne must never look backward now—only forward" (205).

Here, as elsewhere, Tito denies the very temporal continuum that is the logic of the novel—a narrative system that relies on connections of past to present for its meanings. The play between past and future is a fundamental part of the temporal continuum of meaning that makes up the plotted whole, in which particular events are not read in their specificity but "point beyond themselves to a coordinating system."[16] And so indeed the past persistently returns, much as Tito tries to bury it. According to the paradoxical logic of plotted narrative, the past *must* return, since it is mentioned only in its relation to subsequent unfolding, the causes included for the sake of their effects, the choices for the sake of their consequences. Tito's immoral desire to bury the past is something like denying the most fundamental structure of narrative meanings, which necessarily entail links between past and present simply in order to preserve comprehensibility. Implicit, then, is again the alliance of plotted narrative and bourgeois morality: knowing that the past has an ineluctable claim on the present is both the substance of individual responsibility and the very fabric of plotted narrative.

"You have changed towards me," Tito says to Romola, "it has followed that I have changed towards you. It is useless to take any retrospect. We have simply to adapt ourselves to altered conditions" (418). Aside from the fact that this is not the whole story—since it is Tito, after all, who first changes toward Romola, rather than the reverse[17]—

what is most telling is Tito's dismissal of the use of retrospection in favor of adaptation: one must change to suit the circumstances, but without looking backward. This is the opposite of Romola's empirical education, which moves toward knowledge by containing the results of past trials within the present. It is also the survival of the fittest with a vengeance. For Tito, the extinction of earlier forms is relentless and unsentimental, and the future alone holds a monopoly on interest and value.

In short, Tito tries to bury the past that generates or informs subsequent moments. Romola knows that this forgetting is impossible, because memories simply do not disappear. Of course, the difficulty of forgetting is particularly important within a narrative sequence, where our readerly presumption is that details are included only if they are worthy of being remembered. Thus Tito's insistence that Romola forget Dino's crucifix ironically functions as a *reminder* for the reader. Indeed, Romola will later unbury the crucifix, as this moment presumably leads us to suspect.

If Romola is concerned to remember past images and ties, and Tito entirely dismisses the value of the past, we might formulate a simple dichotomy to describe the difference between their perspectives: the moral and responsible heroine recognizes the importance of the past and traces a path that connects the experiences of the past with choices in the present, making her a perfect student of narrative. By contrast, her masculine counterpart, in pursuit of pleasure, neglects and betrays past promises and keeps his eye entirely on the future, unable to construct true narratives to account for his experiences. Thus it is Romola who tells the story of Tito's life to his own son at the end of the novel, Romola who understands temporal links between choices and their consequences. Her husband's inability to make the proper connections between past and present makes him unable to grow into moral maturity, unable, therefore, to gather knowledge and equally unable to construct true narrative sequences that make valid sense of the ways of the world. Ethics, epistemology, and plotted narrative unite in Eliot's novelistic world.

But, of course, the place of Dino's dream in the novel functions as a way of unraveling the narrative's own persuasive structure: Romola tries, in the exceptional case of her brother's prophecy, to forget the past, to dismiss a moment that has been chosen as meaningful within the narrative, and her dismissal is corroborated by the narrator. But the image returns, again and again—as irrepressible as Tito's denials of Baldassarre.

no way to reject narrative of past

In other words, there is no way to reject the past *of narrative,* no matter
how unfounded it might be. The narrator represents the dream as a relentless return: "She could not prevent herself from hearing inwardly the
dying prophetic voice. . . . She could not prevent herself from dwelling
with a sort of agonized fascination on the wasted face" (328). This inability to dispose of Dino's dream might lead the reader to believe that
Romola is actually *mistaken* to dismiss the quintessentially narrative voices
of prophecy. Perhaps they cannot be forgotten because, like old ties, they
have a valid claim on the present. Mary Wilson Carpenter's apocalyptic
reading of the novel is based, in part, on this assumption:

> If Dino's prophecy, despite its accuracy, is not worth heeding,
> why is it given such importance in the narrative? Or to put it an-
> other way, if the prophecy is only part of a world of "phantoms"
> and "disjointed whispers," why should Dino nevertheless appear
> to have been correct in his prediction of events? [18]

Carpenter frames the question perfectly. But rather than proposing an intricate symbolic scheme to account for the workings of the novel, as Carpenter does, I would contend that at this point the realist text reaches its
crucial tension. The narrative actually invalidates the production of narrative meaning. In the novel's attempts to dismiss the voices of prophecy,
the form and the purpose of plotted suspense come into conflict.
   The reasonable narrator tells us that Dino's dream is important to
Romola's education because it allows her to sympathize with those who
succumb to the force of visions:

> The persistent presence of these memories, linking themselves
> in her imagination with her actual lot, gave her a glimpse of un-
> derstanding into the lives which had before lain utterly aloof
> from her sympathy—the lives of the men and women who were
> led by such inward images and voices.
>   "If they were only a little stronger in me," she said to herself,
> "I should lose the sense of what that vision really was, and take
> it for a prophetic light. I might in time get to be a seer of visions
> myself." . . . Romola shuddered at the possibility. (328–29)

Thus Romola and the narrator seem to agree that prophecies are powerfully persuasive but ultimately fallacious. It is this rationalist theme,
however, that is necessarily undercut by the *nonrational* structure of

narrative, which cannot distinguish true from false temporal patterns within the temporal continuum that makes narratives persuasive. Roland Barthes contends that "the mainspring of narrative is precisely the confusion of consecution and consequence, what comes *after* being read in narrative as what is *caused by;* in which case narrative would be a systematic application of the logical fallacy denounced by Scholasticism in the formula *post hoc, ergo propter hoc.*"[19] To put this another way: narrative suspense produces a sense that there are resolutions to come, and if they do come as expected, they necessarily take on narrative validity, whether or not a voice—even an authoritative voice—dismisses them in no uncertain terms.

Suspense in the novel is a way of asserting the truth-value of narrative as a form; we cannot tell how to interpret a meaningful moment in the present, and we need to read on to find out how it should have been read. But this epistemological process is dangerously similar to arbitrary prophetic authority: neither offers us valid proof of actual connections between hypothesis and event, and both persuade us simply by claiming a link between interpretive hints and later events. Given this structural analogy, we clearly face the same interpretive dilemmas with the novel as we did with the visionary. Remember, for example, that conflicts among visionaries made it impossible to tell which was the better seer. With the Franciscans predicting one outcome, and the Dominicans another, both aiming to validate their predictions after the fact by some intricate interpretive "stretching," only prior faith in one or the other would allow us to choose to believe one rather than the other. The same is true of narrative. After all, there are other narratives out there, equally concerned with the problems of appearance and essence, of truth and morality. And perhaps if we turned to other narratives with different outcomes to the same debates as those we find in *Romola,* the "knowledge" we have gathered in this narrative would begin to look dubious indeed. What, after all, would make one fictional plot more persuasive than another?

But we do not actually need to turn our attention as far afield as other novels to find alternatives to the empirical lessons taught to us by this text. As in the other suspenseful fictions we have considered, there are alternative narratives implied within *Romola* itself. The suspense crucial to our desire for knowledge actually requires that there be more than one plausible outcome to any narrative mystery. Tito almost undeceives Tessa about their marriage and thus almost remains faithful to Romola. In his moment of deliberation both options seem possible. But if he were to decide to be faithful to Romola, his beauty would be a sign of his goodness, Piero would be wrong, and we readers would have no reason to cast off Romola's proverbial correlation between outer and inner beauty. Surely the novel invites such speculations, and the fact that he chooses the immoral path within the novel does not make the experience of the text conform to the "real" more than it would if he were allowed to follow the moral course. Crucial to the ideological lessons of the novel, he must be entirely capable of choosing the moral direction. Given the necessary openness of suspenseful narrative, then, it must be possible to write equally convincing narratives to support conflicting general claims. And the condemnation of prophecy on the grounds of its conflicting declarations—its profusion of epistemologically undifferentiated possibilities—can be turned back on the plotted text.

As we have seen, the text also suggests that it is not valid to assert the legitimacy of religious prophecy simply because it happens to come true subsequently, for two reasons: on the one hand, the fulfillment of the prediction might be an accidental, inauthentic connection, in no way proving the validity of the prophecy; and on the other, interpretations can always be stretched, after the fact, to confirm the prophetic voice. But how does the narrative establish the validity of its own empirical knowledge? We have seen that plot works in part by setting up cryptic suggestions and unresolved debates, which, since narrative is told from the perspective of the future, are actually incorporated for the sake of their later resolution. Thus our "empirical" conclusions, which seemed to involve the testing of interpretive paradigms against the hidden realities of the world, are in fact there before they were ever arranged to be tested. We might say, in this context, that Tito, far from being a free moral agent, is absolutely destined to a treacherous future, and we, far from being autonomous and skeptical readers, have acquired a knowledge that is as preordained as the miraculous interventions of the divine will.

This brings us, then, to the union of narrative, epistemology, and ethics—the lesson that Romola learned, that we were meant to learn, and that Tito did not learn at all—namely, that moral maturity calls for an understanding of the power of the human choices in the world. In place of arbitrary divine predestination, the text favors an empirical causal model: "the inexorable law of human souls, that we prepare ourselves for sudden deeds by the reiterated choice of good or evil which gradually determines character" (224). Importantly, the text simply states this law and then offers substantiation of it: both Romola and Tito follow precisely this pattern. But if the novel suggests that it is not valid to assert the legitimacy of religious prophecy simply because it happens to come true subsequently, then is it ever valid to assert the legitimacy of a *novel's* events, simply because its hypotheses are validated by the unfolding of its own plot?

This is of course a question of correspondence, that quintessentially realist problem. How can we tell whether our hypotheses and representations really fit the world? In *Romola,* the monk's vision occurred and the event that followed it may seem to correspond to that vision, but according to Romola, there is no causal link between the two. All too similarly, however, the debate about Tito suggested that he might turn treacherous, which indeed he does. Just as a nonbeliever in prophecy would probably dismiss its persuasive force, a skeptical reader might contend that events like Tito's treachery are not caused by conscious, individual human choice, as we are told, but by the forces of material production, or by unconscious drives of desire, or by divine fiat. In the context of these other causal models, the novel shows that it is persuasive only within a sequence that it proceeds to explain on the basis of its own, previously established interpretive paradigm. What reasonable warrant could we have for believing in such a vision and acting on it?

Far from skeptical, we readers are actually guided, blind, by a narrative that establishes clear questions and then provides allegedly "empirical" responses to those questions, based on its own prior theory of causality. Far from free, we too are led by phantoms and disjointed whispers in a narrative that incorporates its own mysteriously prophetic moments into the text, only after having already arranged for their realization. Written in the knowledgeable future, the Bildungsroman, like prophecy, allows us readers no independent ways of learning connections in the world. Hence the validity of the causal model of choice and its consequences is, like prophecy, authoritative and self-justifying, confirmed only by the evidence that the text describes.

Romola herself, unwilling to accept the interpretive stretching involved in this form of persuasion, simply rejects the truth-value of the visionary even once it has come true. And perhaps we—who have learned from the plot to be skeptical readers—might choose to imitate her. With revolutionary gusto, that is, we could take the very same freedom in interpretation that Romola does when she refuses to be persuaded by the authoritative voices of prophecy. Rejecting the causal model implicit in the text, we could simply dismiss the novel's lessons, claiming that they represent an arbitrary connection between interpretive possibilities and narrative unfolding. The law of narrative might be sacred, but the rebellion might be sacred too.

PART IV

Unraveling the Rhetoric of Suspense: James, Pater, and Wilde

8   Losing the Plot

Henry James's "Travelling Companions"

Henry James's characters are famous for engaging in acts of suspending—hesitating, deferring knowledge, "hanging fire." Indeed, James's fiction repeatedly hints at its debts to the realist experiment, from the haunting suspense of *The Turn of the Screw* and the avid detectives of *The Aspern Papers* and *The Figure in the Carpet* to the interweaving of time, ethics, and hidden truth in *What Maisie Knew, The Ambassadors, The Wings of the Dove,* and *The Golden Bowl.* Indeed, while James's career is rich in generic and narrative complexity, he returns again and again to the problem of narrative knowledge. Tzvetan Todorov argues that in James, the "narrative is always based on *the quest for an absolute and absent cause.* . . . The secret of Jamesian narrative is precisely the existence of an essential secret, of something not named, of an absent and superpowerful force which sets the whole present machinery of the narrative in motion."[1] But if this "absent cause" brings to mind the madwoman in the attic or the long-forgotten convict, James's texts do not reward the suspension of judgment with shocking truths and unconventional certainties. Rather, as a number of critics have claimed, James deliberately departs from the traditions of Victorian plotting. "Secrets in James appear at first to be lures for the reader and devices of suspense," John Carlos Rowe explains, "but the revelation of the secret in James almost always ends in radical ambiguity." Narrative indecision then throws attention back on the activity of reading itself: "a character's very desire to know the truth . . . reveals the secret of that character's personality rather than the truth of the ostensible secret of the plot." In her brilliant reading of *The Turn of the Screw,* Shoshana Felman offers a similar conclusion. The governess's attempt to find out the truth and "impose meaning" on mysterious events ultimately reveals her as capable of a kind of violence: "imposing sense both as a *directive* and as a *direction* upon the others." For Felman, the governess's drive to make sense of events also implicates the reader, and thus our experience of reading "becomes, in effect, itself nothing other than a repetition of the crime."[4] From this perspective, James departs from his suspenseful precursors by foregrounding the act of interpretation, which then doubles back on the reader—prompting a self-reflexive relation to narrative mysteries rather than a newfound knowledge of the otherness of the world.

This chapter traces James's interest in narrative reflexivity to one of his first published short stories, "Travelling Companions" (1870–71), which performs a careful and devastating critique of the realist experiment. In this tale James's narrator informs us that he has been experiencing the world "in defiance of reason and Ruskin" (*Complete Tales,* 186).[5] It is my contention that the "defiance of Ruskin" is one of the more crucial purposes of this experimental narrative. On the one hand, James uses Ruskin's experiments as a model for his own narrative while, on the other, he unsettles their power to teach us a skeptical relationship to the world. Drawing on George Eliot's critique of suspense as a circular, self-confirming form, he suggests that even Ruskin's own experiments might end up producing a confirmation of conventional texts and images, generating not unsettling doubt but political and ethical complacency. Following Eliot, too, James assumes that the suspense adopted by his realist precursors had always been an attempt to describe the narrative unfolding of the world. Extending Eliot's insights into the formal artifices of suspense, he employs two kinds of narrative time in the same text: a "realist" model of temporal succession set alongside a plotted version of narrative time—which seems uncomfortably artificial by comparison. In this skeptical context—and in a deliberate attempt to defy Ruskin—James lays the groundwork for his reflexive later works.

Realism and the Critics

Scholarly interest in "Travelling Companions" has focused almost exclusively on biographical matters. Leon Edel's famous biography of James calmly quotes passages from the story as if they came from James's diaries or letters. Indeed, Edel avoids giving source information for these excerpts, which means that only the reader who recognizes this little-known story can catch Edel depending on a fictional narrative for his facts. Kenneth Churchill's more recent reading of the story also involves taking a piece from it to illustrate James's feelings for Italy. "The 'I' of this passage is not, indeed, James, but the hero of one of his early tales. The passage, however, is clearly closely autobiographical." And James Buzard claims that "there is little discernible distance between the first-person narrator . . . and the 27-year-old Henry James."[6]

It is true that James and his fictional hero have at least one significant experience in common: the meandering narrator of the story completes his artistic tour of Italy just as James himself had done in the year that the story appeared. But there is a difference between James and his narrator, and it is a plotted one: the hero of the fiction meets an eligible American woman, a Miss Evans, also visiting the sites of Italy with her father. As they come to know Venice together, the narrator begins to fall in love with Miss Evans. She rejects him, telling him that his feelings are merely a reflection of the romance of their surroundings, rather than true and lasting love. Then in Rome, some time later, her father dies, and she accepts the narrator's offer of marriage, acknowledging that his initial "passion that fancies" has become instead "the passion that knows" (225). This is, in other words, a love story as well as a travelog, a marriage plot as well as a record of the author's life. Indeed, as if to flaunt its kinship with other fictions, the story mimics the path of previous plots. A compromising night spent by the two protagonists in Padua reenacts a scene from George Sand's *La dernière Aldini,* a novel that Miss Evans reads on the journey.[7] And the narrator describes his travels as though they were a novel: "With an interest that hourly deepened as I read, I turned the early pages of the enchanting romance of Italy" (184).

Yet the impulse to read the story as a record of real experience is not surprising. Curiously for a plotted fiction, the hero's movements in

"Travelling Companions" are prompted almost entirely by Murray's *Handbook for Travellers,* a real guidebook, and one used by thousands of English-speaking tourists.[8] The story follows the guidebook's itinerary, and the narrator repeatedly feels sure that he will meet Miss Evans because the two travelers are following similar prescribed trails. One might say, in fact, that James's narrative actually obeys the plotless pattern of tourism more closely than it observes the plotted patterns of fiction: the guidebook recommends all that is of value to the visitor, and the narrator's movements are prompted by his desire to look at these sights, one after another, as he moves from one city to the next. The only major events of the narrative are the chance meetings between the narrator and his beloved, who are brought to the same places by the recommendations of the guide. Murray's *Handbook* is both the model for this narrative and the generator of its plot.

The story is thus an eccentric fiction—an odd combination of love story and travelog, marriage plot and plotless description. The protagonist simply happens upon his beloved repeatedly: she, like him—and like other "real" travelers—with Murray in hand. The plotted side of the narrative actually trails along behind its tourism, as the hero follows the advice of the guidebook rather than the impulses of the heart. In fact, since guidebooks are often called "companions," one might imagine that the title of the story works more convincingly as a reference to Murray's guide than to Miss Evans. In this itinerant context, the love story emerges as strangely dissatisfying. The guidebook narrative, motivated by the nomadic, unteleological time of tourism, is not organized around patterns of desire. Thus the acceptance of marriage in the final lines of the story, which brings to a close what little narratable desire this story musters, is curiously unmotivated, abrupt, apparently *unnatural.* The end of the love story, familiar to every reader of the conventional marriage plot, has become a baffling, arbitrary end tacked on to an itinerant narrative. After having been refused twice by Miss Evans—first because he is blinded by romance, then because he proposes out of a sense of duty rather than real love—James's narrator does nothing to change the situation but simply waits for true love to happen, doing exactly what he has done throughout the narrative: sight-seeing. The love plot of "Travelling Companions" seems therefore both dissatisfying and perplexing, apparently uncaused. Why does Miss Evans agree to marry the narrator in the end? Is it because her father has died and she is alone? Is it because she believes that the narrator is really in love with her? Is it because he has finally seen the whole length and breadth of Italy? And how might we account for any of these possibilities based on the evidence of the text?

The narrative gives no certain answers. Consequently, the very same scholars who have plundered the story for its autobiographical content have criticized James for its awkwardness, the author's failure to give it the shape and interest of a real *story*. Sergio Perosa begins to plumb the tale for its thematic depths, only to conclude that its themes are more or less irrelevant: "Love at first denied is, after the experience of Italy, accepted: but the story does seem a mere pretext for the description of cherished places." James Buzard writes: "All the sightseeing in 'Travelling Companions' would have been difficult to combine with any very sophisticated plot." Leon Edel complains that James was actually committing a kind of impropriety: "the time was to come when he would either divorce his travelogs from his imaginative writings, or properly combine the two." And Jeff Steiger sees it as "understandable" that critics have largely ignored "Travelling Companions" because it "is an ungainly attempt to hybridize a tour of Italian art with a story of courtship that is in truth a thinly disguised and, ultimately, not very palatable amorous fantasy."[9]

It would be easy to dismiss those critics eager to graft the biography onto the fiction, just as it would be easy to criticize those readers who are disappointed in the generic mixture of the narrative—an itinerant love story, too much polluted by travel, or an imaginative travelog, too much contaminated by fiction. But I want to suggest that these various critical responses actually emerge from the very problem of narrative that concerns us in this chapter: it is the distinctly unteleological character—the shapelessness itself—of the guidebook-story that makes it seem close to the real and thus easily read as autobiography. Indeed, the plot is not so much shapeless as shaped by a "real" model—the tourist's itinerary. It is in its very kinship with the pattern of travel that the narrative comes to imitate the real. But if it is this reliance on the itinerant time of real travelers that makes the story ring true and hence autobiographical, it is the same process that denies the love story its shape as an integrated plot. Just as James employs a new and more "real" pattern of narrative time, the plotted side of the narrative comes to seem arbitrary and unnatural.

By insisting on a more realistic version of narrative time, which is disconcertingly unplotted, James denies plot itself its realism.

In this context, the critics' refusal to read "Travelling Companions" as anything other than a record of the author's life begins to make sense. Realism's twentieth-century detractors have pointed to the artifices of plotted narrative as untrue to the shapelessness of life's contingencies.[10] In mimicking the goalless path of "real" travelers, James's story lends itself neatly to the twentieth-century conception of what realist narrative should be—a temporal structure that strives to imitate the passage of time in the world. James therefore displaces the doubts and tests of the realist experiment by introducing a new version of narrative realism, one that emphasizes directionless, itinerant time, unconstrained by teleology.

Rewriting the Realist Experiment

Formally speaking, guidebook travel appears, at first, surprisingly similar to the realist experiment: the tourist turns his attention back and forth between the book's representation of the world and his own experience, reading the scenes in his guidebook and then setting out to see the real scenes for himself. And like Ruskin, James's tourist describes his vision as if we readers could share the experience: "You will know what I mean," he tells us, "if you have looked upward from the Piazza at midnight" (177). Crucially, however, there is a Ruskinian element that is missing from the guidebook, and that is the impulse to test, to stir up skeptical doubt and forward-looking desire. After all, the tourist does not read the guidebook in order to interrogate its truthfulness but rather pointedly and deliberately sets out to reexperience the images it describes. For the tourist, the real does not precede the representation, as the infinitely various original that reveals the failures of mimesis. Instead, the protagonist organizes his experience to correspond to the representations given by the guidebook, which in turn arrange the world so that it will conform to the terms of conventional representation—the picturesque.

Consider, for example, the narrator's description of Venice at sunset:

> There is no Venice like the Venice of that magical hour. For that brief period her ancient glory returns. . . . The dead Venetian tone brightens and quickens into life and lustre, and the spectator's enchanted vision seems to rest on an embodied dream of

the great painter who wrought his immortal reveries into the ceilings of the Ducal Palace. (204)

If the spectator has a vision of the city that seems to rest on a painting, the painting in turn represents the city. But although Venice resembles a painting for a single hour, the painting is characterized as immortal. Thus it would seem that the real temporarily imitates the timeless picture, rather than reverse. And this is a moment of perfect touristic satisfaction. In dramatic contrast to Ruskin, the traveler is content when he has managed to make his lived experience conform to the frames of Old Master painting.

At an early point in the story, the narrator happens upon a painting, alleged to be by the painter Correggio:

> It was pretty, it was good; but it was not Correggio. There was indeed a certain suggestion of his exquisite touch; but it was a likeness merely, and not the precious reality. One fact, however, struck swiftly home to my consciousness: the face of the Madonna bore a singular resemblance to that of Miss Evans. The lines, the character, the expression, were the same; the faint half-thoughtful smile was hers, the feminine frankness and gentle confidence of the brow, from which the dark hair waved back with the same even abundance. All this, in the Madonna's face, was meant for heaven; and on Miss Evans's in a fair degree, probably, for earth. But the mutual likeness was, nevertheless, perfect. (188)

The picture is first compared to other works of art by Correggio and then compared to a living woman. The woman turns out to be a better likeness. Indeed, Miss Evans is the "perfect" image of the painting. The painted Madonna may not be the "precious reality" of a Correggio representation, but then perhaps it is the precious reality of Miss Evans.

Not surprisingly, the heroine begins to worry that she has been too thoroughly incorporated into the narrator's aesthetic experience:

> "Listen," said Miss Evans, after a pause. "It's not with me you're in love, but with that painted picture. All this Italian beauty and delight has thrown you into a romantic state of mind. You wish to make it perfect. I happened to be at hand, so you say, 'Go to,

I'll fall in love.' And you fancy me, for the purpose, a dozen fine
things that I'm not." (203)

Like a good Ruskinian, Miss Evans is wary of the seductions of representation, mistrustful of their power to corrupt our relationship to the
real. So apprehensive is she, in fact, that she refuses the narrator's offer of
marriage, suggesting that his cheerful acceptance of the conventions of
representation forms a proper obstacle to the marriage plot.

But her companion is content to enjoy the correspondence between
the world and its images. "Yes, incontestably, Miss Evans resembled my
little Vicenza picture," he says, upon meeting her again in Venice (193).
It is this tendency to see the real as if it always already conformed to a
work of art that characterizes what we might call the narrator's *aestheticizing eye*.[11] It is the clear purpose of the tourist to set up his experience
to coincide with preexisting representations. And if both the Ruskinian
experimenter and the Jamesian tourist move their eyes back and forth between representations and realities, the tourist is satisfied to make the real
fit the cultural images he has inherited.

So: what has happened to Ruskin's skepticism about the correspondence between pictures and the world? The realist experiment depends
on a faith that the data emerging from the world can constrain the hypotheses posed by cultural images. Ruskin assumes that the world of nature is fundamentally other to the world of human culture. Nature, separate from culture, is thus able to defy the claims of culture to represent
it. James's guidebook, by contrast, does not imagine the real as standing
outside of cultural representation to challenge or resist it, but rather produces an experience of the real, inviting the reader to bring the world
into conformity with its own descriptions.

The guidebook shapes not only the tourist's vision of the world but
also the identity of the tourist himself. Murray's *Handbook for Travellers* is
so standard that it allows tourists to recognize and identify with one another. In Milan, the narrator notices that an American "had perceived
my Murray." This recognition of a shared culture provides the excuse for
an introduction. Mr. Evans makes the first move: "English, sir?" (174).
In fact, both parties are American, but Murray's guide, here, is the point
of recognition for those who share an identity—English speakers tour-
ing Italy—and it literally brings them together.

Although this shared identity might seem at first to be based solely on language, Murray's guide ultimately constructs an experience of Italy for its readers; it suggests itineraries, offers specific information, recommends sights and facilities. When the two protagonists are stranded in Padua, Murray even recommends the hotel in which they are forced to spend the night (212). In other words, English speakers in Italy may share more than their language—with Murray in hand, they observe the *same* Italy, from the vantage point of the same store of knowledge, accompanied by the same range of comforts and advice. The guidebook incorporates a knowledge not only of the area traveled but also of the site from which the travelers come—which, in this case, is not a geographical location, but a linguistic one: the English-speaking world.

James's narrator depends on Murray for his own experience and then invites us readers to participate in the construction and reinforcement of Murray's Italy. Although much of the narrative is told in the past tense, the narrator takes on the voice of the second-person present when he discusses the sights of Italy, as if we too could repeat the traveling experience recorded by the fiction: "You feel that art and piety here have been blind, generous instincts" (185); "This spot at Vicenza affords you a really soul-stirring premonition of Venice" (186); and on seeing the Tintoretto Crucifixion, "You breathe a silent prayer of thanks that you, for your part, are without the terrible clairvoyance of genius" (206). Thus the character's experience of the real consists in the act of re-presenting the scene recommended by the guidebook, which can in turn be re-experienced by the reader. Indeed, this is a text that not only reinforces the guidebook but also imitates it. There are striking similarities between the language of James's descriptions and the language of Murray's *Handbook*. At the Lido, for example, Murray explains that the visitor will find "ancient Jewish sepultures, moss-grown, and half covered with drifted sand, adding to the gloomy feeling of the solitude; the few trees are old and stunted, the vegetation is harsh and arid, all around seems desolate." [12] James echoes this description, as if standing on the same spot: "beyond these [fortifications], half over-drifted with sand and over-clambered with rank grasses and coarse thick shrubbery, are certain quaintly lettered funereal slabs, tombs of former Jews of Venice" (200). In the spirit of Murray's guide, James's fictional narrative imagines an endless experience of repetition, hinting that the reader might replicate the experience recounted by the narrative, which itself repeats the experience of the guidebook.

James's narrative thus gives a twist to the realist experiment. Rather than encouraging us to unsettle the representations, the guidebook invites us simply to repeat them. And this replication, far from provoking us to new doubts and desires, has its deeply complacent satisfactions. With repetition comes a stable sense of shared identity and a deliberate reinforcement of traditional aesthetics. It is, in other words, profoundly self-confirming. Indeed, the tourist's goal is to ignore any evidence of a world that lies outside the guidebook, and so he compels the real to be endlessly experienced and reexperienced as a substantiation and repetition of the text.

The Politics of Realism

The repetition of entrenched cultural perceptions, Ruskin warned, carries with it disturbing political and ethical consequences. We can see these consequences at work in "Travelling Companions," where, with Murray in hand, the guidebook reader duplicates a culturally authorized aesthetic experience with worrying political overtones. At one point, the narrator and his companion contemplate a passing stranger in Venice:

> "Is he English?" asked Miss Evans, "or American?"
> "He is both," I said, "or either. He is made of that precious clay that is common to the whole English-speaking race." (196)

To be a speaker of English is to belong to a "race." And it is Murray's guide that allows English speakers to find one another, to recognize fellow members of the "race." Thus the narrator—with his Murray's *Handbook* leading him from place to place—carries his fixed identity with him, always identifying himself with other English speakers and differentiating himself from the country he observes.

In this process, the native Italians become objects of visual interest much like the works of art that form the ostensible purpose of the journey:

> At a neighboring table was a group of young Venetian gentlemen, splendid in dress, after the manner of their kind, and glorious with the wondrous physical glory of the Italian race.

"They only need velvet and satin and plumes," I said, "to be subjects for Titian and Paul Veronese."

They sat rolling their dark eyes and kissing their white hands at passing friends, with smiles that were like the moon-flashes on the Adriatic. (195–96)

Earlier, in Milan, the narrator and Miss Evans agreed that they are going to Venice to see "Titian and Paul Veronese" (179). Here, then, the Italians fall just short of presenting exactly the pictorial spectacle that the Americans have come to see. The Italians are "picturesque" in the strictest sense—they are explicitly perfect for picture-ing.[13] All they require is some further adornments—velvet, satin, and plumes—to become worthwhile aesthetic objects.[14] And if the "physical glory" of the Italians is aesthetically suitable, it is entirely unlike the beauty of the native English speaker, whose demeanor suggests the demands of the spirit rather than the senses:

> The young [Anglo-Saxon] man was rather short of stature, but firm and compact. His hair was light and crisp, his eye a clear blue, face and neck violently tanned by exposure to the sun. He wore a pair of small blonde whiskers. . . . The young man's face was full of decision and spirit; his whole figure had been moulded by action, tempered by effort. He looked simple and keen, upright, downright. (196)

Italian beauty appears in all its artificial and superficial resplendence against the truthfulness of the Anglo-Saxon visage: physical glory as opposed to moral radiance; marvelous costumes as opposed to a clear simplicity of spirit. The Anglophone face is honest and legible; the Italians need velvet and satin and plumes—yet more layers of clothing on top of their already splendid dress—to look like their paintings.

In this contrast between English speakers and native Italians, the narrator upholds a distinction between active subjects and passive objects. Of course, it is this difference between active perception and passive display that typically marks the power of the gaze.[15] And our narrator is clearly identified with the active Anglo-Saxon he describes: "'he looks like you, sir,'" says Mr. Evans to our hero (196). Never offered a straightforward description of the narrator, we learn about his appearance only through his resemblance to a fellow English speaker. And this indirection is not insignificant: through this circuitous process, the narrator remains always the spectator, never the spectacle.[16]

Without fail, the narrator carefully distinguishes his own "race" from the one he has come to see, happily turning Italians into pictures, English speakers into complex and active subjects. And the world of nature is similarly constructed as a passive and picturesque other. As the Italian landscape becomes the object of the narrator's aestheticizing gaze, it turns into a world to be conquered and possessed. Mary Louise Pratt argues that visual description took its place in Victorian travel writing as the ultimate aim of conquering territory and mastering new dominions: "In the end, the act of discovery itself, for which all the untold lives were sacrificed and miseries endured, consisted of what in European culture counts as a purely passive experience—that of seeing."[17] But this "passivity" hides all the usual activity of busy ideology, and James's narrator, from the top of Milan Cathedral, neatly fits Pratt's paradigm of the "monarch-of-all-I-survey" traveler[18]:

> To the south the long shadows fused and multiplied, and the bosky Lombard flats melted away into perfect Italy. This prospect offers a great emotion to the Northern traveller. A vague, delicious impulse of conquest stirs in his heart. From his dizzy vantage-point, as he looks down at her, beautiful, historic, exposed, he embraces the whole land in the far-reaching range of his desire. "That is Monte Rosa," I said; "that is the Simplon pass; there is the triple glitter of those lovely lakes." (179)

"Perfect Italy" is gendered: the exposed and beautiful "she"—passive, prostrate object of the narrator's lofty and active visual embrace. It is noteworthy, too, that our hero shifts momentarily into the timeless present tense of the guidebook, as if his description would be of use to any "Northern traveller" observing the panoramic view. Italy is the passive woman's body, melting and fusing out of the range of ordered description; but it is also the mapped, circumscribed territory that is both to be conquered and known.

James's story is, in two senses, eminently realist. It is full of visual representations that can be matched up with the real. And historically mimetic, too, the narrator's experience is composed of moments that belong to the ordinary life of the nineteenth-century tourist, come to consume the visions of a foreign land. He is simply doing what nineteenth-century travelers do.[19] Yet this very act of conformity to a common experience emerges as far from ethical and far from innocent. The repetitions of tourism construct and preserve the distance between self and other: Italy, the other, is constantly differentiated from its tourist visitor, whose Anglophone identity is forged in the process.

"Travelling Companions" thus hints at potential political dangers haunting the realist experiment. If Ruskin wanted us to move our eyes back and forth between conventional representations and the world they represented, he assumed that this process would necessarily disrupt our faith in the representations and offer us a new appreciation of the otherness of the real. But James's narrator suggests that there are powerful temptations to let the images hold sway. After all, what is to prevent the viewer from celebrating conventional representations, even when fully conscious of their conventionality, seeking to fit the world to the images he most enjoys? If the world is his own to be conquered and possessed, what impulse is there for him to suspend himself in the face of its otherness?   *what motivates suspense?*

The Contingency of Perception

It might be tempting to assume that James himself was unaware of the subtle political concerns associated with tourism and simply colluded with his colonizing contemporaries to produce a vision of traveling conquest. But it is impossible to overlook the dissenting vision of Miss Evans. She is also a tourist, but one who pointedly gives up the guidebook and aims to blur the boundaries between self and other. While the narrator constantly differentiates himself from the objects of his vision, Miss Evans aims to go native—to "become for a while a creature of Italy" (180). So: is the feminine spectator—in good realist fashion—a better reader of the world than her masculine counterpart?

It is no doubt obvious to any reader of "Travelling Companions" that the narrator and his beloved approach Italy with rather different standards for judgment. The aesthete-tourist relishes the effusive prolixity of descriptive language, while his more spiritual companion registers deep but silent emotion. Throughout the narrative, the woman appreciates the iconographical force of religious paintings as if she identified with them.

In front of a Tintoretto Crucifixion, she "burst into an agony of sobs" (206); and Leonardo's *Last Supper* renders her speechless with emotion, as if in imitation of the fixity of the picture. She is also found in prayer in St Mark's, no guidebook in sight, more like a sincere worshipper than a tourist. Refusing the distance between tourist and native, between observer and observed, Miss Evans is also the one of the pair deemed capable of deep feeling and sympathy—the "divine gift of feeling" that the narrator admires in the first scene of the story (175).[20] Like her realist predecessors, it is the woman reader who attempts to forge the anti-conventional, ethical relationship to the not-self. And thanks to Miss Evans, there is no need to accept the narrator's perspective as either the voice of the implied author or as a necessary and natural way of seeing, an ideological vision espoused unwittingly by the text as a whole. Miss Evans's rejection of the arbitrary division between tourists and natives renders suspect both the "knowledge" of Italy presented by the guidebook and the complacently aestheticizing vision of the narrator.

But in the process, Miss Evans entirely abandons the realist experiment. Rejecting the guidebook, she also gives up the back-and-forth movement between representation and the world. Indeed, she may be an ethical reader, but she is hardly a Ruskinian one, since her impulse is to fuse with the otherness of the world rather than to appreciate it across the gap that separates self from other. Tellingly, then, neither of the two protagonists engages in the activity of self-suspending: the narrator persistently reaffirms himself, while his companion loses herself altogether in alterity. Moved not by cultural skepticism but by spontaneous sympathy, she performs no tests. And her experience of otherness intensifies as the story unfolds: Miss Evans grows progressively more intent on abandoning the ordinary practices of the tourist until the narrator is actually unable to distinguish her from her Italian counterparts. In short, her ethical move is not to suspend herself in the face of the other but to "become for a while" that other. Like George Eliot—herself, intriguingly, a Miss Evans—James suggests that a respectful, feeling appreciation for otherness requires something other than the doubts and tests of suspense.

The narrative consequences of Miss Evans's refusal to experiment are suggestive. Neither character offers us hypotheses to be tested, intriguing conjectures to be set against the real. Thus the few mysteries that the text generates remain frustratingly unsolved. For example, at an early point in the story, the two characters observe a mysteriously unhappy Italian woman. The narrator evaluates her in terms of conventional aesthetics. "This poor woman is the genius of the Picturesque. She shows us the essential misery that lies behind it," the narrator explains. "Look at her sweeping down the aisle. What a poise of the head! The picturesque is handsome, all the same" (183). If the narrator is lured momentarily by the ethical demand to recognize misery, he returns almost immediately to the pleasures of the aesthetic. Meanwhile, his companion is more compelled by the enigma, showing a lingering interest in the mystery of the woman's life: "What in the world does she mean? . . . I do wonder what is her trouble" (183). But if Miss Evans, here, seems like a familiar realist reader, interested in the hidden truths of the world, she never speculates, suggesting possible solutions. And she never pursues the truths buried beneath the visual surface. If we readers are tempted to generate some guesses about the hidden facts, we too are left to wonder, since the narrative never returns to the woman to solve the mystery. And without the impulse to know the buried truths of the real, the text offers very little in the way of forward-looking desire.

The ethical reader, in James, is no solver of puzzles, no canny reader of enigmatic appearances. And although Miss Evans emerges in the text as both gentle and sympathetic, the narrative gives us no grounds for accepting her vision as a more reliable picture of the real than that of the narrator. There is no test to assure us that her approach to the world allows her a more trustworthy, more *accurate* relation to alterity. For example, while the narrator is relishing a sensuous pleasure in Veronese's "Rape of Europa," a depiction of a god made beast, his companion prefers a vision of "deified human flesh"—Tintoretto's "Bacchus and Ariadne" (207). And although the narrator abruptly decides to cast off his own opinion in order to agree with Miss Evans, it is not because her choice has unsettled the narrator's paradigm. She merely proposes an alternative, and he accepts. Miss Evans invites us to question the ethical dangers of her lover's perspective, but she never proposes her own vision as more *true*.

Indeed, there seems to be no way of establishing any picture of the world as more accurate than another. The narrator emphasizes his own frustrated attempts to distinguish between sincerity and affectation, between fancying and knowing, and he repeatedly maintains that his own perceptions are "colored" by circumstance and emotion, the romance of the setting and his feelings for Miss Evans. This epistemological uncertainty becomes more conspicuous as the narrative proceeds; shifts in time and space call earlier perceptions into question, without affirming one view and canceling others. The whole experience of Italy is affected by the narrator's changing location, and early on his starting point in Germany is evoked to enhance his sense of the exotic: "I rather enjoyed the heat," he tells us, "it seemed to my Northern senses to deepen the Italian, the Southern, the local character of things" (175). But then his view of Italy shifts as he travels southward. When he first arrives in Milan, he repeats insistently: "'It's the South, the South. . . . the South in nature, in man, in manners.' It was a brighter world. 'It's the South,' I said to my companion'" (181). Later, when he reaches Naples, he corrects himself: "I discovered the real South, the Southern South—in art, in nature, in man, and the least bit in woman" (220). From this new vantage point, Milan seems to represent something other than its original hot southern brightness. In Naples, "As I looked upward at Northern Italy, it seemed, in contrast, a cold, dark hyperborean clime, a land of order, conscience, and virtue" (220).

What, then, is the reality of Milan—hot or cold, northern or southern, orderly or chaotic? The only factor altering each hypothesis is a further impression, itself constrained and affected by the relative location and experience of the observer. Indeed, the contingency of perception haunts even the first few lines of the narrative, as the narrator ascribes some of the force of Leonardo's *Last Supper* to its location: "A part of its immense solemnity is doubtless due to its being one of the first of the great Italian masterworks that you encounter in coming down from the North" (171)—as if intrinsic to the experience of the painting was its place in the shared journey of its viewers. In another example, the Lido, in itself, is unimpressive, and there are certainly scenes of comparable intrinsic beauty in America: "In my own country I know many a sandy beach . . . of little less purity and breadth of composition." But these, according to the narrator, claim "far less magical interest." The solution to this mystery is its relative location: "The secret of the Lido is simply your sense of adjacent Venice" (200).

Perceptions of alterity shift endlessly, never coming to rest in an impression that can be shown to be more reliable than any other. If movement through time brings new perceptions, then perception itself may endlessly shift with respect to other times and places, past, present, and even the future beyond the narrative's end. And since the real is not set up as a solid foundation that generates a single lasting vision and cannot be summoned as the epistemological base against which to compare representation, then reading the world must produce endlessly shifting reflections of the interpreting self, rather than a stable knowledge of the other. Thus the shift back and forth between mimesis and the world, which brought us to increasing skepticism in *Modern Painters,* brings only a gathering of impressions in James.

In this context, the guidebook—which strives to shape a common, shared, repeatable experience—suggests a focused critique of Ruskin. The tourist repeats a conventional experience of otherness that has been written into existence. Indeed, the only stable knowledge of the other that is possible stems from a carefully arranged scheme of aesthetically traditional images. Implicitly, then, all consensus about the world is orchestrated by the repetitive conventions of representation. Carefully replacing the driving anxieties of the scientific experiment with the itinerant satisfactions of the tourist, James hints at the impossibility of gaining access to a world uncontaminated by culture, ideology, and convention.

The Disappearance of Suspense

"Travelling Companions" denies the priority of the real in the relationship between reality and its representations. There is no way to stand outside of representation to evaluate its claims: assorted interpretive paradigms construct the otherness of the world according to their own criteria and might perpetually conflict without ever reaching resolution, crisis, or compromise. Thus the hope of knowledge proffered by the realist text—the expectation that with experience we will be able to decipher mysterious appearances and reject conventional assumptions—recedes, replaced by the very process of shifting perspective itself.

This shift brings with it some critical consequences for narrative form. In a text that insists that perception may shift endlessly with every change in perspective, there can be no expectation that some hypotheses can be verified and others discarded. Thus James leaves us simply to witness the tourist in the repeated act of constructing his experience so that it will match its representations. This is hardly a suspenseful experience. What kind of suspicions and hesitant hopes can arise, after all, if we live with the assurance that the world will always come to match the assumptions we bring to it? Tourism, as any reader of Murray's guide will tell you, is a plotless experience.

This conclusion suggests once again that suspense and realism rise and fall together. Just as suspenseful plotting took force alongside the development of a new realist aesthetic, a cogent critique of realism brings with it a critique of suspense. If James's world is perceptible only through the lenses of a culturally specific observer, then we can never verify or discredit representation through the evidence of a culturally independent lived experience. This means that we lose the intriguing doubts of the realist experiment, which suggest the hope of access to a world that lies outside the conventions of representation. And it means, too, that we lose the impulse to suspend the self, since there is no world outside of the self to constrain or challenge the assumptions we bring to it. With the loss of the gap between culture and alterity, in other words, narrative suspense itself must disappear.

To take this narrative argument a step farther, I want to suggest that James deliberately unsettles the marriage plot—that prototypical plot of desire—by subjecting it to the logic of the guidebook narrative. According to Miss Evans, always the wiser of the two travelers, the love story is threatened by the shifting contextual perspective of the tourist; she argues that the narrator's confession of love for her is simply a reflection of the romance of their surroundings: "Other places, Mr. Brooke, will bring other thoughts" (215). She suggests, in other words, that the narrator's love for her is just like his access to the otherness of the real: it varies with shifts in time and space and is set up to conform to conventional expectations.

It is one of the tasks of the classic marriage plot to distinguish between true love and its untrue pretenders. Miss Evans, here, is worried about the contingency of romance and sees the shifting perspective of travel as producing an equally shifting emotional bond—one not at all appropriate to the permanency of marriage. But by implication she hints at a model of truer love, one more suited to matrimony. That is, Miss Evans suggests that if the narrator's love for her does not, in fact, alter with shifts in location, then his feeling for her will be real. The narrator confirms these doubts when he asks himself whether he is feeling temporary romance or lasting love: "Did I in truth long merely for a bliss which should be of that hour and that hour alone?" (201). Uncertain about the transience of the feeling, he does not pursue his proposal. True love in this narrative would seem to be defined by an absence of change, a capacity to endure despite shifts in time and space.

But can a narrative structured around shifting perspectives ever assure perceptions that will outlast the contingencies of context? "If I promise to be faithful to my wife," J. Hillis Miller writes, "it is always possible that after a lifetime of faithfulness I shall at the last minute betray her."[21] This is the uncertainty that troubles the closure of a narrative concerned with problems of constantly shifting perspective: if there is always another, newer way of seeing, colored by context, how can we be sure of the continuity of the narrator's love, which is its only reality? At one curious moment, he claims that the shift from romantic sentimentality to true love will emerge out of the experience of travel itself, as if the stuff of tourism led to marriage: "The reality [of love] I believed would come. The way to hasten its approach was, meanwhile, to study, to watch, to observe,—doubtless even to enjoy" (219). Just as the reader is invited to recognize tourism's disturbing ideological investments and conservative aesthetic conventions, the narrator imagines that he will sightsee his way into true love.

The text ends in marriage, suggesting that the narrator and his companion have both come to believe in the promise of lasting love. And of course, we have been prepared for this conclusion by the conventions of the marriage plot. The solitary male hero and the presence of a suitably attractive and virtuous woman of the narrator's nationality and social class have indicated a conventional novelistic future from the outset. But then the shifting and uncertain experiences of tourism unsettle every claim to lasting perception, and by the end of the story the marriage we have been expecting feels disquieting. Perhaps this is because there has been no way, in a story that suggests that all experience is contingent on convention and perspective, to guarantee the permanence of feeling so crucial to the narrative of "true" and enduring love, tested by experience. Miss Evans is right to worry that the love story is threatened by the experience of travel. The reality of love, like the real more generally, has fallen prey to James's comprehensive destabilizing.

It may be true that the author's loving attention to travel makes the love story look, as Edel complains, like a strange addition to a travelog, a too-conventional storyline attached to a plotless itinerary. But it is precisely the unlikely achievement of James's story that it makes the love story look excessively conventional. The classic marriage plot calls for such a faith in the reality of love that the reader must imagine it will exist in the same stable form forever. But the kind of lasting love that guarantees the happiness of the happy ending is rendered radically insecure if experience shifts according to culture, location, and ideology, never grounded in a reality that transcends perspective and convention and never able to promise permanence. Thus the marriage that closes "Travelling Companions" looks startlingly abrupt, doubtful—even unpromising—because it is attached to a story about the necessary instability of perception.

The consequences of this shift for narrative are far-reaching. Rejecting plotted suspense as epistemologically unsound, James's story finally offers its readers only the dissatisfying accumulation of perspectival difference. Thus the narrative defamiliarizes the closure of the marriage plot, while it throws suspicion on all intermediate conclusions as shifting and untenable. And James casts his intermittent, itinerant narrative as more "real" than its plotted counterparts, following a path that actual travelers have taken before and will take again. His narrative inconclusiveness has persuaded the critics of its truthfulness, and yet it has frustrated them at the same time—perhaps even helping to relegate this story to relative obscurity. But frustrating or not, this Jamesian skepticism about Victorian plotting helps to launch the deliberately reflexive plots of Modernism. James's own late novels, *The Ambassadors* and *The Golden Bowl*, are like "Travelling Companions" in that they repeatedly investigate the weight of culture in the activities of perception and interpretation, and also like "Travelling Companions," they draw attention to the careful artifices of narrative time. James's skepticism about plot in his early guidebook-narrative is therefore not far from his own mature works. And all of the doubts that attend the narrator's insights in "Travelling Companions" can be seen as emerging from a rethinking of Ruskin's narrative paradigm: James's critical rewriting of the realist experiment.

If Eliot and James helped to usher in a skeptically unsuspenseful art by defying Ruskin, they were not the only nineteenth-century thinkers to cast doubts on the persuasiveness of plot. Indeed, the double narrative model of "Travelling Companions," simultaneously plotted and itinerant in form, has a curious corollary in another text, which, like James's story, stands at the point where Victorian and Modernist sensibilities cross, and like James's work, suggests that there are two ways of writing—and read-ing—events in the world, one as plotted narrative, the other as a kind of skeptical and perspectival bricolage. I am referring to a passage from James George Frazer's *The Golden Bough*—"The Scapegoat"—which concludes with the Crucifixion of Christ:

> In the great army of martyrs who in many ages and many lands, not in Asia only, have died a cruel death in the character of gods, the devout Christian will doubtless discern types and forerun-ners of the coming Saviour—stars that heralded in the morning sky the advent of the Sun of Righteousness—earthen vessels wherein it pleased the divine wisdom to set before hungering souls the bread of heaven. The skeptic, however, with equal con-fidence, will reduce Jesus of Nazareth to the level of a multitude of other victims of a barbarous superstition, and will see in him no more than a moral teacher, whom the fortunate act of his ex-ecution invested with the crown, not merely of a martyr, but of a god. The divergence between these views is wide and deep. Which of them is the truer and will in the end prevail? Time will decide the question of prevalence, if not of truth. Yet we would fain believe that in this and in all things the old maxim will hold good—*Magna est veritas et praevalebit.*[22]

Can we read meaning as converging toward a consensual endpoint, or must we imagine that it shifts according to the location, cultural back-ground, and political investments of the spectator? Is the Crucifixion of Christ the last, triumphant moment of the most meaningful story we have, or is it simply another moment in an increasingly global collection of examples?

9   Pater's Plots

The Renaissance and *The Picture of Dorian Gray*

The suspense plot was losing its radical force in the 1860s and 1870s. George Eliot and Henry James struggled to unsettle realism's claims to skeptical knowledge, replacing the tests of suspense with new narrative experiments that cast doubt on the aims of their precursors. Eliot narrativized the world and rendered the idea of the real radically unstable when she began to worry about narrative's claims to truth; James, building on her critique, suggested that plot always molds the world in its own artificial image.

But it is Walter Pater and Oscar Wilde who push this insight to its most radically unsettling conclusion, laying bare the rhetorical construction of narrative time itself. Pater, like Eliot and James, makes use of the realist experiment while drawing attention to the artifices that make realist claims to knowledge possible, but moving beyond his precursors he investigates the figures and patterns that make the apprehension of both time and alterity possible at all. Oscar Wilde then uses Pater's unveiling of realism's narrative strategies for his own critique of realism—blithely turning its discursive structure upside-down to expose its formal workings.

Plotting the Renaissance

By focusing his attention on the art and culture of the Renaissance, Pater could hardly have offered a more pointed challenge to Ruskin's work.

The Stones of Venice had prized the irregular, self-effacing aesthetics of the Gothic and denounced the pride and precision of Renaissance artists. The Pre-Raphaelite movement readily adopted Ruskin's distinction, as did numerous architects who deliberately chose the Gothic style for new buildings in the period. Thus it was not hard for contemporaries to read Pater's *Renaissance* as a polemical answer to Ruskin's praise for the Gothic.[1] But I would like to suggest that such a reading runs its own risk—the risk of overlooking Pater's profound debt to Ruskin. What happens, that is, if we read Pater not against but *through* Ruskin's work?

Carolyn Williams's compelling study of Pater dramatically unsettles a number of conventional beliefs about Pater's aesthetics. It has been tempting to read Pater as a thoroughgoing relativist, intent on undoing all grounded, empirical, historical knowledge, and as an inward-looking aesthete, concerned only with the evidence of his own sensuous experience. But Williams reads Pater's historicist skepticism and his aestheticism together, as "strategies of epistemological self-consciousness and representation" that together build a program—even a systematic program—for the construction of knowledge. As Williams argues, both historicism and aestheticism presuppose that objects begin at a distance from their observers and must be brought into consciousness. Pater constantly shifts the placement of his objects—both works of art and historical data—changing their relative distance with respect to each other and to the observing consciousness so that each object comes into focus through multiple mediations. Constantly shifting the relations between past and present, object and subject, figure and ground, Pater allows a radically skeptical knowledge to take shape.[2] My own question is as follows: if, as Williams makes clear, Pater is concerned with precisely the questions that have preoccupied the realists—epistemological skepticism, the relation between subject and object, and the problem of representation— then what is Pater's relationship to realism?

Pater twice invokes realism explicitly in *The Renaissance*. In "Leonardo da Vinci" he refers to the painter's return to nature, "with its realism, its appeal to experience" (86). If this sounds like *Modern Painters,* Leonardo's realism carefully eludes the demands of truth telling:

> Vasari's story of . . . [Leonardo's] Medusa, painted on a wooden shield, is perhaps an invention; and yet, properly told, has more of the air of truth about it than anything else in the whole legend.

For its real subject is not the serious work of a man, but the experiment of a child. The lizards and glowworms and other strange small creatures which haunt an Italian vineyard bring before one the whole picture of a child's life in a Tuscan dwelling—half castle, half farm—and are as true to nature as the pretended astonishment of the father for whom the boy has prepared a surprise. (83)

Vasari's description of the image is probably fictional, but it seems true. And if the narrative is "properly told," it will arrange itself quite literally into a picture: Leonardo's own painting of the Medusa, as well as our picture of the young painter's life. (There is an intriguing inversion of Ruskin's plots here: while *Modern Painters* began with deceptive paintings and then produced narratives to bring us to tested truth, Pater's image of Leonardo begins with Vasari's story and from that produces a painting.) Although neither the story nor the painting may be based on fact, if the story is told well, it will still provide us with a valuable representation of Leonardo's childhood.

There is a further twist on the problem of truth in this passage. The painter's image is as true to nature as the pretended astonishment of his father.[3] In Pater's analogy, both the paintings of the small creatures and the father's surprise aim to look true, while both are, in fact, only imitations of the real thing. But if each is as persuasive as the other—if the father's pretended surprise is as "true to life" as Leonardo's *Medusa*—then we readers have no fixed, external standard for truth. While Ruskin appealed to the realities of the natural world as the ground of truth for representation, Pater moves back and forth from one to another without allowing the process to come to rest. The painting is only as true as the father's reaction, which, in turn, is only as true as the painting. In the work of the analogy, there is no solid ground for comparison.

In a similar moment in the collection, Pater interprets a portrait by Botticelli. According to legend, Botticelli's painting seems to "embody" a poem by Matteo Palmieri (43). But along the way, we learn that Palmieri may not be a poet at all: he is only "reputed" to be the poem's author (42). At this point, Pater explicitly relinquishes the aim of truth telling: "True or false," he writes, "the story interprets much of the peculiar sentiment with which [Botticelli] infuses his profane and sacred persons"

(43). Legend—be it true or false—offers us a good reading of the portrait. Notably, Pater here reverses the path of interpretation suggested by the legend—using the poem to interpret the painting instead of the other way around.

But perhaps the direction of the comparison does not matter much, since painting and poem are in a relationship of interpretative reciprocity. The only possible way to justify Pater's reading would be to turn to the painting itself, to judge the fitness of the poem to the portrait, or the portrait to the poem. We find ourselves in a kind of hermeneutic *mise-en-abîme,* where each work equally illustrates and is illustrated by the other—each alternately the representation and the object of representation. As in Ruskin's experiments, Pater's comparisons play back and forth between two objects to determine their correspondences and differences: but unlike Ruskin's plots, Pater celebrates the back and forth movement of comparison itself, interested in the ways that each side illuminates the other.

In the example from "Leonardo," the painting and the father's feigned surprise were mutually representational, both expressions of an attempt to mirror nature. Yet surely this is a circuitous route to a description of the painter's attempt at "realism." Why not simply assert that the painting strove to imitate nature? And why use Vasari's false legend to give us a "picture" of Leonardo's life? Partly, of course, Vasari's legend is useful because the picture itself is lost. But then Pater informs us that the legend may have invented the picture altogether. Indeed, according to a false but convincing story, Leonardo tries to produce a false but convincing picture of nature, to which his father responds with false but convincing surprise. They are analogous and can illustrate each other, but none offers us the fixed ground of knowledge.

The work of analogy produces an understanding that arises out of a movement back and forth between two instants. Rather than locating the true in a single moment, Pater produces a "picture" from the very process of relation—the play between two moments. The specifically *narrative* consequences of this two-way movement are not necessarily different from the kinds of models we encountered with Ruskin: after all, they too required the constant comparison between representation and the real, a movement in two directions. But Ruskin's plots demand a faith in the stable otherness of the world. In response to these experiments,

George Eliot suggested that the truths of the world were themselves shifting and developing—eluding all attempts to fix as stable—and Henry
James made it clear that reality emerged only in light of its images. Pushing a step beyond Eliot and James, Pater seems to refuse conclusions
about the real altogether, interested in the process of relating itself.

To put this another way, Pater hints that the persuasive force of the
realist experiment is actually reliant on nothing other than the potentially
infinite possibilities of mutual illumination and definition. His comparisons do not look single-mindedly for similarity between an image and a
fixed ground but point to the productive nature of differentiation itself.
Not surprisingly, then, knowledge itself takes the form of analogy in *The
Renaissance*. Pater tells us, for example, that Leonardo "brooded over . . .
the correspondences which exist between the different orders of living
things, through which, to eyes opened, they interpret each other" (81).
Knowledge lies neither in one order nor the other, but in the understanding that is possible through the movement back and forth between
the two.

Like knowledge and representation in *The Renaissance,* Pater's narratives are also typically caught between two moments. Leonardo's work,
for example, recalls and repeats the methods of the past while prefigur-
ing the new: "much of the spirit of the older alchemy still hangs about
it, with its confidence in short cuts and odd byways to knowledge" (84);
but he also "anticipat[es] long before, by rapid intuition, the later ideas
of science" (86). The relationship between pupil and teacher is likewise
one of reciprocal temporality: "as in a sense [Verrocchio] anticipates Leonardo, so, to the last Leonardo recalls the studio of Verrocchio" (80). At
the center of these descriptions is a movement in two directions: as the
past anticipates the future and the future recalls the past, the present has
collapsed into a play of temporal forces moving in opposite directions.

Significantly, Pater makes the movement of analogy central to the
collection as a whole, writing in the preface that his Renaissance figures
"unconsciously illustrate each other" (xxiii–xxiv). So it is, perhaps, that
the peculiarly disconnected form of the entire collection takes on its validity: Pater sets up individual figures of the Renaissance to throw light
on one another and, through the conceptual work of their emergent similarities, to illustrate the Renaissance as a whole. No single figure more
truly belongs to the Renaissance than any other; rather, each joins the

Renaissance in his analogous relationship to the others. The disjointed nature of the collection suggests that the historical period can only be conceived through the crossing and comparing of its parts. Pater's rhetorical focus on the gaps and spaces between the figures is constitutive of our understanding of the Renaissance. Synecdoche and analogy, both broken and partial devices, form the content of our knowledge of the period—and so, as a period, the Renaissance is never fully present to representation.

Perhaps this should not surprise us. After all, the Renaissance is defined as a moment caught between ancient and modern, anticipating the future just as it recalls and reenacts the past. Caught in the junction where past and future meet, it can be represented only as a crossing. Thus the larger narrative of *The Renaissance* is no sweeping story of development, no plotted pursuit of knowledge. Pater, a reader of Eliot's *Romola,* combines her critique of plotted narrative with her interest in the Renaissance to suggest that the crossing of old and new in the Renaissance raises— inevitably—the question of narrative transition.[4] Each of Pater's essays is presented as if it took its place in sequence, but the artists do not build on the achievements of their forebears: rather, they look forward and backward at once—all invoking the Middle Ages and antiquity at the same time that they anticipate Goethe and Victor Hugo. Thus the Renaissance is a narrative middle, an instant of passage.

The consequences of this emphasis on the middle are telling. Eschewing origins and endpoints, Pater's narratives suspend time without withholding. Take Michelangelo's image of the Creation, for example: "the beginning of life has all the characteristics of resurrection; it is like the recovery of suspended health or animation, with its gratitude, its effusion, and eloquence" (58). In the moment of his own origin, Adam is "suspended," inhabiting the pause between death and new life. Thus the creation of man turns out to be not only an emergence but a "resurrection," not only an origin but also a renewal. In other words, creation— the consummate beginning—is itself a moment, to borrow a phrase from *Adam Bede,* "in which the story pauses a little," as if even the most famous of narrative beginnings must be conceived as an interruption.

This eccentric interpretation of Michelangelo brings us to Pater's second reference to "realism." In the middle of the *Renaissance* collection there are two essays that together build a history of sculpture, "Luca della

Robbia" and "The Poetry of Michelangelo," where Pater argues that the crucial problem for sculpture as an art is its inflexible materiality. Stone itself produces "a hard *realism,* a one-sided presentment of mere form, that solid material frame which only motion can relieve" (50–51; my emphasis). Pater's sculptural "realism" refers to the material reality of the medium rather than the imitation of an object in the world.[5] It is this realism that sculpture must strive always to avoid: "Against this tendency to the hard presentment of mere form trying vainly to compete with the reality of nature itself, all noble sculpture constantly struggles" (51). Desperately fighting against "presentment," sculpture makes it clear that being present is not the aim of the Paterian aesthetic.[6] Realism is not the goal, but the impediment to art in stone.

But what would allow sculpture to escape its own hard "realism"? Stone has a tendency to become a "thing of heavy shadows, and an individuality of expression pushed to caricature" (51). In "Luca della Robbia," Pater describes the ways that "three great styles in sculpture" have freed sculpture from its own heaviness. The Greeks represented generalized, impersonal types of humanity, until they distilled something timeless in the stone: "like some subtle extract or essence, or almost like pure thoughts or ideas" (51). Much later, Michelangelo pushed sculpture to the opposite extreme, representing "the special history of the special soul" (52). And "midway between" these two poles were the early Renaissance sculptors: "the system of Luca della Robbia and the other Tuscan sculptors of the fifteenth century, partaking both of the *Allgemeinheit* of the Greeks . . . and the studied incompleteness of Michelangelo" (53–54). On the one hand, Pater presents this as a kind of Hegelian narrative of sculptural development, in which each phase both incorporates and supersedes the knowledge of the one before on the path to freedom, as stone is progressively released from "its stiffness, its heaviness, and death" (51). But on the other hand, this is a narrative told in the wrong order: from the extremity of breadth and universality to the extremity of individualism, and from this opposition to its mean or midpoint, marking what might seem to be the synthesis of antiquity and modernity before modernity has actually happened. After all, Luca della Robbia and his fellows are allowed to "partake" of their successors as much as they do of their forerunners. Just as the first essay ends with its focus on the middle of the narrative, "The Poetry of Michelangelo," which follows it, ends with the middle, too. It finishes with a reference to the "tradition of those earlier, more serious Florentines, of which Michelangelo is the inheritor, to which he gives the final expression" (72). Both essays end with a look backward in time.[7]

If we were to reorder the narrative, of course, we would find a progression: from the anonymous Greeks to the shadowy, named but unknown Tuscans to the apex of individual expression found in Michelangelo. But even when we take Michelangelo as the end of the story of sculpture, Pater refuses to provide the rounded conclusion of narrative closure that we might expect of a tale of consummation: Michelangelo leaves "his sculpture in a puzzling sort of incompleteness, which suggests rather than realises actual form" (53). This incompleteness is the triumph of the Michelangelesque. Indeed, the two essays repeatedly emphasize his skill at presenting the feeling of an imminent eruption: "some spirit of the thing seems always on the point of breaking out" (52–53); "an energy of conception . . . seems at every moment about to break through all the conditions of comely form" (57); "the brooding spirit of life itself is there; and the summer may burst out in a moment" (60). If Michelangelo represents the victorious end of a progressive narrative of freedom, his work does not so much embody that freedom as suggest its emergences, stopping at the point between the deathly stasis of blank rock and the realization of completed form. Ironically, Pater calls this studied incompletion Michelangelo's "perfect finish," as if the end were never ending, the completion incomplete.

Since Michelangelo's sculpture provides an escape from the presentment of the real—with its deathly heaviness—Pater suggests that in order to resist "realism" we must focus on the middle of the story, refusing to reach closure, dwelling on transition and incompletion. To put this another way: when Pater explicitly refuses realism, he does so by writing a story that celebrates the suspensions of the middle as the whole content of narrative. In a sense, Pater simply takes Ruskin further down his own path by emphasizing the imperfections of representation, its inability to do anything other than strive to get beyond its own limitations to the other. In narrative terms, this means endless suspending. But Pater also pointedly departs from Ruskinian realism in these essays on sculpture. Pater's Michelangelo, like Ruskin, celebrates the activity of mediation—the painstaking effort to move beyond the materiality of representation to the living breath of the world. But Pater changes the place of the real in this process. The real is no longer alterity, the not-self, but the materiality of sculpture itself. In other words, the goal of sculpture is to become something other than itself—other *to* itself. Pater relies on Ruskin's structural oppositions, setting art against reality, self against other, and life against death, but he fundamentally alters the role of the real in these oppositions: now it is no longer the other and the source of life in art, but rather art's most rigid self and its potential death.

Can we bring together Pater's two references to realism—Leonardo's childish experiments and Michelangelo's efforts to relinquish the real—as critical responses to Ruskin? It may seem an eccentric conclusion, but in both cases realism is tied to a version of suspense. Leonardo moves between reality and representation, between truth and falsehood, between image and text, never able to come to rest on firm ground. For Michelangelo, meanwhile, realism is hard, deathly stone, the burden of art, and the proper response to this real is to emerge from it. But this does not mean leaving the real behind altogether; it means, instead, life coming out of death, the space between stone and not-stone, the process itself of emergence. In both cases it is the interruption—the suspension—that gives the Renaissance its character.

If the realist experiment has always emphasized the middle of the story, Pater's essays seek to mark *only* the experience of rupture, the fractured consciousness of the in-between. In *The Renaissance,* understanding emerges, in large part, from the work of analogy, moving back and forth between two moments, each of which throws light on the otherness of the other. The difference between representation and the "real" in Ruskin was all about the failures of representation; in Pater, those differences themselves become fruitful, allowing us to see both poles in new ways, each in light of new comparisons. Refused any epistemological resting place, we are offered the rupture between perspectives as itself crucial to the production of understanding. As Jonathan Loesberg writes, the "experience itself" of Pater's work calls for a "friction between sensations, a friction necessary for an experience to take shape."[8]

Given the centrality of transition in the production of meaning, it is perhaps not surprising that the narrative of resurrection is one of the most common motifs in the collection: death looking forward to new life, which must look back on death to acquire its significance. Temporal shifts are, of course, integral to narrative. But Pater's narratives, with their emphasis on the middle, are particularly focused on the representation of narrative *transition,* which cannot be perceived without the movement in two directions. Narrative, like the back-and-forth movement of analogy, requires past and future to act as other to one another.

Indeed, Pater hints at a potential link to be forged between the split understanding born of analogy and the fragmentary perception of narrative time, both of which imagine that meaning is born of division and difference. If this is a conclusion now widely recognized in poststructuralist writing, it is my contention that it works, in Pater's essays, as a response to realism, both pictorial and narrative. Far from replacing the experimental paths of *Modern Painters* with startlingly new narrative forms, Pater can be read as drawing attention to the structural fissures of the realist text. With hindsight, that is, we can read Pater back on to Ruskin to discover that *Modern Painters* also rested on analogous relations: the real threw light on the duplicity of painting, just as painting permitted the reality of the real to take shape. Even in grounded Ruskinian realism, respective identities were forged out of the act of their differentiation. Similarly, in a narrative such as *Jane Eyre,* a single mystery, appearing repeatedly, helped to make the apprehension of temporality possible, the future illuminating the past and the past the future, but with Paterian lenses we might see that each was perceptible only in light of the otherness of the other. Thus Pater's unconventional uses of the same patterns of persuasion potentially reveal the work of realism as the rhetorical production of understanding, haunted by the self-divided moment of perception.

If rhetoric is temporal, temporality is rhetorical, both conceived in the fracturing of perspective, and both, in Pater, crucial to perception. In analogy and narrative transition alike, consciousness is made aware of the divided construction of knowledge itself, which occurs only by way of otherness—representation in light of the real, the past in light of the future. In the end, the analogy between narrative and analogy is not simply formal: it concerns the temporally divided operation of understanding itself, in which object and temporal moment can only be perceived in relation to an other. If Pater's work is not such a fundamentally new narrative model, it is a new and more radical *epistemology* than the Ruskinian model, deliberately ungrounded in a fixed and knowable world.

Pater, rather than inventing new forms, remains firmly in the tradition of the realist experiment, but focuses our attention on its rhetorical gaps, fissures, and suspensions, which have always permitted meaning to emerge only out of difference.

Wilde's End of Realism

In *The Picture of Dorian Gray,* Wilde sardonically rewrites *Adam Bede* to throw its ethical claims into question. Dorian returns from a spell in the country, late in the novel, to tell Lord Henry that he has "altered." Having apparently learned a moral lesson from the death of Sibyl Vane, he has decided to commit only "good actions," beginning by resisting the temptation to seduce a beautiful young village girl. "Hetty was not of our own class, of course," he tells Lord Henry. Intent on reforming himself, Dorian virtuously chooses self-denial, leaving Hetty "as flower-like" as he has found her (204). But if Dorian—and the reader of *Adam Bede*—believe that this is precisely what Arthur Donnithorne should have done with his own Hetty, Lord Henry is there to scoff at the futility of the gesture: "Do you think this girl will ever really be contented now with any one of her own rank? . . . The fact of having met you, and loved you, will teach her to despise her husband, and she will be wretched. I can't say I think much of your great renunciation" (204). Perhaps, as Lord Henry suggests, it is not sexual seduction that can ruin either Hetty, since class difference is what does the really profound and irrevocable damage. Quite seriously, it would seem, Wilde shifts the blame from Eliot's emphasis on personal responsibility to the hierarchies of social class, inviting us to revise our reading of the individualist ethics taught by *Adam Bede*.

Eliot was not the only target of Wilde's caustic reconsideration. The young Wilde had been an enthusiastic student of both Ruskin and Pater at Oxford, but in 1888 he insisted on his "departure from Mr. Ruskin," boasting that this shift marked "an era in the aesthetic movement."[9] And this was true. Explicitly rejecting both ethics and truth telling as aims for art, Wilde refused the basic tenets of realism, embracing Pater's reflexivity far more unreservedly than Ruskin's epistemology. But although it is true that Wilde was critical of Ruskin, *The Picture of Dorian Gray* can be read as a careful response to *Modern Painters.* Following in Pater's footsteps, Wilde echoes the patterns of Ruskin's realist experiments while questioning and destabilizing their claims.

In the novel, Dorian Gray moves his eye back and forth between his image in the mirror and his portrait and recognizes a difference. The real and the image of the real, contrasted, reveal the passage from the old Dorian to the new. When he first spies a difference between the real and the representation, he develops "a feeling of almost scientific interest" (118). Here, then, we find all of the familiar ingredients of the realist experiment: reliant on the comparison between the representation and the "real" and feeling something like a scientist, Dorian comes to see—quite literally—the ethical consequences of his actions.

If Dorian models the back-and-forth movement between representation and the real, which we have seen so many times before, experimentation is also an explicit theme in the novel. Lord Henry Wotton sees Dorian as a perfect experimental subject: "It was clear to him that the experimental method was the only method by which one could arrive at any scientific analysis of the passions; and certainly Dorian Gray was a subject made to his hand, and seemed to promise rich and fruitful results" (92). In this light, we could read the entire novel as the unfolding of Lord Henry's experiment: it is under the sway of Lord Henry's theories, after all, that Dorian first utters his wish to switch places with the portrait. But it is also worth noting that Lord Henry does not actually have the opportunity to witness the "rich and fruitful" results of his speculations, because the experiment oddly changes hands: it is Dorian himself who repeatedly tests the painting against his image in the mirror, and it is he who begins to try out actions in the world to see how they are reflected in the painting. Like a good scientist, he even begins to speculate about different outcomes: "might not his nature grow finer, after all? . . . Perhaps, some day, the cruel look would have passed away from the scarlet sensitive mouth" (138–39).

Lord Henry's initial experiment has somehow changed its course—slipping into Dorian's life as if it were his own—and thus the text hints at a new and unsettling path for experimental activity. Suddenly it is unclear where experiments begin and end, who initiates them, and how and where they develop. Representing Lord Henry's thoughts in free indirect speech, the narrator says: "It often happened that when we thought we were experimenting on others we were really experimenting on ourselves" (92). The test doubles back, implicating the experimenter, suddenly bringing in the self where it had seemed to be about the other.

Something like free indirect speech itself, which slips from narrator to character and does not come to rest in either voice, experimentation slips from subject to subject, supplanting one in favor of another without warning, without apparent cause.

The dislocation of the experimental subject hints at a larger pattern of displacement in the narrative. Ed Cohen asks how *The Picture of Dorian Gray* can be both a successfully homoerotic narrative and one that never actually connects men's bodies to one another; how it can seem like a proud example of an emerging gay aesthetic and a closeted text that says nothing explicit and so escapes otherwise active censure. Cohen claims that the text's doubleness emerges from its repeated—even systematic—displacements. Desire is routinely displaced from bodies onto representations: this is certainly the case for Basil Hallward when he translates his passion for Dorian into an aesthetic event; and Cohen argues that it is the case for all of the male desire in the novel.[10] Intriguingly, it is also the case for Dorian himself when his self-love, prompted by the image of himself, becomes a love of the picture, which then becomes a love of the self again. Self and other have become indistinguishable in a kind of endlessly displaced cycle. "Once, in boyish mockery of Narcissus, [Dorian] had kissed, or feigned to kiss, those painted lips" (126). Is it himself Dorian kisses or an other? Is he kissing or merely feigning to kiss? Selves and others, actions and imitations: these have all become inextricable and interchangeable. Consequently, it is no longer clear who is the subject and who the object of experimentation. This pervasive confusion produces, circuitously, the representation of male-male desire, just as it fragments and displaces the moments of the Ruskinian experiment. And so, we might say, Wilde queers Ruskin.

Wilde also turns Ruskin upside-down. The "real" and the image have switched places in *The Picture of Dorian Gray*. The real is now the silent, deceptive mask, while the painting has become a narrative teller of truths. It is in this context that we recognize Wilde as a more faithful student of Pater than of Ruskin. In *The Renaissance,* Pater suggested that it did not matter which side of the comparison took priority—since each could throw light on the other. And he hinted that Ruskin's realism was not, after all, so different: far from seeking the perfect identity between representation and the "real," the realist experiment simply required the space between them to generate its plots. Similarly, Dorian, shifting his eye back and forth between the picture and the face in the mirror, like his textual predecessors, gathers understanding from the contrast between the "real" and the representational, despite the fact that the two poles have been inverted. It is the contrast itself—not the priority of one side or the other—that makes the comparison fruitful.

But why does Dorian Gray need the experiment at all? What kind of knowledge does it offer? In part, Wilde uses the distance between the representation and the reality to emphasize that contrast—difference— is what generates the desire crucial to narrative itself. The exact equivalence between the real and the image at the beginning of the novel yields a circular, distinctly nonnarrative relationship: "Morning after morning [Dorian] had sat before the portrait wondering at its beauty, almost enamoured of it, as it seemed to him at times" (126). As long as the real coincides with its image, there is no room for plot because there is difference and no desire; "morning after morning" gestures to this endless repetitiveness. But as soon as the gap between the real and its image appears, the plot can get under way.

Two early moments in the narrative make this point clear. Dorian is first startled into desire when Lord Henry presents him with the contrast between present and future. That contrast takes shape through two visual images: Dorian recognizes himself in the portrait, and then he is moved to utter his fatal wish when Lord Henry offers a horrifying picture of a future of disintegration. For a few chapters thereafter, we return to a state of stasis, marked by Dorian's perfect identification with his portrait: picture and reality correspond, and Wilde marks this as the nonnarrative redundancy of both perfect mimesis *and* self-love. Then the difference between the portrait and Dorian's face appears once again, and the cycle of repetition is broken. The gap between the real and its image, between self and other, is absolutely essential to the production of narrative desire.

If this process sounds remarkably like the realist experiment, Wilde alters the results of the character's experimental tests. Indeed, I want to suggest that the crucial lesson learned by both reader and character in *The Picture of Dorian Gray* is the passage of time itself. Even if the character behaves ethically and well, after all, it is clear that time will take its toll: "Hour by hour, and week by week, the thing upon the canvas was growing old. It might escape the hideousness of sin, but the hideousness of age was in store for it" (105). It is surely in part for this reason that Dorian never reforms: there is no point in changing his ways, since ugliness is invariably the product of time, its effects tempered only somewhat by the moral life.

To return to the experiment: the character's face marks the beginning of the narrative, while the painting registers its growing difference from that starting point, and thus the text marks its temporal trajectory for us by making difference recognizable—or *cognizable*—through a contrast between two visual images. In place of realist knowledge—figured as developing correspondences between interpretive models and the real—the knowledge that both reader and character glean from Wilde's experiments is the growing recognition of insurmountable difference. Even if there were a way to resist a life of sin, there is no way to resist the passage of time. Brevity, the promise of change, is the generator of this narrative—and perhaps of all narrative, since the narratable lies in the perceptible imminence of change, "a cluster of latent potentialities . . . disequilibrium, suspense, and general insufficiency."[11] In this context, it becomes plain that Wilde makes the form of narrative into its own content. What we learn from the growing distance between the real and the representational is nothing other than the interval that has elapsed since the novel began. The fruits of the realist experiment, here, consist in the recognition of *narrative time itself.*

The Picture of Dorian Gray emerges as a quintessentially reflexive narrative project, where narrative representation has taken itself as its own object. Indeed, Wilde hints at his debt to a tradition of narrative theory. In the eighteenth century, Gotthold Ephraim Lessing distinguished narrative from pictorial representation by arguing that only poets could represent time's unfolding. Lessing writes: "By countless devices [Homer] presents this single object in a series of moments, in each of which it has a different form."[12] Narrative time emerges through the recurrence of the same signs, each time with a difference, which together permit the recognition of temporal passage.[13] *The Picture of Dorian Gray* reads like a demonstration of Lessing's theory of narrative, using the figure of the experiment to mark the increasing distance between the past and the present of narrative. But then Wilde unceremoniously overturns Lessing's central conclusions. After all, Lessing is the first thinker to reject the classical logic of *ut pictura poesis,* separating static images from moving narrative in order to analyze the different capabilities of the two forms.[14] Wilde all too obviously upsets this distinction, his whole text a staging of their inversion. Indeed, I would like to suggest that Wilde was fully intending to wreak havoc with Lessing.[15]

On the very first page of the novel, the reader is invited to remember the terms of Lessing's formalism:

> the fantastic shadows of birds in flight flitted across the long tussore-silk curtains that were stretched in front of the huge window, producing a kind of momentary Japanese effect, and making [Lord Henry Wotton] think of those pallid jade-faced painters of Tokio who, through the medium of an art that is necessarily immobile, seek to convey the sense of swiftness and motion. (47)

Lessing would surely agree that painting as an art is "necessarily immobile." But then, moving birds recall Japanese painting, which in turn tries to convey motion in a motionless medium. The real resembles static representations, which then seek to imitate the flux of life. If static pictures try to represent moving realities, living birds recall Japanese pictures, and in good Paterian fashion, neither the real nor the representational is clearly in possession of the founding moment.

If formalism has already reached its limits on the first page of the novel, an implicit critique of formalism is found at the heart of the text. In all of the texts we have considered up to now static image and narrative time have taken their places in a hierarchy: narrative has repeatedly claimed epistemological superiority over visual appearance, using the stasis of the image to provoke desire in hidden mysteries and future revelations—in short, to affirm its own truth-telling value. But the dependence of the image on narrative time cannot entirely mask its curious, equally significant antithesis, and this other side of the formalist hierarchy is crucial to the Wildean text. If pictures rely on narrative, narrative is dependent on the static frames of visual representation, which, thanks to their very stasis, provide not only the stimulus to narrative knowledge, inviting readers to put their faith in the truth-telling powers of the plotted text, but also the static moments necessary to the apprehension of discursive time.

Significantly, no one is ever present when the picture of Dorian Gray

actually undergoes its transformations.[16] Thus it retains its status as a motionless frame. The recognition of narrative time is thus produced by
the movement back and forth between two motionless pictures. Consequently, an apprehension of narrative time seems to *require* the stasis of
the visual image in order to generate its illusion of temporality. If *Modern Painters* made it clear that static visual appearances required the passage of narrative time to tell their truths, *The Picture of Dorian Gray* reveals
the reliance of narrative time on the static image. Wilde is uncannily
close, here, to the invention of cinema: the making of narrative out of a
sequence of frozen visual frames.[17]

But then, it is also true that the stasis of Dorian's beauty takes on significance only in relation to narrative temporality, to its own brevity or
promise of change. To come to a quintessentially Paterian conclusion,
then, the still image and the shifts of narrative are actually dependent
upon one another. If the realist experiment taught us that painting is incapable, on its own, of conveying knowledge, Wilde shows that narrative is likewise unable to register the value of its own epistemological
claims without relying on the frames of static pictures.

Coda

Intrigued by the rhetorical form of the realist experiment, Pater and
Wilde focused on the discursive practices that allowed narrative temporality to take place. They drew attention away from the truths to be
affirmed by narrative and pointed instead to the artifices of the form.
Disregarding the fruits of the experiment, they invited their readers to
investigate the rhetorical complexities of the experiment itself.

This attention to the artifices of narrative had two significant consequences for the alliance of realism and suspense. First of all, it allowed the
recognition of reflexivity to act as the pleasurable aim of the exercise of
reading. If Ruskin understood the seductive pleasures of investigating
the artifices of art, he urged his readers to pass quickly over the reflexive
moment in favor of a focus on the relationship between representation
and its objects. Eliot, James, Pater, and Wilde moved the attention back
to the artifice, investigating the activity of reading and the artifice of the
art object as the most interesting moments in the story. In so doing, they
also foregrounded the conclusion that highly plotted narrative was artificial. And if plot was artificial, it was therefore also unrealistic, unable to

document the chaotic and inaccessible realities of lived experience. But this meant that the role and purpose of suspenseful plotting had shifted: suspense was no longer understood as a method for approaching the real; it had become an effort to replicate the real. The attempt at verisimilitude, as Ruskin himself well knew, was a project doomed to failure. Thus Eliot, James, Pater, and Wilde—for all their sophistication—misleadingly recast the alliance of realism and suspense as a hopelessly naive mimetic exercise. Realism, ex post facto, became the very sort of imitation it had intended to put on trial.

Ruskin, Brontë, Dickens, and Collins were self-conscious about the need to probe conventional representations—exposing their limitations and insisting on the need to test all images, all surfaces, all beliefs. Ironically, their project could be said to have led to its own demise, turned back on itself by writers trained into skepticism by the very suspense of the realist experiment. But in the process realism was misread, interpreted with hindsight as a descriptive model rather than an epistemological method. The realists seemed, looking backward, to have trusted innocently to marriage plots and detective fictions to render successful pictures of the world. To James, Pater, and Wilde, realist narrative appeared remarkable, in retrospect, for a naive ingenuousness, an uncritical struggle for transparency.

This misreading might not have surprised the realists. After all, it was they who argued that we readers are inclined to project our own assumptions onto the other, unable to rein them in except when compelled to suspend our judgment. It was the realists who counseled a thoroughgoing skepticism to counter the powerful temptation to trust our own conjectures and inclinations. And it was they who recognized both the labors and the pleasures of putting our most cherished convictions to the test. Whenever we are relieved of the pressure to suspend judgment, the realists argued, we are only too quick to see the world as a reflection of our own expectations and desires.

Eliot, James, Pater, and Wilde turned the skepticism of the realist experiment back onto itself and left us the legacy of their critical reading. But their response to realism calls for a corresponding skepticism. If the fin de siècle grew accustomed to representing realism as a too-trusting faith in mimesis, the time has come for the realist experiment to offer its critical reply.

Notes

Introduction

1. Forster, *Aspects of the Novel*, 46, 53, 66.
2. Ibid., 46.
3. Barthes, *S/Z*, 76.
4. Barthes, *Pleasure of the Text*, 14.
5. Belsey, *Critical Practice*, 82.
6. Miller, *Novel and the Police*.
7. Peter Thoms and Elizabeth Deeds Ermarth are two recent examples. Thoms writes: "the unrest of narrative incompletion is tolerated only in the hope that it will soon dissipate. [Suspense] is a subtle method of social- and self-management, a repressive exercise in which a criminal . . . is located and fenced round by society's boundaries." *Detection and Its Designs*, 106. Ermarth argues that "the 'solution' of a crime . . . reaffirms the existence of a single social system of explanation and interpretation." *English Novel in History*, 2.
8. Barthes opposes the passive "readerly" pleasures of suspense fiction against the *jouissance* of the demanding "writerly" text (*Pleasure of the Text*, 14). Two narrative theorists in particular have helped to influence my conclusion that suspense is more "writerly" than Barthes allows. Robert Caserio argues that plotted narrative is developmental and dynamic, shaped by "a commitment and openness to change and transformation." *Plot, Story, and the Novel*, 24. Peter Brooks extends this insight in *Reading for the Plot*.
9. See Jonathan Smith's excellent account of nineteenth-century responses to Bacon in *Fact and Feeling*.
10. John Stuart Mill and William Whewell famously disagreed about how to tell when a scientific hypothesis had been verified, but both acknowledged the necessary role

of the hypothesis. See Achinstein, *Particles and Waves*, 117; and Losee, *Historical Introduction to the Philosophy of Science*, 160.

11. [Whewell], "Spedding's *Complete Edition of the Works of Bacon*," 316.

12. Quoted in Smith, *Fact and Feeling*, 12.

13. Ibid., 8.

14. Jevons, *Principles of Science*, 577. Peter Medawar argues that "the account of the scientific method which became recognized as the official alternative to Mill's was not Whewell's but Stanley Jevons'." *Art of the Soluble*, 149.

15. From Huxley's *Scientific Memoirs*, quoted in Block, "T. H. Huxley's Rhetoric," 210; Jevons, *Principles of Science*, 508; Tyndall, "Scientific Use of the Imagination" (1870), in *Fragments of Science* 2: 128.

16. Quoted in Jevons, *Principles of Science*, 591. Huxley offered a similar warning: "if I might impress any caution upon your minds, it is the utterly conditional nature of our knowledge,—the danger of neglecting the process of verification under any circumstances; and the film upon which we rest, the moment our deductions carry us beyond the reach of this great process of verification." "On the Educational Value of Natural History Sciences" (1854), in *Science and Education*, 55.

17. Jevons, *Principles of Science*, 593; Huxley, *Science and Education*, 55.

18. Huxley, "On the Advisableness of Improving Natural Knowledge," 230.

19. Huxley, "Scientific Education: Notes of an After-Dinner Speech" (1869), in *Science and Education*, 128.

20. Letter to the *Times* (30 June 1853); in Faraday, *Philosopher's Tree*, 183. For a consideration of the relationship between Faraday's Sandemanian Christianity and his science, see Cantor, *Michael Faraday*.

21. Jevons, *Principles of Science*, 592: "it is most frequently the philosophic mind which is in doubt."

22. Jonathan Crary has recently suggested that suspension might be crucial to the idea of modernity itself. He points to an intriguing relationship between suspension and a growing nineteenth-century concern with the capacity to pay attention, a concern coterminous, Crary argues, with the definition of modern subjectivity. As one deliberately pays attention to an object or spectacle, one undergoes a double suspension, suspending awareness of irrelevant and extraneous sensory data and suspending time, pausing to take in the world of objects. *Suspensions of Perception*, 10.

23. Lewes, *Problems of Life and Mind* 1: 433–34.

24. Ibid., 433.

25. From an 1840 letter. Faraday, *Life and Letters* 2: 106.

26. Quoted in Ryals, *World of Possibilities*, 2–3.

27. Mill argues that the only "rational position" is the "suspension of judgment": "unless [a person] contents himself with that, he is either led by authority, or adopts, like the generality of the world, the side to which he feels most inclination." *On Liberty*, 36.

28. Stephen, "Relation of Novels to Life," 98.

29. Notably, Stephen here does not cast fiction as a trivial pastime for women but represents it as a serious epistemological project on a par with philosophy and natural science, even emphasizing the masculinity of the readers who will benefit from it.

30. Ruskin, *Works* 11: 65.

31. Levine, "Objectivity and Death," 287. See also Levine's "Dying to Know," 1–4, and "Two Ways Not to Be a Solipsist," 7–41.

32. Eliot, "Leaves from a Note-Book," 444–45.

33. It could be argued that suspense produces more pain than pleasure—we might think of Lucy Snowe's lament against her own intense anxiety in *Villette*—but the extraordinary popularity of suspense plots suggests that readers willingly subject themselves to whatever pain suspenseful plotting inflicts. In his engaging work on Trollope, Christopher Herbert suggests that both Victorian writers and contemporary theorists have privileged the "serious" and have consequently missed the potential for joining pain and pleasure in fiction. For Herbert, Trollope is the unusual Victorian who tried to marry comic delight with the seriousness of significant thought and value. I would like to suggest that the suspenseful plots of Victorian fiction do something rather similar: bringing together excitement and stimulation with "duty, work, self-control, and self-denial." *Trollope and Comic Pleasure*, 11, 33.

34. One classic source for the history of European realism is René Wellek, who argues that although there were Victorian fictions that one could call realistic, "there was no realist movement of that name before George Moore and George Gissing, late in the eighties." *Concepts of Criticism*, 229. For Erich Auerbach—to cite another memorable source—European realism found its roots in Balzac and Stendhal, and it involved a rejection of classical aesthetics, a deliberate mixing of registers, and a desire "to represent man . . . as embedded in a total reality, political, social, and economic, which is concrete and constantly evolving." *Mimesis*, 468, 463.

35. Levine, *Realistic Imagination*; Ermarth, *Realism and Consensus in the English Novel*; Knoepflmacher, *George Eliot's Early Novels*, 35; Jameson, *Political Unconscious*, 104; Shaw, *Narrating Reality*; Armstrong, *Fiction in the Age of Photography*; Brantlinger, *Reading Lesson*, 122.

36. See, for example, Armstrong, *Fiction in the Age of Photography*; Knoepflmacher, *George Eliot's Early Novels*; and John Rignall, *Realist Fiction and the Strolling Spectator*.

1. Ruskin's Radical Realism

1. Rigby's review of *Modern Painters* appeared in the *Quarterly Review* (March 1856), reprinted in Bradley, *Ruskin*, 187; Mather, *John Ruskin*, xi; Wilenski, *John Ruskin*, 192. John Rosenberg claims that *Modern Painters* "would be less perplexing if Ruskin had known more when he began it, or learned less in the course of its composition" (*Darkening Glass*, 2). Elizabeth Helsinger makes the case that *The Stones of Venice* marks a new direction for Ruskin, launching his preoccupations with history and social criticism (*Ruskin and the Art of the Beholder*, 141). Gary Wihl emphasizes Ruskin's "textual fragmentariness" in *Ruskin and the Rhetoric of Infallibility*, xi.

2. In the final volume of *Stones*, for example, Ruskin writes: "It was noticed, in the second volume of *Modern Painters*, p. 187, that the principle which had most power in retarding the modern school of portraiture was its constant expression of individual vanity and pride" (*Works* 11: 73–74).

3. Examples are too extensive to list. To have a sense of the interweaving, however, we might consider the problem of "Sensualist" artists, which Ruskin introduces midway through *Stones*. He writes: "I propose to work out the subject fully in the last volume of *Modern Painters*." The last volume turned out to be three volumes, but Ruskin made good on his promise in all three (*Works* 10: 229).

4. Lukacs, *Meaning of Contemporary Realism*, 19–20.

5. See Levine, *Realistic Imagination*; McGowan, *Representation and Revelation*; Kearns, *Nineteenth-Century Literary Realism*; and Lloyd, *Crises of Realism*.

6. Armstrong, "Fiction in the Age of Photography," 40.

7. Russo, *Skeptical Selves,* 13.

8. Eliot, *Letters* 4: 43.

9. Eliot, *Adam Bede,* 150–51; Brontë, *Shirley,* 39; Lewes, *Principles of Success in Literature,* 105. Linda Nochlin argues that realist art was associated with work because the revolutions of 1848 had raised the issue of labor as a central political problem for the first time. She focuses on the content of representation, rather than the labor of the artist, affirming that after 1848 "the worker becomes the dominant image in Realist art." *Realism,* 113.

10. Ruskin is responding, so he claims, to a culture in which "Brilliance and rapidity of execution are everywhere sought as the highest good" (*Works* 3: 620). This climate encourages "glitter and claptrap," discouraging "the man of industry," who is capable of great and serious truths when allowed the time to work to achieve them (3: 620–21).

11. Even in the very first draft of *Modern Painters,* the young Ruskin insists that truth is the greatest aim of art and asserts that "man shall have nothing worthy of . . . possession without labouring for it." *Modern Painters: "First Draft",* 19.

12. The *Oxford English Dictionary* cites the fourth volume of *Modern Painters,* published in April 1856, as the earliest instance of the word "realism" to mean "close resemblance to what is real; fidelity of representation, rendering the precise detail of the real thing or scene." Ruskin did not in fact use the word in this way in *Modern Painters* 4, but it is not surprising that the *OED* made such an error: in *The Three Colours of Pre-Raphaelitism* (1878), Ruskin suggests that he has been widely credited with the invention of realism and points the reader to two places in *Modern Painters* where they can find realism defined—the third volume and the preface to the second edition of the first volume (see *Works* 34: 162). Clearly, in the 1870s, Ruskin was being seen as the father of realism. See also his letter to J. A. Froude (*Works* 37: 83). Richard Stang locates the first uses of the word "realist" in 1851 and 1853, followed by "realism" in 1856. *Theory of the Novel in England,* 148. More recently, David Skilton claims simply that "The word 'realism' entered the language in the late 1850s." *Early and Mid-Victorian Novel,* 86. The *Oxford English Dictionary* distinguishes between a philosophical realism, the uses of which date as early as the seventeenth century, and representational realism, which catches on in the mid-nineteenth century.

13. [George Eliot], unsigned review, *Westminster Review* 9 (April 1856), in Bradley, *Ruskin,* 180; emphasis in original.

14. In the context of recent writing on realism, my Ruskinian definition of Victorian realism comes closest to that of Harry Shaw, who writes: "nineteenth-century realist fiction makes most sense when it is viewed as an attempt to deal with situations which involve partial knowledge and continual approximation." *Narrating Reality,* 29.

15. *Churchman* (October 1843), 671–73; quoted in Ruskin, *Works* 3: xxxv–xxxvi; [John Eagles], unsigned review, *Blackwood's Magazine* 54 (October 1843), in Bradley, *Ruskin,* 56; unsigned review, *Athenaeum* (3 February 1844), 105, in Olmsted, *Victorian Painting,* 463; [Walt Whitman], unsigned review in *Brooklyn Eagle* (22 July 1847), in Bradley, *Ruskin,* 76; Rigby, in Bradley, *Ruskin,* 185; *Fraser's Magazine* (March 1846): 358–68, quoted in Ruskin, *Works* 3: xxxvi.

16. Bradley, *Ruskin,* 185.

17. Jarves, "Pen Likenesses of Art Critics," 5.

18. In 1838, R. H. Horne wrote: "The Discourses of Sir Joshua Reynolds have long borne a high and extensive reputation: private libraries have been considered incomplete without them, and the favourite 'precepts' of their accomplished author continue at the present time not only to be frequently quoted as 'authority,' but to influence artists in their practice, their opinions of themselves, and their most ardent hopes." "British Artists and Writers on Art," 613. Ruskin himself feels bound to respond to Reynolds's *Discourses* at length in the third volume of *Modern Painters* (*Works* 5: 20ff.).

19. Reynolds, *Discourses on Art*, 124, 127, 122.

20. Samuel Taylor Coleridge likewise rejects "mere painful copying" in favor of an accord between the world and the mind: "[The artist] must out of his own mind create forms according to the severe laws of the intellect, in order to generate within himself that co-ordination of freedom and law . . . which assimilates him to nature and enables him to understand her." "On Poesy or Art," 47–48.

21. Kant, *Critique of Judgment*, 53–54.

22. As Kant explains, the sublime tells us about a subjective experience of the world but does not offer up an understanding of objects in the world: "in what we are accustomed to call sublime there is nothing at all that leads to particular objective principles and forms of nature corresponding to them. . . . We must seek a ground external to ourselves for the beautiful of nature, but seek the sublime merely in ourselves and in our attitude of thought, which introduces sublimity into the representation of nature." Kant, *Critique of Judgment*, 84.

23. For a fine account of the distinction between the Augustan emphasis on ideal, general, universal truths and the Victorian focus on particularity, see Christ, *Finer Optic*, 1–15.

24. Lewes, "Criticism in Relation to Novels," 356.

25. Christian Socialist F. J. Furnivall invited Ruskin to teach at his new Working Men's College and requested permission to reprint "The Nature of Gothic" chapter of *The Stones of Venice* as a pamphlet for working-class readers. A number of critics disagree with the conclusion that Ruskin's text was radical, however. Robert Hewison argues *The Stones of Venice* was, in fact, an "Ultra-Tory" treatise. "Notes on the Construction of *The Stones of Venice*," 149. And Judith Stoddart sees Ruskin's refusal to sanction the communal International Working Men's Association as evidence of his faith in an implicitly aristocratic "familial notion of society passed down from father to son." "Conjuring the 'Necromantic Evidence,'" 166.

26. Morris, "How I Became a Socialist," 35. Morris also prophesied that the discussion of labor in *The Stones of Venice* would be seen in future years as "one of the few necessary and inevitable utterances of the century." Preface to "The Nature of Gothic," i.

27. Glasier, *William Morris*, 11, 67.

28. Only two named Marx and nine Shakespeare. See Goldman, "Ruskin, Oxford, and the British Labour Movement," 58, and Rose, "Rereading *The English Common Reader*," 56.

29. Furnivall wanted to see Ruskin's message about labor spread widely. He tells the story in the *Daily News* (4 April 1899, in Ruskin, *Works* 10: ix). See also Benzie, *Dr. F. J. Furnivall*, 41–70.

30. For discussions of the gendering of the audience in Ruskin's work, see Helsinger,

"Ruskin and the Politics of Viewing," especially 134–40, and Marsh, "'Resolve to Be a Great Paintress,'" 177–85.

31. We have seen the close links between Ruskin and George Eliot. As for Brontë, after reading the first volume of *Modern Painters,* she wrote: "Hitherto I have only had instinct to guide me in judging art; I feel now as if I had been walking blindfold—this book seems to give me eyes. I *do* wish I had pictures within reach by which to test the new sense. Who can read these glowing descriptions of Turner's works without longing to see them?" See Wise, *Brontës* 2: 240. Brontë also writes glowingly of *The Stones of Venice* (Wise, *Brontës* 3: 195–96, 233). In 1868, James paid homage to Ruskin as the "single eminent representative" of art criticism in England and claimed that it was surprising that Ruskin could have so great an influence on artists, and so little on critics. See James, *Painter's Eye,* 33–34. Proust's biographer calls Ruskin the novelist's "salvation" and describes Proust's Ruskinian education in prose that sounds wonderfully like Ruskin's: "Except that it brought him joy unspoilt by suffering, Proust's passion for Ruskin took precisely the same course as his love-affairs or ardent friendships. There was a prelude of tepid acquaintance; a crystallization and a taking fire; and a falling out of love, from which he emerged free, but changed and permanently enriched." Painter, *Marcel Proust* 1: 256.

32. Ruskin's "naturalism" has nothing to do with the movement of literary naturalism called by that name that emerged later in the century best characterized by the determinist narratives of Emile Zola. Ruskin's naturalism entails "the love of natural objects for their own sake, and the effort to represent them frankly, unconstrained by artistical laws" (*Works* 10: 215).

33. "To the Gothic workman the living foliage became a subject of intense affection, and he struggled to render all its characters with as much accuracy as was compatible with the laws of his design and the nature of his material, not unfrequently tempted in his enthusiasm to transgress the one and disguise the other" (*Works* 10: 236).

34. In the library edition of Ruskin's works, the attention to "naturalism" runs to twenty-four pages (*Works* 10: 215–39).

35. Ruskin, *Unto This Last, and Other Essays,* 321 n 25.

36. In "The Two Paths" (1859), Ruskin puts this point even more vehemently: we see "the visible operation of the human intellect in the presentation of the truth." If you stop imitating natural forms, "there is but one word for you—Death:—death of every healthy faculty, and of every noble intelligence" (*Works* 16: 285, 289).

2. Ruskin's Plots

1. Eagles, "British Institution," 544.
2. Hazlitt, *Essays on the Fine Arts,* 267–68.
3. Ruskin, "Danger to the National Gallery," letter, *Times* (7 January 1847), in *Works* 12: 397.
4. "The principle of universal suffrage, however applicable to matters of government, which concern the common feelings and common interests of society, is by no means applicable to matters of taste, which can only be decided upon by the most refined understandings." Hazlitt, *Essays on the Fine Arts,* 16.
5. It is one of Ruskin's assumptions that visual representation must reproduce the experience of human vision, which cannot focus on two distances at once, and which sees some aspects confusedly and others distinctly in any single glance. This

assumption is nowhere more obvious than in his discussions of perspective, where the location of the viewer must determine the appearance of the painting: "If a thing has character upon its outline, as a tree, for instance, or a mossy stone, the farther it is removed from us, the sharper the outline of the whole mass will become, though in doing so the particular details which make up the character will become confused in the manner described" (*Works* 3: 442).

6. As Ruskin puts it, "The picture which is taken as a substitute for nature had better be burned" (*Works* 3: 12).

7. By the 1870s, when "sensation fiction" had become a staple of popular English fiction, reviewers sometimes distinguished the literature of character from the literature of plot, calling the first "realistic" and the second "sensational." Anthony Trollope said this distinction was a "mistake" arising "from the inability of the imperfect artist to be at the same time realistic and sensational. A good novelist should be both, and both in the highest degree." Quoted in Skilton, *Early and Mid-Victorian Novel*, 138. It was a "mistake" in another sense, too: if plot was aligned with sensation and against realism and character, this alignment came about only in the late 1860s, after the heyday of the realist experiment. Plot and character were absolutely intertwined in the suspense model of the 1840s, lasting well into the 1860s, when the activities of hypothesizing, speculating, and testing were thought to reveal character just as it much as they launched the events of plot.

8. The terms "scientists" and "philosophers of science" are anachronistic. William Whewell is credited with the invention of the terms "scientists" and "physicists" in the 1840s, but these are not the words typically used to describe scientific investigators in the period. Instead they are called "philosophers" or "natural philosophers." There is much less of a distinction between scientists and philosophers of science in the early Victorian period than our own terms would suggest.

9. Tyndall, "On the Study of Physics" (1854), in *Fragments of Science* 1: 291.

10. Ibid. 1: 292, 293.

11. Ruskin and Tyndall were on friendly terms through the composition of *Modern Painters,* and Ruskin sent Tyndall a copy of his *Queen of the Air* in 1869, but the two later argued about James Forbes's theory of glaciers, and their exchange was heated in the 1870s. See Sawyer, "Ruskin and Tyndall," 220–24. I agree with Jonathan Smith that although Ruskin and Tyndall argued about experimentation, "the broad methodology developed in *Modern Painters* was consistent with the scientific methodology being articulated in the same period, a method combining the inductive observation of the facts with the operation of the imagination, with hypotheses, hunches, and guesswork." *Fact and Feeling,* 152–53. Ruskin recommends at least three experiments to his readers in *Deucalion,* where he criticizes Tyndall explicitly. See *Deucalion,* 36, 59–60, 72.

12. Tyndall, *Faraday as a Discoverer,* 175, 117, 30. Faraday's own words confirm Tyndall's description. Throughout his long career as a scientist, he continually worried about the danger of relying on favorite hypotheses and failing to attend to the evidence of the world. In 1844, he said: "He is the wisest philosopher who holds his theory with some doubt." See his *Life and Letters* 2: 175.

13. Tyndall, *Faraday as a Discoverer,* 49–50.

14. Thomas Kuhn argues, famously, that scientists are more inclined to confirm pre-existing assumptions than to indulge in fundamental doubts: "In science . . . novelty emerges only with difficulty, manifested by resistance against a background provided

by expectation." *Structure of Scientific Revolutions,* 64. This resistance may describe the general practice of science, but Tyndall, Faraday, and Lewes show that Victorian thinkers were deeply concerned with the necessity—in theory at least—of subjecting their most basic presumptions to radical mistrust.

15. Even John Stuart Mill, who tried to reduce the role of hypotheses in science, agreed. He wrote that the experiment was "necessarily tentative": "we begin by making any supposition, even a false one, to see what consequences will follow from it; and by observing how these differ from the real phenomena, we learn what corrections to make in our assumption." *System of Logic,* 326.

16. Lewes, *Problems of Life and Mind* 1: 433.

17. Herschel, *Preliminary Discourse,* 72. Eighteenth-century scientists and novelists appear to have been much more likely to cast suspense as difficult, painful, or even intolerable. John Gregory, the first physician to write a code of medical ethics, wrote in 1772 that "a state of suspence is always disagreeable" because "it is difficult for men to give up favorite opinions, and to think from a state of security and confidence into one of suspence and skepticism." *Lectures on the Duties and Qualifications of a Physician,* 202, 232.

18. Quoted in Crease, *Play of Nature,* 39. This quotation suggests that the marriage of doubt and pleasure lasted better into the twentieth century in scientific circles than in literary ones.

19. Beer, *Darwin's Plots,* 90.

20. Ronell, "Test Drive," 213.

21. Watt, *Rise of the Novel,* 12–30.

22. Elizabeth Deeds Ermarth writes that the codes of suspense are "evident in almost all Victorian novels . . . from the superlative achievements of Charles Dickens and George Eliot to the lesser ones of Charles Reade, Wilkie Collins, and Conan Doyle." *English Novel in History,* 2.

23. See the introduction to this book for a fuller discussion of the critical response to suspense.

24. Miller, *Novel and the Police,* 54.

25. Ibid., 45–46.

26. Marianna Torgovnick offers an elegant description of the difference between first and second readings, giving this difference a realist spin: "The process of reading without knowing endings is . . . rather like the process of day-to-day living: we make tentative guesses at direction and meaning by applying our experience of what the data we encounter usually lead to and mean. . . . Second or subsequent readings— when the question of 'what happens next' no longer pertains with urgency, differ fundamentally from first readings and resemble the ways in which we experience the past." *Closure in the Novel,* 8. Harry Shaw, too, works with this distinction, critical of the ways that literary scholars typically read literary plots with hindsight, as "templates with a pre-given ideological meaning." *Narrating Reality,* 128.

27. Geraldine Jewsbury, unsigned review, *Athenaeum* (25 July 1868), 106; in Page, *Wilkie Collins,* 170. Reviewers who disliked the novel—and there were quite of few of those—complained that it was a mere puzzle or conundrum, mysterious but superficial, offering nothing more than suspense. A review in the *Nation* had it that "nobody ever reads [Collins's novels] twice, and that when the end of the first perusal is reached, everybody thinks his time has been wasted." *Nation* 7 (17 September 1868),

235; in Page, *Wilkie Collins*, 175. The *London Review* predicted that "Most of those who read 'The Moonstone' are likely to regard it less as a work of literature than as an elaborate puzzle, at the explanation of which they will endeavour to arrive with all possible haste." "The Moonstone," unsigned review, *London Review* 17 (25 July 1868), 116.

28. It is worth noting that second readings may actually be capable of generating suspense. Noël Carroll argues that suspenseful endings often put our larger sense of justice in question. Even on second readings then, when an immoral ending is presented as likely, we must entertain the possibility that good does not always prevail: "the audience is given a stake in the outcome of certain events in the fiction when the relevant outcome is presented as morally righteous, at the same time that the rival outcome is presented as evil. When the righteous outcome appears improbable, relative to the information provided in the story up to that point, suspense is a fitting or intelligible reaction." "Paradox of Suspense," 84.

29. Frank Kermode, for example, criticizes the "consoling" and "crude" formal coherence of the nineteenth-century novel, which offers us a falsely soothing sense of order: "if [novels] mitigate our existential anguish it is because we weakly collaborate with them." For Kermode, *Ulysses,* with its resistance to plot, comes closer to asserting "human freedom and unpredictability." *Sense of an Ending,* 113, 140, 144.

30. See notes to the *Moonstone,* 527–28. Jenny Bourne Taylor argues that Collins's two scientific sources represent two poles of the scientific world, "the respected voice of mainstream physiological psychology" and "the marginalized advocate of mesmerism." Taylor makes the case that by bringing them together, Collins is revealing their shared belief in an unconscious. *In the Secret Theatre of Home,* 183.

31. Collins, Preface, 500.

32. Unsigned review, *Times* (30 October 1860), 6; see also unsigned reviews in *Critic* 21 (25 August 1860), 233–34, and *Guardian* 15 (29 August 1860), 780–81; all reprinted in Page, *Wilkie Collins,* 98, 82, 89–91.

33. Patricia Frick argues that artists in a number of Collins novels follow Ruskin's aesthetic prescriptions, and she points out that the two writers met more than once, beginning as early as 1846. "Wilkie Collins and John Ruskin," 11–22. Collins himself described the controversial reception of *Modern Painters* in a letter to R. H. Dana in 1849: "The violent paradoxes in the First volume had the effect which violent paradoxes, when cleverly argued, usually produce:—they amused some, displeased others, and startled everybody. . . . [Readers saw Ruskin] as a man, who having determined to say something new on every subject he touched, resolutely overlooked or dogmatically contradicted, any received and tested principle of intellectual or critical truth that came in his way." *Letters* 1: 53–54.

34. Sidgwick, "Poems and Prose Remains," 363–87.

35. Beer, *Darwin's Plots,* 8, 159–60, 90.

36. Ibid., 7.

37. At the very end of *The Origin of Species,* Darwin shows us a future filled not with the surprises of unpredictable otherness but with the continued dominance of the strong: "We can so far take a prophetic glance into futurity as to foretell that it will be the common and widely-spread species, belonging to the larger and dominant groups within each class, which will ultimately prevail and procreate new and dominant species." Darwin, *Origin of Species,* 559–60.

38. George Levine argues that realist narrative is closer to Darwinian evolution than it ever intended, structured by the attempt to avoid the accidents of Darwinian contingency but doomed to failure: "Realism is programmatically antagonistic to chance, but like Darwin almost inevitably must use it to resolve its narrative problems." Like Beer, Levine sees evolution rather than experimentation as the model for Victorian suspense. *Darwin and the Novelists,* 19–20.

39. In his diaries, Ruskin mentions his frequent attendance at the Geological Society, his acquaintance with prominent Victorian scientists, and his participation in debates about scientific methods and theories. See *Diaries of John Ruskin* 1: 74, 82, 239, 244. See also Ruskin's explicitly scientific works from the 1870s and 1880s: *Love's Meinie* and *Proserpina,* both in *Works,* and *Deucalion.* For contemporary scholarly accounts, see Weltman, "Myth and Gender in Ruskin's Science," 153–73, and Sawyer, "Ruskin and Tyndall," 217–46.

40. For an overview of these debates, see Greene, *Geology in the Nineteenth Century,* especially 53–67. In *Deucalion,* Ruskin defended James Forbes's theory of glaciers against Tyndall's by using experiments with piecrust and treacle. See Sawyer, "Ruskin and Tyndall," 220.

41. For example, Ruskin staunchly defended his own right to speak on scientific matters in his article titled "The Distinctions of Form in Silica" by affirming that "precisely the same faculties of eye and mind are concerned in the analysis of natural and of pictorial forms" (*Works* 26: 386).

42. Even when imitation produces its most convincing illusion of actual space, Ruskin explains, it still reveals that it is a trick when we touch the surface of the canvas: "one sense is contradicted by another . . . the eye says a thing is round, and the finger says it is flat" (*Works* 3: 100–101).

43. In *Illusion in Art,* M. L. D'Otrange Mastai also calls attention to this aspect of trompe l'oeil.

44. "Irony" is, of course, a term with a long and complex history, but a working definition may come from Gary Handwerk, who claims that "The identifying trait of irony is that there be an *incompatibility* between competing meanings, between a proferred and an implied alternative." *Irony and Ethics in Narrative,* 1. Jean Baudrillard also points to the irony of trompe l'oeil in *De la séduction,* 87: "Apparences pures, elles ont l'ironie de trop de réalité" (Pure appearances, they have the irony of too much reality [my translation]).

45. Echoing Ruskin on this point, Gerrit Henry writes on photo realism: "[R]eality is made to look so overpoweringly real as to make it pure illusion." In Battcock, *Super Realism,* 11.

46. Richard Wollheim claims that trompe l'oeil "incite[s] our awareness of depth, but . . . in a way designed to battle our attention to the marks upon the surface." This sounds like Ruskin at first, but then Wollheim's "battle" turns out to be hardly a fight: the illusion of depth immediately conquers the recognition that the illusion is created out of paint and canvas and repels attention to "the marked surface." *Painting as an Art,* 62. For Ruskin, trompe l'oeil ends up focusing our attention on the marked surface, not repelling it.

47. This category is not limited to art that tells truths; it clearly contains examples of deceptive images. In fact, truthful art prompts us to test its *claims* to truth. Imitation is the alternative category, provoking no experimentation.

48. E. H. Gombrich uses this analogy in his discussion of mimesis: "the correct portrait, like the useful map . . . is not a faithful record of visual experience but the faithful construction of a relational model." *Art and Illusion*, 78.

49. Homi Bhabha's reading of "mimicry" is uncannily like Ruskin's "imitation." Mimicry "problematizes the signs of racial and cultural priority, so that the 'national' is no longer naturalizable. What emerges between mimesis and mimicry is a *writing*, a mode of representation." *Location of Culture*, 86, 87–88.

50. With its emphasis on skeptical testing, the plot of the realist experiment is therefore largely untroubled by the difficulty of choosing between free will and determinism, which Catherine Gallager defines as the central problem for the realism that emerges in the mid-Victorian period. *Industrial Reformation of English Fiction*, 3–110.

3. "Harmless Pleasure"

1. Brontë, "Biographical Notice," 134.

2. Gaskell, *Life of Charlotte Brontë*, 271.

3. G. H. Lewes could hardly contain his shock: "Curious enough is it to read *Wuthering Heights* and *The Tenant of Wildfell Hall*, and remember that the writers were two retiring, solitary, consumptive girls! Books, coarse even for men, coarse in language and coarse in conception, the coarseness apparently of violent and uncultivated men—turn out to be the productions of two girls living almost alone, filling their loneliness with quiet studies, and writing these books from a sense of duty, hating the pictures they drew, yet drawing them with austere conscientiousness!" See Lewes's unsigned review, *Leader*, 953. Harriet Martineau tried to justify the disharmony, explaining that the novels reveal a commitment to lived experience and asking readers not to "pass criticism on the coarseness which, to a certain degree, pervades the work of all the sisters, and the repulsiveness which makes the tales of Emily and Ann really horrible to people who have not iron nerves." *Biographical Sketches*, 363–64.

4. For example, Tom Winnifrith and Edward Chitham point to Charlotte's "shyness and depression" as the reason for her refusal to make the most of her fame. *Charlotte and Emily Brontë*, 11. John Kucich claims that Charlotte "cultivates psychic withdrawal," but he argues that this is not so much a sign of vulnerability as a kind of power. "Passionate Reserve and Reserved Passion," 74, 82.

5. Janet Gezari emphasizes Charlotte's "uneasiness" rather than her pleasure in this passage. See *Charlotte Brontë and Defensive Conduct*, 17.

6. Brontë, "Biographical Notice," 135.

7. So compelling was the metaphor of the veil that two of the reviewers who responded to the "Biographical Notice" echoed it in the first lines of their reviews. The *Examiner* wrote: "In a preface to this volume the author of *Jane Eyre* partially lifts the veil from the history and mystery of authorship which has occupied the Quidnuncs of literature for the past two years." In Allott, *Brontës*, 288. The opening of the *Athenaeum* review read: "The lifting of that veil which for a while concealed the authorship of *Jane Eyre* and its sister-novels excited in us no surprise." Unsigned review, *Athenaeum* (28 December 1850), 1368.

8. Brontë, "Biographical Notice," 135.

9. Ibid., 134. Catherine A. Judd puts to rest the misconception that women writers took male pseudonyms in order to find publishers, and she points out that a number

of male writers in the period—including Shelley, Thackeray, Ruskin, and Swinburne—chose women's names to publish their work. See "Male Pseudonyms and Female Authority," 251.

10. Eve Sedgwick writes: "the veil that conceals and inhibits sexuality comes by the same gesture to represent it, both as a metonym of the thing covered and as a metaphor for the system of prohibitions by which sexual desire is enhanced and specified." *Coherence of Gothic Conventions*, 143.

11. Barthes, *S/Z*, 75.

12. This "checking," for Roland Barthes, is one of the prototypical delays of the hermeneutic code; narratives pique our curiosity, provoking our desire for closure, when they offer a "*suspended answer* (the aphasic stoppage of the disclosure)." *S/Z*, 75.

13. Miller, *Narrative and Its Discontents*, 21.

14. As Jerome Beaty puts it, "though 'edited by' would not necessarily have indicated the kind of novel being presented, what it might have been expected to indicate was a work by a well-known novelist, acknowledged by name, pseudonym, or the titles of that novelist's other works." *Misreading Jane Eyre*, 12.

15. Unsigned review, *People's Journal* (November 1847), in Allott, *Brontës*, 81.

16. Unsigned review, *Christian Remembrancer* (April 1848), in Allott, *Brontës*, 89.

17. [G. H. Lewes], unsigned review of Brontë, *Jane Eyre, Fraser's Magazine* (December 1847), in Allott, *Brontës*, 84.

18. Bodenheimer, "Jane Eyre in Search of Her Story," 102.

19. [Elizabeth Rigby], unsigned review, *Quarterly Review* 84 (December 1848), 175–76.

20. Unsigned review, *Christian Remembrancer* (April 1848), in Allott, *Brontës*, 89.

21. [Edwin Percy Whipple], "Novels of the Season," *North American Review* (October 1848), in Allott, *Brontës*, 97–99.

22. Unsigned review, *Era* (14 November 1847), 9.

23. Brontë, *Letters* 1: 564; my emphasis.

24. Barthes, *S/Z*, 100.

25. Sedgwick points to the importance of the veil in Gothic fiction more generally, arguing in part that it comes to represent "sexuality itself—sexuality as error, as the driving, transitory illusion that a specific object can adequately answer to desire." *Coherence of Gothic Conventions*, 145.

26. Robert Heilman claims that Brontë updates and mocks Gothic conventions in *Jane Eyre,* strategically employing anti-Gothic details and rewriting the stock characters of the "sex villain" and the "clerical hero" in the figures of Rochester and St. John. But Heilman also argues that the invocation of Gothic "intensity" frees Brontë to explore passions and impulses not permitted in the novel of society. "Charlotte Brontë's New Gothic," 165–80. Susan Wolstenholme's more recent *Gothic (Re)Visions* makes the case that Brontë is more indebted to her Gothic forebears than Heilman allows, arguing that she uses gendered Gothic conventions of performance and spectatorship to defy masculine authority (57–78).

27. Radcliffe, *Mysteries of Udolpho* 1: 118. All subsequent quotations from this text will refer to page numbers from this 1973 edition.

28. Haggerty, *Gothic Fiction/Gothic Form*, 18.

29. Wilson, "Who Cares Who Killed Roger Ackroyd?" 264.

30. Barthes, *S/Z*, 15–16.

31. Barthes, *Pleasure of the Text*, 14.

4. Realism as Self-Forgetfulness

1. [Edwin Percy Whipple], unsigned review, *Atlantic Monthly* (September 1861); in P. Collins, *Dickens*, 428.

2. [E. S. Dallas], unsigned review, *Times* (17 October 1861), in P. Collins, *Dickens*, 432; [H. F. Chorley], unsigned review, *Athenaeum* (13 July 1861), in Dickens, *Great Expectations*, ed. Law and Pinnington, 54; [Margaret Oliphant], "Sensation Novels," *Blackwood's Magazine* (May 1862), in Collins, *Dickens*, 439.

3. Eco, "Overinterpreting Texts," 48–49. For a reading of the relationship between science and detection that focuses on their shared capacity to control and discipline, see Thomas, *Detective Fiction and the Rise of Forensic Science*.

4. Bloom, "Capitalising on Poe's Detective," 17; Bersani, *Future for Astyanax*, 63.

5. The list of critics who have faulted both suspense and realism for imposing too limiting a structure on the frightening disarray of the world is long. Gary Day, for example, sees "Realism, with its emphasis on order, coherence, and limitation" as the "dominant" Victorian mode. He writes: "Although the Victorians were troubled with uncertainty, they preferred to repress their doubts and cling instead to the view that ultimate truths did exist." In "Figuring Out the Signalman," 26.

6. "The Purloined Letter" has attracted a great deal of critical attention in the past few decades. My own brief look at Poe, here, is intentionally condensed and specific. For a rich range of other readings, see Muller and Richardson's *The Purloined Poe*, an excellent critical collection that includes Poe's story, Lacan's famous "Seminar on 'The Purloined Letter,'" Derrida's response to Lacan, and others. All references to the text are taken from this edition.

7. Ibid., 39.

8. Dickens, *Great Expectations*, ed. Margaret Caldwell, 137. All subsequent quotations refer to page numbers from this edition.

9. "He perceives the witch of his life as his godmother; just as that upside-down vision perceives the godfather of his life as his witch." Stone, *Dickens and the Invisible World*, 317.

10. As Graham Daldry puts it, "what [Pip] does not see" is that "the retrospect of the narrative does not necessarily include its anticipation." *Charles Dickens and the Form of the Novel*, 142.

11. Katherine Kearns suggests a similar conclusion, arguing that the alterity of the real gives rise to the novel's concern with legal trials: "The realistic novel's preoccupation with lawyers, court cases, and trials reflects the apprehension of a reality that must be pled into existence." *Nineteenth-Century Literary Realism*, 10.

12. Mrs. Joe is, of course, wrong about this, as we learn later, when Magwitch describes his own childhood, a childhood composed not of questions but of unfair accusations.

13. Biddy's working-class status and initially unkempt appearance might seem to disqualify her from the title of domestic angel, but the trajectory of her plot brings her to become an ideal wife and mother, and this ending is certainly fitting: she has always shown a willingness to sacrifice herself for others, an enthusiasm for education (particularly for literacy), and an industrious, respectable self-reliance. If she does not begin in the middle class, she certainly meets all of the requirements to join it.

14. Intriguingly, Gail Turley Houston argues that Estella too is "self-forgetful": "groomed to be the absent center of the Victorian male's affections." See her *Consuming Fictions*, 159.

15. Jaggers's "fair" system convicts Magwitch, who has indeed broken the law—but who is "innocent" of wrongdoing as far as the reader is concerned. Biddy's more flexible system of knowledge gathering suggests an alternative to the courtroom.

16. Martine Hennard Dutheil argues that Pip "evolv[es] from a naïve reading of signs to a much more skeptical view of language according to which there is more to words than necessarily meets the eye." I would suggest that this argument overlooks the fact that the "naïve" reading is helpful in the effort to make sense of Mrs. Joe's cryptic language, and also that it is reading *flexibility,* a willingness to pull from many competing paradigms of interpretation, that solves the mystery. In other words, the text does not advocate replacing the "naïve" with the sophisticated, but rather it advocates using all tools available for unearthing the secrets of the real. See "*Great Expectations* as Reading Lesson," 166.

17. Kathleen Sell claims that women in the novel repeatedly fail to live up to the model of "selfless" femininity, and Pip blames his own flaws on the failures of Mrs. Joe, Miss Havisham, and Estella. A look at Biddy, it seems to me, must shift Sell's conclusions. "Narrator's Shame," 222.

18. Sharon Aronofsky Weltman argues that Ruskin's science relied on a culturally feminine model rather than a masculine one: "The feminine type is Ruskin's model for scientists who perceive without piercing; who need no phallic swords or dissection tools or engines of war; and who open their hearts to receive the knowledge nature provides." "Myth and Gender in Ruskin's Science," 157.

19. In his impressive look at the theme of reading and interpretation in the novel, Peter Brooks overlooks Biddy altogether, suggesting that Pip learns to read thanks to Mr. Wopsle's aunt and mentioning Mrs. Joe's "aphasic" symbols without discussing who deciphers them. See his *Reading for the Plot,* 131.

20. Robert Garnett suggests that the logic of the text will not permit a marriage to Biddy, since only the emotionally "moderate" men in the novel—Joe, Herbert, and Wemmick—can be paired with moderate women. Pip's passions soften over the course of the narrative, but he never becomes a thoroughgoing moderate and so cannot be properly paired with Biddy. For Garnett, Estella is the more credible companion: "Estella plainly does not belong among the novel's temperate homebodies . . . She is the very antithesis, for example, of Biddy's contented domesticity." "The Good and the Unruly in *Great Expectations,*" 34.

21. From a letter to Wilkie Collins (23 June 1861), in Dickens, *Letters* 9: 428.

22. In this respect, *Great Expectations* is a clear exception to Robert Caserio's claim that "However much Dickensian plot cultivates diverse meanings and multiple directions . . . the ending, considered not as finale but as *telos,* organizes all that precedes, explains all suspenseful mysteries and indeterminacies, marshals every detail and contingency, every event and character, into a structure revealed at the last—as purposeful." *Plot, Story, and the Novel,* 169.

23. Brooks, *Reading for the Plot,* 136.

24. When he revised the text, Dickens changed the final phrase, "I saw the shadow of no parting from her," to the more ambiguous ending, "I saw no shadow of another parting from her" (480).

25. Thus suspense troubles Frank Kermode's conclusion that "plotting presupposes and requires that an end will bestow upon the whole duration and meaning." *Sense of an Ending,* 46.

5. The Gender of Realism Reconsidered in *Adam Bede*

1. "[Women] must be . . . instinctively, infallibly wise—wise, not for self-development, but for self-renunciation." Ruskin, *Works* 18: 123.

2. In her popular conduct books, Sarah Stickney Ellis insisted that women should be taught "to forget themselves, and to cultivate that high tone of generous feeling to which the world is so much indebted." *Women of England,* 73.

3. Chapter 17 has been anthologized as the most important articulation of British realism in many sources, including George Becker's *Documents of Modern Literary Realism* and Lilian Furst's *Realism.*

4. For example, Daniel Borus writes: "Realist narration disdained the intervening narrator, who paused and commented on the action. Such a device, realists generally thought, only called attention to the artificiality of the text and undermined its credibility as an authentic document." *Writing Realism,* 23.

5. Mitchell, *Stone and the Scorpion,* 97.

6. Fuss, *Identification Papers,* 4, 9, 39.

7. J. Hillis Miller, for example, calls attention to the "rifts" and "fissures" between the theory and the novel's unfolding, while Stephen Gill's introduction to the novel reads Eliot's sympathetic descriptions of rural life as an illustration of her developing theory of realism. Miller, *Ethics of Reading,* 80; Gill, introduction, xvi–xxxvii.

8. I am using the masculine pronoun following J. Hillis Miller, who writes: "the putative speaker . . . is not Mary Ann Evans, the author of *Adam Bede,* but a fictive personage, 'George Eliot,' who narrates the story and who is given a male gender." *Ethics of Reading,* 66.

9. Book 1 ends with a chapter called "Links," and we are reminded of this by a chapter in book 4 entitled "More Links."

10. Fuss, *Identification Papers,* 2.

11. David Carroll suggests that Dinah's selflessness can be read "as a kind of self-indulgence." *George Eliot and the Conflict of Interpretations,* 82–83.

12. Fuss, *Identification Papers,* 2.

13. Mitchell, *Stone and the Scorpion,* 96; Paxton, *George Eliot and Herbert Spencer,* 59.

14. "I'm half a mind t' ha' a look at her to-night . . . a uncommon pretty young woman," says Wiry Ben in the first pages of the novel (8). "She looked like St. Catherine in a Quaker dress," says Arthur (54).

15. "Adam, unconscious of the admiration he was exciting, presently struck across the fields" (8).

16. "After the passage of the 1870 Education Act, a child's experience of school was increasingly likely to be shaped by gender. . . . The Board School curriculum was increasingly organized along sexist lines, with girls being taught domestic subjects such as home economics, sewing, cooking and child care, while boys were offered new options such as animal physiology, algebra, chemistry, and physics." Reynolds, *Girls Only?* 23–24. Similarly, children's books and stories generally specify an exclusively male or female readership only after 1870, with the publication of periodicals such as the *Boy's Own Paper.* See Bristow, *Empire Boys,* 53–64; and Knowles and Malmkjaer, *Language and Control in Children's Literature,* 9.

17. Both Bristow's *Empire Boys* and Reynolds' *Girls Only?* cite Thomas Hughes's *Tom Brown's Schooldays* (1857) as the first major text of boys' fiction.

18. Eliot, *Mill on the Floss*, 45, 30, 33, 35.

19. Homans, "Dinah's Blush," 155–70.

20. "Hetty blushed a deep rose-color when Captain Donnithorne entered the dairy and spoke to her; but it was not at all a distressed blush, for it was inwreathed with smiles and dimples, and with sparkles from under long curled dark eyelashes" (71). Hetty's "cheeks never grew a shade deeper when [Adam's] name was mentioned" (85). "Dinah's sexualization is limited to blushing" (Homans, "Dinah's Blush," 168).

21. A similar visual exchange marks the erotic connection between Maggie and Stephen in *The Mill on the Floss:* "[Stephen] only wished he dared look at Maggie, and that she would look at him,—let him have one long look into those deep strange eyes of hers and then he would be satisfied and quite reasonable after that. He thought it was becoming a sort of monomania with him, to want that long look from Maggie, and he was racking his invention continually to find out some means by which he could have it." *Mill on the Floss*, 519.

22. Kant, *Critique of Judgment*, 54.

23. Hegel, *Phenomenology of Spirit*, 111.

24. "If Arthur had had time to think at all, he would have thought it strange that he should feel fluttered too, be conscious of blushing too" (112).

25. "The vainest woman is never thoroughly conscious of her own beauty till she is loved by the man who sets her own passion vibrating in return" (129).

26. Homans makes a persuasive argument that the novel favors the marriage between Adam and Dinah as the realization of middle-class ideology, which Eliot "universalizes . . . by making its peculiar characteristics appear natural, generically human ones." "Dinah's Blush," 156.

27. At the very moment that Hetty is dressing up before her bedroom mirror, Dinah is looking outside: "the first thing she did on entering her room was to seat herself . . . and look out on the peaceful fields" (134).

28. Bryson, *Vision and Painting*, 87, 89.

29. In his overview of literary realism, René Wellek gives a great deal of attention to the realism of detail, "the minute description of costumes and customs." *Concepts of Criticism*, 227.

30. For example: "I confess I have often meanly shrunk from confessing to those accomplished and acute gentlemen what my own experience has been," "he" claims (156).

6. Realist Narrative in Doubt

1. Flint, "Blood, Bodies, and *The Lifted Veil*," 456.

2. According to Millie Kidd, most critics "agree that [Latimer] is deliberately painted as unattractive, that he is the cause of his own demise, and that his nihilistic views are not those of the author." "In Defense of Latimer," 37. Beryl Gray explains that Latimer's "spiritual predicament is created through his misinterpretation or misapplication of what is revealed to him," in her afterword to the story, 73. Jennifer Uglow describes Latimer's "self-obsession and refusal to engage actively with other people," in *George Eliot*, 119.

3. A notable exception is Charles Swann, "Déjà vu, déjà lu," 40–57. Swann reads the story as a deliberate undermining of Eliot's own usual insights and practice—a kind of thought experiment. "Latimer is given everything a good George Eliot character

usually asks for: he knows how others feel and he has visions of what will happen to him—and much good it does him" (48). Swann argues that George Eliot's horrified recognition of the limits of her ethics brings with it consequences for the text's form: "narrative suspense is virtually eliminated" (45).

4. Flint points out that the male scientist infuses his blood into a female patient, which enables her to speak, much like George Eliot herself, a "woman author writing with masculine authority" ("Blood, Bodies, and *The Lifted Veil*," 470). Latimer also behaves as if he has an uncontested claim to dispose of a servant's body as he wishes.

5. Knoepflmacher, *George Eliot's Early Novels*, 158.

6. Flint, "Blood, Bodies, and *The Lifted Veil*," 456; Uglow, *George Eliot*, 116.

7. Jane Wood describes Latimer as poised between two improper extremes: "We are constantly reminded of an 'excess' of sensitivity, passion, imagination, susceptibility, and of 'superadded consciousness,' and equally, of a 'deficiency' of physique, of social skills, and of the power of self-regulation." "Scientific Rationality and Fanciful Fiction," 163.

7. The Prophetic Fallacy

1. There is little critical consensus about the political force of the novel's ending. Susan Bernardo claims that Romola throws off masculine authority when she "creates a household of meaning and takes control at the end of the novel," whereas Shona Simpson, who focuses on the role of the intellectual woman in the novel, insists that the narrative closes with "silence, silent acceptance of duty and work; children, and the perpetuation of a system in which boys learn and women do not. . . . The image of the intellectual woman is subordinated to that of the caring nurse, the Madonna, the mother, even if that mother is a stepmother and the children adopted." See Bernardo, "From Romola to *Romola*," 101; Simpson, "Mapping *Romola*," 64.

2. Bonaparte, *Triptych and the Cross*, 10.

3. Carpenter, *George Eliot and the Landscape of Time*, 76.

4. Corner, "Telling the Whole," 68.

5. For Bratti Ferravecchi, he is literally illegible: "I picked up a stranger this morning as I was coming in from Rovezzano, and I can spell him out no better than the letters on that scarf I bought from the French cavalier" (22). Even the visionary Dino, who sees Tito as the "Great Tempter" in a dream, cannot make out his features: "And at the *leggio* stood a man whose face I could not see—I looked, and looked, and it was a blank to me, even as a painting effaced" (161).

6. Making a similar case, Alison Byerly argues that nineteenth-century narrative strives to make itself seem more real by exposing the artifices of the other arts. See her *Realism, Representation, and the Arts*.

7. Harris, *Omnipresent Debate*, 7.

8. Strauss, *Life of Jesus Critically Examined* 1: 88. See also Feuerbach, *Essence of Christianity*, 207.

9. Bonaparte, *Will and Destiny*, 48–62.

10. Rimmon-Kenan, *Narrative Fiction*, 39.

11. Beer, *Darwin's Plots*, 185.

12. Critics have agreed that human choice is crucial to Eliot's epistemology. Bonaparte writes that there is no escaping the "web of events" that connects each action to a larger whole (*Will and Destiny*, 55); and Elizabeth Deeds Ermarth argues that "The

far-reaching consequences of every action and the growing weight of conditions that the sum of actions entails are . . . powerfully present facts." "Incarnations," 273. John Reed argues that "Eliot wanted to represent a world governed by the laws of invariant causation unaffected by any supernatural power." *Victorian Will,* 309.

13. Beer, *Darwin's Plots,* 185.

14. Brooks, *Reading for the Plot,* 23. Or as Frank Kermode puts it: "all that seems fortuitous and contingent . . . is in fact reserved for a later benefaction of significance in some concordant structure." *Sense of an Ending,* 148.

15. Norris, *Deconstruction,* 133.

16. Ermarth, *Realism and Consensus,* 42.

17. Four serial issues earlier, the narrator tells us: "this morning for the first time [Romola] admitted to herself not only that Tito had changed, but that he had changed towards her" (280).

18. Carpenter, *George Eliot and the Landscape of Time,* 76.

19. Barthes, "Introduction to the Structural Analysis of Narratives," 94.

8. Losing the Plot

1. Todorov, *Poetics of Prose,* 145; emphasis in original.

2. Rowe, "Use and Abuse of Uncertainty," 57.

3. Ibid.

4. Felman, "Grasp with Which I Held Him," 199, 205.

5. The story was first published in the *Atlantic Monthly,* beginning late in 1870 and continuing into 1871.

6. Edel, *Henry James,* 305; Churchill, *Italy and English Literature,* 158; Buzard, *Beaten Track,* 239.

7. Adeline Tintner points out this connection in "Rococo Venice," 109. See also George Sand, *La dernière Aldini,* 168ff.

8. For the rise of Murray's guides and the competition between Murray and Baedecker, see Buzard, *Beaten Track,* 67–77.

9. Perosa, "Italy in Henry James's International Theme," 51; Buzard, *Beaten Track,* 241; Edel, introduction, 10; Steiger, "Fall of Conversion," 128.

10. For example, Tom Lloyd argues that realism always needs to avoid "emplotment" because "experience, like history, is messy, chaotic, not easily given to organization." *Crises of Realism,* 11.

11. Mary Louise Pratt argues that a particular kind of aesthetic vision was crucial to nineteenth-century tourism: "sight is seen as a painting and the description is ordered in terms of background, foreground, symmetries. . . . The esthetic pleasure of the sight singlehandedly constitutes the value and significance of the journey." *Imperial Eyes,* 204.

12. Murray, *Handbook for Travellers,* 433.

13. As Peter Howard explains, "The most distinctive feature of Picturesque ideas was that all exterior objects were to be judged by whether or not they contributed to a verisimilitude with a fine picture." *Landscapes,* 56–57. For a fuller history of the Picturesque, see Hipple, *Beautiful, the Sublime, and the Picturesque.*

14. Here James's protagonist tidily fits a description given of nineteenth-century tourists by Louis Turner and John Ash: "Loving and understanding the Italians remains an intellectual pose, they can only be loved as picturesque objects, kept at a suitable distance." *Golden Hordes,* 48.

15. Laura Mulvey offers this famous formulation in "Visual Pleasure and Narrative Cinema": "According to the principles of the ruling ideology and the psychical structures that back it up, the male figure cannot bear the burden of sexual objectification. Man is reluctant to gaze at his exhibitionist like. Hence the split between spectacle and narrative supports the man's role as the active one of advancing the story, making things happen." *Visual and Other Pleasures,* 20.

16. The only other instance of a visual description of the narrator is similarly oblique, emerging when a dying Italian girl compares him to a figure she has seen in a dream: "The stranger had light hair, light eyes, and a flowing beard like you" (190).

17. Pratt, *Imperial Eyes,* 204. See also 201–19.

18. Although Pratt's work is largely concerned with accounts of European exploration into "unknown" territory, she points out that "It is not surprising . . . to find German or British accounts of Italy sounding like German or British accounts of Brazil" (ibid., 10).

19. To quote Sergio Perosa again: "in 'Travelling Companions' . . . most of Italy is 'done'—from Milan to Venice, from Florence to Rome—with extensive descriptions that read like tourist guidebooks." "Italy in Henry James's International Theme," 51.

20. Steiger makes the case that Charlotte Evans launches James's concern with the American girl as a figure peculiarly capable of both suffering and redemption and argues that in "Travelling Companions" she shows the narrator what it means to feel. Her efforts to become Italian, according to Steiger, have everything to do with her attempts to feel like a Catholic, in contrast to the narrator's less responsive Protestantism. "Fall of Conversion," 127–39.

21. Miller, *Ethics of Reading,* 33.

22. The truth is great and will prevail. Frazer, *Golden Bough,* 676.

9. Pater's Plots

1. Williams, *Transfigured World,* 79.

2. Ibid., 3, 81–85.

3. The father's pretense is an invention of Pater's, since Vasari tells the story as if Leonardo's father was genuinely surprised. "Ser Piero nel primo aspetto non pensando alla cosa, subitamente si scosse, non credendo che quella fosse rotella, nè manco dipinto quel figurato ch'è vi vedeva; e tornando col passo addietra, Lionardo lo tenne dicendo: Questa opera serve per quel che ella è fatta." Vasari, *Le vite,* 493. (Ser Piero, not expecting anything at first, was suddenly startled, not thinking that what he saw was a shield, or even a painted figure; and he turned his steps in the opposite direction, but Leonardo stopped him, saying, "This work will serve the purpose for which it was made" [my translation].)

4. David DeLaura establishes that Pater read *Romola,* and he even goes so far as to claim that "the reading of *Romola* may well have been the impetus that set Pater on the road to the essays which were gathered in 1873 as *Studies in the History of the Renaissance.*" DeLaura, "*Romola* and the Origin of the Paterian View of Life," 226. David Carroll also links *Romola* to Pater's *Renaissance,* claiming that Pater's work "reads at times like an extended commentary on *Romola.*" *George Eliot and the Conflict of Interpretations,* 177.

5. This might be seen to anticipate a modernist version of realism, where art is "not to be conceived of . . . as a copy . . . of reality, but instead as an independent object

with the same degree of 'thingness' as objects in the world." Steiner, *Colors of Rhetoric*, 17.

6. Pater carefully distinguishes the term "presentment," which has connotations of heavy materiality, from his use of the word "representation," which refers to the expression of personal feeling in sculpture (52).

7. J. B. Bullen argues that Pater locates Michelangelo in this fifteenth-century tradition as a polemical response to Ruskin, who characterized the Renaissance as a break from the past. Ruskin lectured on "The Relation between Michelangelo and Tintoret" in 1871, several months before Pater's "Poetry of Michelangelo" appeared in the *Fortnightly.* "Pater and Ruskin on Michelangelo," 55–73.

8. Loesberg, *Aestheticism and Deconstruction,* 18.

9. Wilde, *Letters,* 96. Wilde acknowledged his debt to Pater in an 1897 letter to Alfred Douglas, referring to *The Renaissance* as "that book which has had such a strange influence over my life." *Complete Letters,* 735.

10. Cohen, "Writing Gone Wilde," 806.

11. D. A. Miller, *Narrative and Its Discontents,* ix.

12. Lessing, *Laocoon,* 93.

13. Even Wendy Steiner, who counts herself among Lessing's contemporary critics, recognizes as fundamental to narrative this "all-pervasiveness of the need for a repeated subject." For other discussions of the repeated sign in narrative, see also Ricoeur, *Time and Narrative* 3: 246; White, *Content of the Form,* 16; and Steiner, *Pictures of Romance,* 17–22.

14. Lessing writes: "The rule is this, that succession in time is the province of the poet, co-existence in space that of the artist. . . . Painting and poetry should be like two just and friendly neighbors, neither of whom is allowed to take unseemly liberties in the heart of the other's domain, but who exercise mutual forbearance on the borders." *Laocoon,* 109–10.

15. Wilde read Lessing's *Laocoon* while he was at Oxford, writing in his notebook that Lessing was not the first writer to discuss "the limitations of the sculptor who has to deal merely with form," but had been anticipated by the ancients. *Oscar Wilde's Oxford Notebooks,* 114.

16. As far as we know, that is, no one ever does, although Dorian calls attention to the possibility when he hopes "that some day he would see the change taking place before his very eyes" (83).

17. For a recent, highly sophisticated reading of the relation between the still image and the motion picture, see Stewart, *Between Film and Screen.*

Bibliography

Achinstein, Peter. *Particles and Waves: Historical Essays in the Philosophy of Science*. New York: Oxford University Press, 1991.

Allott, Miriam, ed. *The Brontës: The Critical Heritage*. London: Routledge and Kegan Paul, 1974.

Armstrong, Nancy. *Desire and Domestic Fiction: A Political History of the Novel*. Oxford: Oxford University Press, 1987.

———. "Fiction in the Age of Photography." *Narrative* 7 (January 1999): 37–55.

———. *Fiction in the Age of Photography: The Legacy of British Realism*. Cambridge: Harvard University Press, 1999.

Auerbach, Erich. *Mimesis: The Representation of Reality in Western Literature*. Trans. William R. Trask. Princeton: Princeton University Press, 1953.

Barthes, Roland. "Introduction to the Structural Analysis of Narratives." In *Image, Music, Text*. Trans. Stephen Heath. New York: Hill and Wang, 1977. 79–124.

———. *The Pleasure of the Text*. Trans. Richard Miller. New York: Hill and Wang, 1975.

———. *S/Z*. Trans. Richard Miller. New York: Hill and Wang, 1974.

Battcock, Gregory, ed. *Super Realism: A Critical Anthology*. New York: E. P. Dutton, 1975.

Baudrillard, Jean. *De la séduction*. Paris: Editions Galilée, 1979.

Beale, Lionel S. *How to Work with a Microscope*. London: John Churchill, 1857.

Beaty, Jerome. *Misreading Jane Eyre: A Postformalist Paradigm*. Columbus: Ohio State University Press, 1996.

Becker, George G. *Documents of Modern Literary Realism*. Princeton: Princeton University Press, 1963.

Beer, Gillian. *Darwin's Plots: Evolutionary Narrative in Darwin, George Eliot, and Nineteenth-Century Fiction*. London: Routledge and Kegan Paul, 1983.

Belsey, Catherine. *Critical Practice*. London: Methuen, 1980.

Benzie, William. *Dr. F. J. Furnivall: Victorian Scholar and Adventurer*. Norman, OK: Pilgrim Books, 1983.

Bernardo, Susan M. "From Romola to *Romola:* The Complex Act of Naming." In Levine and Turner, *From Author to Text:* 89–102.

Bersani, Leo. *A Future for Astyanax: Character and Desire in Literature*. Boston: Little, Brown, 1976.

Bhabha, Homi K. *The Location of Culture*. London: Routledge, 1994.

Birch, Dinah, ed. *Ruskin and the Dawn of the Modern*. Oxford: Oxford University Press, 1999.

Block, Ed, Jr. "T. H. Huxley's Rhetoric and the Popularization of Victorian Scientific Ideas, 1854–1874." In *Energy and Entropy: Science and Culture in Victorian Britain*. Ed. Patrick Brantlinger. Bloomington: University of Indiana Press, 1989. 205–28.

Bloom, Clive. "Capitalising on Poe's Detective: The Dollars and Sense of Nineteenth-Century Detective Fiction." In *Nineteenth-Century Suspense: From Poe to Conan Doyle*. Ed. Clive Bloom, Brian Docherty, Jane Gibb, and Keith Shand. London: Macmillan, 1988. 14–25.

Bodenheimer, Rosemarie. "Jane Eyre in Search of Her Story." In *Charlotte Brontë's Jane Eyre: Modern Critical Interpretations*. Ed. Harold Bloom. New York: Chelsea House, 1987. 97–112.

Bonaparte, Felicia. *The Triptych and the Cross*. Brighton, UK: Harvester Press, 1979.

———. *Will and Destiny: Morality and Tragedy in George Eliot's Novels*. New York: New York University Press, 1975.

Borus, Daniel H. *Writing Realism: Howells, James, and Norris in the Mass Market*. Chapel Hill: University of North Carolina Press, 1989.

Bradley, J. L. *Ruskin: The Critical Heritage*. London: Routledge and Kegan Paul, 1984.

Brantlinger, Patrick. *The Reading Lesson: The Threat of Mass Literacy in Nineteenth-Century British Fiction*. Bloomington: Indiana University Press, 1998.

Bristow, Joseph. *Empire Boys: Adventures in a Man's World*. London: HarperCollins, 1991.

Brontë, Charlotte. "Biographical Notice of Ellis and Acton Bell" (1850). In *The Brontës: Interviews and Recollections*. Ed. Harold Orel. Iowa City: University of Iowa Press, 1997. 133–40.

———. *Jane Eyre*. 1847. Ed. Jane Jack and Margaret Smith. Oxford: Clarendon Press, 1969.

———. *The Letters of Charlotte Brontë*. Ed. Margaret Smith. 2 vols. Oxford: Clarendon Press, 1995.

———. *Shirley*. 1849. Ed. Andrew and Judith Hook. Harmondsworth, UK: Penguin, 1974.

Brooks, Peter. *Reading for the Plot: Design and Intention in Narrative*. Cambridge: Harvard University Press, 1984.

Bryson, Norman. *Vision and Painting: The Logic of the Gaze*. New Haven: Yale University Press, 1983.

Bullen, J. B. "Pater and Ruskin on Michelangelo: Two Contrasting Views." In *Walter Pater: An Imaginative Sense of Fact*. Ed. Philip Dodd. London: Frank Cass, 1981. 55–73.

Buzard, James. *The Beaten Track: European Tourism, Literature, and the Ways to Culture, 1800–1918*. Oxford: Clarendon Press, 1993.

Byerly, Alison. *Realism, Representation, and the Arts in Nineteenth-Century Literature*. Cambridge: Cambridge University Press, 1997.

Cantor, Geoffrey. *Michael Faraday: Sandemanian and Scientist*. New York: St. Martin's Press, 1991.

Carpenter, Mary Wilson. *George Eliot and the Landscape of Time*. Chapel Hill: University of North Carolina Press, 1986.

Carroll, David. *George Eliot and the Conflict of Interpretations*. Cambridge: Cambridge University Press, 1992.

Carroll, Noël. "The Paradox of Suspense." In *Suspense: Conceptualizations, Theoretical Analyses, and Empirical Explorations*. Ed. Peter Vorderer, Hans J. Wulff, and Mike Fridrichsen. Mahwah, NJ: Lawrence Erlbaum, 1996. 71–91.

Caserio, Robert. *Plot, Story, and the Novel: From Dickens and Poe to the Modern Period*. Princeton: Princeton University Press, 1979.

[Chorley, H. F.]. Unsigned review of Dickens, *Great Expectations*. *Athenaeum* 1759 (13 July 1861): 43–45. Rpt. in Dickens, *Great Expectations*, ed. Law and Pinnington: 524–26.

Christ, Carol. *The Finer Optic: The Aesthetic of Particularity in Victorian Poetry*. New Haven: Yale University Press, 1975.

Churchill, Kenneth. *Italy and English Literature: 1764–1930*. London: Macmillan, 1980.

Cohen, Ed. "Writing Gone Wilde: Homoerotic Desire in the Closet of Representation." *PMLA* 102 (1987): 801–13.

Coleridge, Samuel Taylor. "On Poesy or Art." 1818. Rpt. in *Miscellanies, Aesthetic and Literary*. Ed. T. Ashe. London: George Bell, 1885. 47–48.

Collins, Philip, ed. *Dickens: The Critical Heritage*. London: Routledge and Kegan Paul, 1971.

Collins, Wilkie. *Letters*. Ed. William Baker and William M. Clarke. 2 vols. London: Macmillan, 1999.

Collins, Wilkie. *The Moonstone*. 1868. Harmondsworth, UK: Penguin, 1986.

———. Preface. *The Woman in White*. 1860. By Wilkie Collins. Ed. Kathleen Tillotson and Anthea Trodd. Boston: Houghton Mifflin, 1969. 499–500.

Corner, Julian. "'Telling the Whole': Trauma, Drifting and Reconciliation in *Romola*." In Levine and Turner, *From Author to Text*: 67–88.

Crary, Jonathan. *Suspensions of Perception: Attention, Spectacle and Modern Culture*. Cambridge: MIT Press, 1999.

Crease, Robert P. *The Play of Nature: Experimentation as Performance*. Bloomington: University of Indiana Press, 1993.

Daldry, Graham. *Charles Dickens and the Form of the Novel*. London: Croom Helm, 1987.

[Dallas, E. S.]. Unsigned review of Dickens, *Great Expectations*. *The Times* 17 October 1861: 6. Rpt. in P. Collins, *Dickens*: 432.

Darwin, Charles. *The Origin of Species*. 1859. London: Oxford University Press, 1951.

Day, Gary. "Figuring Out the Signalman: Dickens and the Ghost Story." In *Nineteenth-Century Suspense: From Poe to Conan Doyle*. Ed. Clive Bloom, Brian Docherty, Jane Gibb, and Keith Shand. London: Macmillan, 1988. 26–45.

DeLaura, David J. "*Romola* and the Origin of the Paterian View of Life." *Nineteenth-Century Fiction* 21 (December 1966): 225–33.

Dickens, Charles. *Great Expectations*. 1861. Ed. Margaret Cardwell. Oxford: Clarendon Press, 1993.

———. *Great Expectations*. 1861. Ed. Graham Law and Adrian Pinnington. Peterborough, ON: Broadview Press, 1998.

———. *Letters*. Ed. Madeline House, Graham Storey, and Kathleen Tillotson. Oxford: Clarendon Press, 1997.

Dutheil, Martine Hennard. "*Great Expectations* as Reading Lesson." *Dickens Quarterly* 13 (September 1996): 164–74.

Eagles, John. "British Institution for Promoting the Fine Arts in the United Kingdom, Etc.—1836." *Blackwood's Edinburgh Magazine* 40 (October 1836): 544.

[Eagles, John]. Unsigned review of Ruskin, *Modern Painters*. *Blackwood's Magazine* 54 (October 1843): 485–503. Rpt. in Bradley, *Ruskin*: 34–64.

Eco, Umberto. "Overinterpreting Texts." In *Interpretation and Overinterpretation*. Ed. Stefan Collini. Cambridge: Cambridge University Press, 1992. 45–66.

Edel, Leon. *Henry James: The Untried Years, 1843–1870*. London: Rupert Hart-Davis, 1953.

———. Introduction. *The Complete Tales of Henry James, 1868–72*. By Henry James. London: Rupert Hart-Davis, 1962.

Eliot, George. *Adam Bede*. New York: Harper and Brothers, 1859.

———. "Leaves from a Note-Book." 1871–79. In *Essays of George Eliot*. Ed. Thomas Pinney. London: Routledge and Kegan Paul, 1963. 437–51.

———. *Letters*. Ed. Gordon S. Haight. London: Oxford University Press, 1956.

———. *The Lifted Veil*. 1859. London: Virago Press, 1985.

———. *The Mill on the Floss*. 1860. Ed. Gordon S. Haight. Oxford: Clarendon Press, 1980.

———. *Romola*. 1862–63. Ed. Andrew Brown. Oxford: Clarendon Press, 1993.

[Eliot, George]. Unsigned review of Ruskin, *Modern Painters*. *Westminster Review* 9 (April 1856): 625–33. Rpt. in Bradley, *Ruskin*: 179–83.

Ellis, Sarah Stickney. *The Women of England: Their Social Duties and Domestic Habits*. London: Fisher, Son, 1839.

Ermarth, Elizabeth Deeds. *The English Novel in History, 1840–1895*. London: Routledge, 1997.

———. "Incarnations: George Eliot's Conception of Undeviating Law." *Nineteenth-Century Fiction* 29 (December 1974): 273–86.

———. *Realism and Consensus in the English Novel*. Princeton: Princeton University Press, 1983.

Faraday, Michael. *Life and Letters*. Ed. Thomas Bence-Jones. London: Longmans, Green, 1870.

———. *The Philosopher's Tree: A Selection of Michael Faraday's Writings*. Ed. Peter Day. Bristol, UK: Institute of Physics Publishing, 1999.

Felman, Shoshana. "'The Grasp with Which I Held Him': A Child Is Killed in *The Turn of the Screw*." In *The Turn of the Screw*. By Henry James. Ed. Peter G. Beidler. Boston: St. Martin's, 1995. 193–206.

Feuerbach, Ludwig. *The Essence of Christianity*. 1841, trans. 1854. Trans. George Eliot. New York: Harper and Row, 1957.

Flint, Kate. "Blood, Bodies, and *The Lifted Veil*." *Nineteenth-Century Literature* 51 (March 1997): 455–73.

———. *The Woman Reader*. Oxford: Oxford University Press, 1993.

Forster, E. M. *Aspects of the Novel*. New York: Harcourt, Brace, 1927.

Franklin, J. Jeffrey. *Serious Play: The Cultural Form of the Nineteenth-Century Realist Novel.* Philadelphia: University of Pennsylvania Press, 1999.

Frazer, James George. *The Golden Bough.* 1890. Ed. Robert Fraser. London: Oxford University Press, 1994.

Frick, Patricia. "Wilkie Collins and John Ruskin." *Victorians Institute Journal* 13 (1985): 11–22.

Furst, Lilian R. *Realism.* London: Longman, 1992.

Fuss, Diana. *Identification Papers.* New York: Routledge, 1995.

Gallagher, Catherine. *The Industrial Reformation of English Fiction, 1832–1867.* Chicago: University of Chicago Press, 1985.

Garnett, Robert R. "The Good and the Unruly in *Great Expectations*—and Estella," *Dickens Quarterly* 16 (1999): 24–41.

Gaskell, Elizabeth. *The Life of Charlotte Brontë.* 1857. Oxford: Oxford University Press, 1978.

Gezari, Janet. *Charlotte Brontë and Defensive Conduct: The Author and the Body at Risk.* Philadelphia: University of Pennsylvania Press, 1992.

Gill, Stephen. Introduction. *Adam Bede.* 1859. By George Eliot. Harmondsworth, UK: Penguin, 1980.

Glasier, John Bruce. *William Morris and the Early Days of the Socialist Movement.* 1921. Ed. Peter Faulkner. Bristol, UK: Thoemmes Press, 1994.

Goldman, Lawrence. "Ruskin, Oxford, and the British Labour Movement, 1880–1914." In Birch, *Ruskin and the Dawn of the Modern:* 57–86.

Gombrich, E. H. *Art and Illusion: A Study in the Psychology of Pictorial Representation.* London: Phaidon, 1972.

Gray, Beryl. Afterword. *The Lifted Veil.* By George Eliot. London: Virago Press, 1985.

Greene, Mott T. *Geology in the Nineteenth Century: Changing Views of a Changing World.* Ithaca: Cornell University Press, 1982.

Gregory, John. *Lectures on the Duties and Qualifications of a Physician.* 1772. Dordrecht, Netherlands: Kluwer Academic, 1998.

Haggerty, George E. *Gothic Fiction/Gothic Form.* University Park: Pennsylvania State University Press, 1989.

Handwerk, Gary J. *Irony and Ethics in Narrative: From Schlegel to Lacan.* New Haven: Yale University Press, 1985.

Harris, Wendell V. *The Omnipresent Debate: Empiricism and Transcendentalism in Nineteenth-Century English Prose.* Dekalb: Northern Illinois University Press, 1981.

Hazlitt, William. *Essays on the Fine Arts.* 1834–44. Ed. W. Carew Hazlitt. London: Reeves and Turner, 1873.

Hegel, G. W. F. *Phenomenology of Spirit.* 1807. Trans. A. V. Miller. Oxford: Oxford University Press, 1977.

Heilman, Robert B. "Charlotte Brontë's New Gothic." In *The Victorian Novel: Modern Essays in Criticism.* Ed. Ian Watt. London: Oxford University Press, 1971. 165–80.

Helsinger, Elizabeth K. *Ruskin and the Art of the Beholder.* Cambridge: Harvard University Press, 1982.

———. "Ruskin and the Politics of Viewing: Constructing National Subjects." *Nineteenth-Century Contexts* 18 (1994): 125–46.

Herbert, Christopher. *Trollope and Comic Pleasure.* Chicago: University of Chicago Press, 1987.

Herschel, John F. W. *A Preliminary Discourse on the Study of Natural Philosophy.* 1830. Chicago: University of Chicago Press, 1987.

Hewison, Robert. "Notes on the Construction of *The Stones of Venice.*" In Rhodes and Janik, *Studies in Ruskin:* 131–52.

Hipple, Walter John. *The Beautiful, the Sublime, and the Picturesque in Eighteenth-Century British Aesthetic Theory.* Carbondale: Southern Illinois University Press, 1957.

Homans, Margaret. "Dinah's Blush, Maggie's Arm: Class, Gender, and Sexuality in George Eliot's Early Novels." *Victorian Studies* 36 (Winter 1993): 155–70.

Horne, R. H. "British Artists and Writers on Art." *British and Foreign Review* 6 (April 1838): 610–57.

Houston, Gail Turley. *Consuming Fictions: Gender, Class, and Hunger in Dickens's Novels.* Carbondale: Southern Illinois University Press, 1994.

Howard, Peter. *Landscapes: The Artists' Vision.* New York: Routledge, 1991.

Hughes, Thomas. *Tom Brown's Schooldays.* Cambridge: Macmillan, 1857.

Hume, David. *A Treatise of Human Nature.* 1739. Ed. Ernest Mossner. Harmondsworth, UK: Penguin, 1985.

Huxley, Thomas H. "On the Advisableness of Improving Natural Knowledge." 1866. In *Essays.* New York: Macmillan, 1929. 210–31.

———. *Science and Education: Essays.* New York: D. Appleton, 1895.

James, Henry. *The Complete Tales.* London: Rupert Hart-Davis, 1962.

———. *The Painter's Eye: Notes and Essays on the Pictorial Arts.* Ed. John L. Sweeney. Cambridge: Harvard University Press, 1956.

Jameson, Fredric. *The Political Unconscious: Narrative as a Socially Symbolic Act.* Ithaca: Cornell University Press, 1981.

Jarves, J. J. "Pen Likenesses of Art Critics: John Ruskin, the Art-Seer." *Art Journal* 36 (January 1874): 5–6.

Jevons, W. Stanley. *The Principles of Science: A Treatise on Logic and Scientific Method.* 1873. London: Macmillan, 1977.

[Jewsbury, Geraldine]. Unsigned review of Collins, *The Moonstone. Athenaeum* 25 July 1868: 106. Rpt. in Page, *Wilkie Collins:* 170.

Judd, Catherine A. "Male Pseudonyms and Female Authority in Victorian England." In *Literature in the Marketplace: Nineteenth-Century British Publishing and Reading Practices.* Ed. John O. Jordan and Robert C. Patten. Cambridge: Cambridge University Press, 1995. 250–68.

Kant, Immanuel. *Critique of Judgment.* 1790. Trans. J. H. Bernard. London: Hafner, 1951.

Kearns, Katherine. *Nineteenth-Century Literary Realism: Through the Looking Glass.* Cambridge: Cambridge University Press, 1996.

Kermode, Frank. *The Sense of an Ending: Studies in the Theory of Fiction.* New York: Oxford University Press, 1967.

Kidd, Millie M. "In Defense of Latimer: A Study of Narrative Technique in George Eliot's 'The Lifted Veil.'" *Victorian Newsletter* 79 (Spring 1991): 37–41.

Knoepflmacher, U. C. *George Eliot's Early Novels: The Limits of Realism.* Berkeley: University of California Press, 1968.

Knowles, Murray, and Kirsten Malmkjaer. *Language and Control in Children's Literature.* London: Routledge, 1996.

Kucich, John. "Passionate Reserve and Reserved Passion in the Works of Charlotte Brontë." In *Critical Essays on Charlotte Brontë.* Ed. Barbara Timm Gates. Boston: G. K. Hall, 1990. 60–88.

Kuhn, Thomas S. *The Structure of Scientific Revolutions.* Chicago: University of Chicago Press, 1962.

Landow, George P. "Ruskin, Holman Hunt, and Going to Nature to See for Oneself." In Rhodes and Janik, *Studies in Ruskin:* 60–84.

Lessing, Gotthold Ephraim. *Laocoon: An Essay upon the Limits of Painting and Poetry.* 1766. Trans. Ellen Frothingham. New York: Noonday Press, 1957.

Levine, Caroline, and Mark W. Turner, eds. *From Author to Text: Re-reading George Eliot's Romola.* Aldershot, UK: Ashgate, 1998.

Levine, George. *Darwin and the Novelists: Patterns of Science in Victorian Fiction.* Cambridge: Harvard University Press, 1988.

———. "Dying to Know." *Victorian Newsletter* 79 (Spring 1991): 1–4.

———. "Objectivity and Death: Victorian Scientific Autobiography." *Victorian Literature and Culture* 20 (1992): 273–91.

———. *The Realistic Imagination: English Fiction from Frankenstein to Lady Chatterley.* Chicago: University of Chicago Press, 1981.

———. "Two Ways Not to Be a Solipsist: Art and Science, Pater and Pearson." *Victorian Studies* 43 (Autumn 2000): 7–41.

Lewes, George Henry. "Criticism in Relation to Novels," *Fortnightly Review* 3 (November–February 1865): 352–61.

———. *The Principles of Success in Literature.* 1865. Boston: Allyn and Bacon, 1891.

———. *Problems of Life and Mind.* 2 vols. Boston: Houghton Mifflin, 1873.

[Lewes, George Henry]. Unsigned review of Brontë, *Jane Eyre. Fraser's Magazine* 36 (December 1847): 686–95. Rpt. in Allott, *Brontës.*

[Lewes, George Henry]. Unsigned review of Brontë, *Jane Eyre. Leader* (28 December 1850): 953–54.

Lloyd, Tom. *Crises of Realism: Representing Experience in the British Novel, 1816–1910.* Lewisburg, PA: Bucknell University Press, 1997.

Loesberg, Jonathan. *Aestheticism and Deconstruction.* Princeton: Princeton University Press, 1991.

Losee, John. *A Historical Introduction to the Philosophy of Science.* Oxford: Oxford University Press, 1993.

Lukacs, George. *The Meaning of Contemporary Realism.* Trans. John and Necke Mander. London: Merlin Press, 1963.

Marsh, Jan. "'Resolve to be a Great Paintress': Women Artists in Relation to John Ruskin as Critic and Patron." *Nineteenth-Century Contexts* 18 (1994): 177–85.

Martineau, Harriet. *Biographical Sketches, 1852–1868.* London: Macmillan, 1870.

Mastai, M. L. D'Otrange. *Illusion in Art: Trompe l'Oeil, A History of Pictorial Illusionism.* New York: Abaris Books, 1975.

Mather, Marshall. *John Ruskin: His Life and Teaching.* London: Frederick Warne, 1897.

McGowan, John P. *Representation and Revelation: Victorian Realism from Carlyle to Yeats.* Columbia: University of Missouri Press, 1986.

Medawar, Peter B. *The Art of the Soluble.* London: Methuen, 1967.

Mill, John Stuart. *On Liberty.* 1859. Ed. David Spitz. New York: W. W. Norton, 1975.

———. *The System of Logic: Ratiocinative and Inductive.* 1843. London: Longmans, Green, 1891.

Miller, D. A. *Narrative and Its Discontents: Problems of Closure in the Traditional Novel.* Princeton: Princeton University Press, 1981.

———. *The Novel and the Police.* Berkeley: University of California Press, 1988.

Miller, J. Hillis. *The Ethics of Reading: Kant, de Man, Eliot, Trollope, James, and Benjamin.* New York: Columbia University Press, 1987.

Mitchell, Judith. *The Stone and the Scorpion: The Female Subject of Desire in the Novels of Charlotte Bronte, George Eliot, and Thomas Hardy.* Westport, CT: Greenwood Press, 1994.

Morris, William. "How I Became a Socialist." 1894. In *William Morris: Selected Writings and Designs.* Ed. Asa Briggs. Harmondsworth, UK: Penguin, 1962. 33–37.

———. Preface. "The Nature of Gothic." Hammersmith, UK: Kelmscott Press, 1892. i–iv.

Muller, John P., and William J. Richardson, eds. *The Purloined Poe: Lacan, Derrida, and Psychoanalytic Reading.* Baltimore: Johns Hopkins University Press, 1988.

Mulvey, Laura. *Visual and Other Pleasures.* London: Macmillan, 1989.

Murray, John. *Handbook for Travellers in Northern Italy.* London: John Murray, 1869.

Nochlin, Linda. *Realism.* Harmondsworth, UK: Penguin, 1990.

Norris, Christopher. *Deconstruction: Theory and Practice.* London: Routledge, 1982.

[Oliphant, Margaret]. "Sensation Novels." *Blackwood's Magazine* May 1862: 564–80. Rpt. in P. Collins, *Dickens.*

Olmsted, John Charles, ed. *Victorian Painting: Essays and Reviews.* New York: Garland, 1980.

Page, Norman, ed. *Wilkie Collins: The Critical Heritage.* London: Routledge and Kegan Paul, 1974.

Painter, George D. *Marcel Proust: A Biography.* 2 vols. New York: Vintage Books, 1959.

Pater, Walter. *The Renaissance: Studies in Art and Poetry, the 1893 Text.* Ed. and annotated by Donald L. Hill. Berkeley: University of California Press, 1980.

Paxton, Nancy L. *George Eliot and Herbert Spencer: Feminism, Evolutionism, and the Reconstruction of Gender.* Princeton: Princeton University Press, 1991.

Perosa, Sergio. "Italy in Henry James's International Theme." In Tuttleton and Lombardo, *The Sweetest Impression of Life:* 48–65.

Poovey, Mary. *Uneven Developments: The Ideological Work of Gender in Mid-Victorian England.* Chicago: University of Chicago Press, 1988.

Pratt, Mary Louise. *Imperial Eyes: Travel Writing and Transculturation.* London: Routledge, 1992.

Radcliffe, Ann. *The Mysteries of Udolpho.* 1794. Ed. R. Austin Freeman. 2 vols. London: Dent, 1973.

Reed, John R. *Victorian Will.* Athens: Ohio University Press, 1989.

Reynolds, Joshua. *Discourses on Art.* 1778. Ed. Robert A. Wark. New Haven: Yale University Press, 1975.

Reynolds, Kimberly. *Girls Only? Gender and Popular Children's Fiction in Britain, 1880–1910.* New York: Harvester Wheatsheaf, 1991.

Rhodes, Robert, and Del Ivan Janik, eds. *Studies in Ruskin.* Athens: Ohio University Press, 1982.

Ricoeur, Paul. *Time and Narrative.* Trans. Kathleen Blamey and David Pellauer. 3 vols. Chicago: University of Chicago Press, 1988.

[Rigby, Elizabeth]. Unsigned review of Brontë, *Jane Eyre. Quarterly Review* 84 (December 1848): 153–85.

[Rigby, Elizabeth]. Unsigned review of Ruskin, *Modern Painters. Quarterly Review* 98 (March 1856): 384–433. Rpt. in Bradley, *Ruskin:* 184–95.

Rignall, John. *Realist Fiction and the Strolling Spectator.* London: Routledge, 1992.

Rimmon-Kenan, Shlomith. *Narrative Fiction: Contemporary Poetics.* London: Methuen, 1983.

Ronell, Avital. "The Test Drive." In *Deconstruction Is/In America: A New Sense of the Political.* Ed. Anselm Haverkamp. New York: New York University Press, 1995. 200–220.

Rose, Jonathan. "Rereading *The English Common Reader:* A Preface to a History of Audiences." *Journal of the History of Ideas* 53 (1992): 47–70.

Rosenberg, John D. *The Darkening Glass: A Portrait of Ruskin's Genius.* London: Routledge and Kegan Paul, 1963.

Rowe, John Carlos. "The Use and Abuse of Uncertainty in *The Turn of the Screw.*" In *The Turn of the Screw and What Maisie Knew.* Ed. Neil Cornwell and Maggie Malone. Houndmills, UK: Macmillan, 1998. 54–78.

Ruskin, John. *The Complete Works.* Ed. E. T. Cook and Alexander Wedderburn. 39 vols. London: George Allen, 1903–07.

———. *Deucalion.* Boston: Dana Estes, n.d.

———. *Diaries.* Ed. Joan Evans and John Howard Whitehouse. 3 vols. Oxford: Clarendon Press, 1956.

———. *Modern Painters: "First Draft."* Ts. T22. Ruskin Library: University of Lancaster, n.d.

———. *Unto This Last, and Other Essays.* 1860. Ed. Clive Wilmer. Harmondsworth, UK: Penguin, 1985.

Russo, Elena. *Skeptical Selves: Empiricism and Modernity in the French Novel.* Stanford: Stanford University Press, 1996.

Ryals, Clyde de L. *A World of Possibilities: Romantic Irony in Victorian Literature.* Columbus: Ohio State University Press, 1990.

Sand, George. *La dernière Aldini.* 1838. Paris: Michel Lévy, 1882.

Sawyer, Paul L. "Ruskin and Tyndall: The Poetry of Matter and the Poetry of Spirit." In *Victorian Science and Victorian Values: Literary Perspectives.* Ed. James Paradis and Thomas Postlethwait. New York: New York Academy of Sciences, 1981. 217–46.

Sedgwick, Eve Kosoksky. *The Coherence of Gothic Conventions.* New York: Methuen, 1986.

Sell, Kathleen. "The Narrator's Shame: Masculine Identity in *Great Expectations.*" *Dickens Studies Annual* 26 (1998): 203–26.

Shaw, Harry E. *Narrating Reality: Austen, Scott, Eliot.* Ithaca: Cornell University Press, 1999.

Shorter, Clement. *The Brontës and Their Circle.* London: J. M. Dent and Sons, 1914.

Sidgwick, Henry. "The Poems and Prose Remains of Arthur Hugh Clough." *Westminster Review* 92 (October 1869): 363–87.

Simpson, Shona Elizabeth. "Mapping *Romola*: Physical Space, Women's Place." In Levine and Turner, *From Author to Text:* 53–66.

Skilton, David, ed. *The Early and Mid-Victorian Novel.* London: Routledge, 1993.

Smith, Jonathan. *Fact and Feeling: Baconian Science and the Nineteenth-Century Literary Imagination.* Madison: University of Wisconsin Press, 1994.

Stang, Richard. *The Theory of the Novel in England: 1850–1870.* London: Routledge and Kegan Paul, 1961.

Steiger, Jeff. "Fall of Conversion: Catholicism and the American Girl in Henry James's 'Travelling Companions.'" *Henry James Review* 18 (Spring 1997): 127–39.

Steiner, Wendy. *Colors of Rhetoric*. Chicago: University of Chicago Press, 1982.

———. *Pictures of Romance*. Chicago: University of Chicago Press, 1988.

Stephen, James Fitzjames. "The Relation of Novels to Life." 1855. In *Victorian Criticism of the Novel*. Ed. Edwin M. Eigner and George J. Worth. Cambridge: Cambridge University Press, 1985. 93–118.

Stewart, Garrett. *Between Film and Screen: Modernism's Photo Synthesis*. Chicago: University of Chicago Press, 1999.

Stoddart, Judith. "Conjuring the 'Necromantic Evidence' of History: Ruskin and the Enlightenment Revival of the 1870s." *Nineteenth-Century Contexts* 18 (1994): 163–76.

Stone, Harry. *Dickens and the Invisible World: Fairy Tales, Fantasy, and Novel-Making*. Bloomington: Indiana University Press, 1979.

Strauss, David Friedrich. *The Life of Jesus Critically Examined*. Trans. George Eliot. 2 vols. London: Chapman, 1846.

Swann, Charles. "Déjà vu, déjà lu: 'The Lifted Veil' as an Experiment in Art." *Literature and History* 5 (Spring 1979): 40–57.

Taylor, Jenny Bourne. *In the Secret Theatre of Home: Wilkie Collins, Sensation Fiction, and Nineteenth-Century Psychology*. London: Routledge, 1988.

Thomas, Ronald R. *Detective Fiction and the Rise of Forensic Science*. Cambridge: Cambridge University Press, 1999.

Thoms, Peter. *Detection and Its Designs: Narrative and Power in 19th-Century Detective Fiction*. Athens: Ohio University Press, 1998.

Tintner, Adeline. "Rococo Venice, Pietro Longhi, and Henry James." In Tuttleton and Lombardo, *The Sweetest Impression of Life:* 107–27.

Todorov, Tzvetan. *The Poetics of Prose*. Trans. Richard Howard. Ithaca: Cornell University Press, 1977.

Torgovnick, Marianna. *Closure in the Novel*. Princeton: Princeton University Press, 1981.

Turner, Louis, and John Ash. *The Golden Hordes: International Tourism and The Pleasure Periphery*. London: Constable, 1975.

Tuttleton, James W., and Agostino Lombardo, eds. *The Sweetest Impression of Life: The James Family and Italy*. New York: New York University Press, 1990.

Tyndall, John. *Faraday as a Discoverer*. 1868. New York: Thomas Y. Crowell, 1961.

———. *Fragments of Science: A Series of Detached Essays, Addresses, and Reviews*. 2 vols. New York: D. Appleton, 1900.

Uglow, Jennifer. *George Eliot*. London: Virago Press, 1987.

Vasari, Giorgio. *Le vite delle più celebri pittori, scultori e architetti*. 1550. Florence: Adriano Salani, 1925.

Vorderer, Peter, Hans J. Wulff, and Mike Fridrichsen, eds. *Suspense: Conceptualizations, Theoretical Analyses, and Empirical Explorations*. Mahwah, NJ: Lawrence Erlbaum, 1996.

Watt, Ian. *The Rise of the Novel: Studies in Defoe, Richardson, and Fielding*. Harmondsworth, UK: Penguin, 1963.

Wellek, René. *Concepts of Criticism*. New Haven: Yale University Press, 1963.

Weltman, Sharon Aronofsky. "Myth and Gender in Ruskin's Science." In Birch, *Ruskin and the Dawn of the Modern:* 153–73.

Whewell, William. *Life and Selections from the Correspondence*. Ed. Mrs. Stair Douglas. London: C. Kegan Paul, 1881.

————. *The Philosophy of the Inductive Sciences.* 2 vols. London: John W. Parker, 1840.

[Whewell, William]. "Spedding's *Complete Edition of the Works of Bacon.*" *Edinburgh Review* 106 (October 1857): 289–322.

[Whipple, Edwin Percy]. "Novels of the Season." *North American Review* 141 (October 1848): 354–69. Rpt. in Allott, *Brontës.*

[Whipple, Edwin Percy]. Unsigned review of Dickens, *Great Expectations. Atlantic Monthly* 8 (September 1861): 380–82. Rpt. in P. Collins, *Dickens.*

White, Hayden. *The Content of the Form: Narrative Discourse and Historical Representation.* Baltimore: Johns Hopkins University Press, 1987.

[Whitman, Walt]. Unsigned review of Ruskin, *Modern Painters. Brooklyn Eagle* (22 July 1847). Rpt. in Bradley, *Ruskin:* 76.

Wihl, Gary. *Ruskin and the Rhetoric of Infallibility.* New Haven: Yale University Press, 1985.

Wilde, Oscar. *Complete Letters.* Ed. Merlin Holland and Rupert Hart-Davis. New York: Henry Holt, 2000.

————. *Letters.* Ed. Rupert Hart-Davis. New York: Harcourt, Brace and World, 1962.

————. *Oscar Wilde's Oxford Notebooks: A Portrait of Mind in the Making.* Ed. Philip E. Smith II and Michael S. Helfand. New York: Oxford University Press, 1989.

————. *The Picture of Dorian Gray.* In *Oscar Wilde.* Ed. Isobel Murray. Oxford: Oxford University Press, 1989. 47–214.

Wilenski, R. H. *John Ruskin: An Introduction to Further Study of His Life and Work.* London: Faber and Faber, 1933.

Williams, Carolyn. *Transfigured World: Walter Pater's Aesthetic Historicism.* Ithaca: Cornell University Press, 1989.

Wilmer, Clive, ed. *Unto This Last, and Other Essays.* By John Ruskin. Harmondsworth, UK: Penguin, 1985.

Wilson, Edmund. "Who Cares Who Killed Roger Ackroyd?" *Classics and Commercials.* New York: Vintage, 1962. 257–65.

Winnifrith, Tom, and Edward Chitham. *Charlotte and Emily Brontë: Literary Lives.* New York: St. Martin's Press, 1989.

Wise, Thomas James, ed. *The Brontës: Their Lives, Friendships, and Correspondence.* 4 vols. Philadelphia: Porcupine Press, 1980.

Wollheim, Richard. *Painting as an Art.* Princeton: Princeton University Press, 1987.

Wolstenholme, Susan. *Gothic (Re)Visions: Writing Women as Readers.* Albany: State University of New York Press, 1993.

Wood, Jane. "Scientific Rationality and Fanciful Fiction: Gendered Discourse in *The Lifted Veil.*" *Women's Writing* 3 (1996): 161–76.

Wulff, Hans J. "Suspense and the Influence of Cataphora on Viewers' Expectations." In *Suspense: Conceptualizations, Theoretical Analyses, and Empirical Explorations.* Ed. Peter Vorderer, Hans J. Wulff, and Mike Fridrichsen. Mahwah, NJ: Lawrence Erlbaum, 1996. 1–17.

Index

Victorian Literature and Culture Series